D0178002

THE WARTIME
KITCHEN AND GARDEN

THE · WARTIME ·
KITCHEN AND GARDEN

JENNIFER DAVIES

BBC BOOKS

ACKNOWLEDGEMENTS

•

I am indebted to each person who took time to relate their wartime memories either to Keith Sheather, the producer of *The Wartime Kitchen and Garden* programme, or to myself. The books, diaries, wartime recipes and photographs loaned have also been invaluable.

I acknowledge with grateful thanks the help of the National Federation of Women's Institutes and BBC *Gardeners' World* magazine, which both made people aware of this project, thus prompting initial contacts. I must also thank the Imperial War Museum who created the splendid exhibition *The Wartime Kitchen and Garden*.

I thank the following for their help in supplying archive material: the Archives and Manuscript Department of the University of Reading; June Price of Bath College of Higher Education, Newton Park Library; the City Museum and Art Gallery, Stoke-on-Trent; *Newbury Weekly News*; the Institute of Agricultural History and Museum of English Rural Life, University of Reading; Long Ashton Research Station, Bristol; the Royal Horticultural Society Library; the BBC Written Archives, Caversham; Guernsey Tomato Museum; the BBC Reference Library, Bristol; Rothamsted Experimental Station, Harpenden; the Floristry Department, Lackham College, Wiltshire; the Flour Milling and Baking Research Association.

Thanks must go to Lord and Lady Iliffe and to Mrs Elizabeth Ward and Captain Gerald Ward for their kindness over film locations and continued interest, for without the television films there would not have been this book.

As always I thank presenters Ruth Mott, Harry Dodson and Peter Thoday, each of whom through kindness and advice has provided valuable help with this book. I thank too all the television team who worked on location and those who later constructed the programmes, for again without their contribution there could not have been a book.

Thanks must also go to stills photographers Robert Hill and John Jefford, both of whom spent long hours on location.

Finally I am grateful to all at my publishers who have guided this book to fruition. In particular I thank editors Heather Holden-Brown, Deborah Taylor and Ruth Baldwin and designer Linda Blakemore.

Published by BBC Books, a division of BBC Enterprises Limited,
Woodlands, 80 Wood Lane, London w12 0tt

First published 1993
© Jennifer Davies 1993

ISBN 0 563 36437 8

Set in 11½ on 13pt Garamond by Ace Filmsetting Ltd, Frome
Printed and bound in Great Britain by BPCC Paulton Books Ltd, Paulton
Colour separations by Technik Ltd, Berkhamsted
Jacket printed by Belmont Press Ltd, Northampton

CONTENTS

•

A BRIEF CHRONOLOGY
OF THE SECOND WORLD WAR

•

────────── 1939 ──────────

March	Germany invades Czechoslovakia.
1 September	German troops move into Poland. In Britain many schoolchildren, mothers and children under school age, expectant mothers, teachers and helpers are evacuated.
3 September	Britain declares war on Germany.
4 September	Start of the 'phoney war': expected bombardment does not come.
10 September	British Expeditionary Force leaves for France.
December	Many evacuees return home for Christmas.

────────── 1940 ──────────

8 January	Food rationing begins.
April	Lord Woolton becomes minister of food.
9 April	Germany invades Denmark and Norway.
May	Churchill heads coalition Government. Germany invades Low Countries.
27 May	Evacuation of British and Allied troops from Dunkirk begins.
10 June	Italy enters war.
14 June	Germans enter Paris.
10 July	Battle of Britain begins: full-scale air attack on south-east England.
7 September	Start of Blitz on London.
10 September	'Dig for Victory' launched.
15 September	RAF wins Battle of Britain.

────────── 1941 ──────────

March	Battle of the Atlantic begins.
April	Germany launches African offensive and invades Yugoslavia and Greece.
May	First Lend-Lease supplies arrive from USA.
June	Germany invades Russia. Clothes rationing begins. Utility scheme for retail goods introduced.
6 December	Japan attacks Pearl Harbor. USA enters the war.

Jan onwards	War in the Pacific.
Oct/Nov	Battle of El Alamein.
December	Leningrad fifteen months under siege, Germans encircled at Stalingrad: Allies believe that the war is turning in their favour.

——————————————————————— 1943 ———————————————————————

31 January	Germans surrender at Stalingrad.
April	Record level of German U-boats operating in the Atlantic.
May	Germany and Italy surrender in North Africa.
September	70% of British population aged 16–64 in war work: more than in Germany.

——————————————————————— 1944 ———————————————————————

January	Red Army breaks siege on Leningrad.
15 February	Battle of Monte Casino.
4 June	US Fifth Army captures Rome.
6 June	D-Day: Allies land in Normandy.
13 June	V1 (flying bomb) attacks on London begin.
August	Paris liberated.
8 September	V2 attacks launched on Britain (from Holland).
8 September	Allies liberate Brussels.
17 September	Allied airborne troops land behind German lines at Arnhem.
27 September	Allied defeat at Arnhem.

——————————————————————— 1945 ———————————————————————

January	Red Army crosses German frontier.
4 February	Yalta talks: Stalin, Roosevelt and Churchill.
March	Allied armies cross the Rhine.
6 April	USA invades Okinawa, south Japan. German retreat becomes a rout.
10 April	Allies break through in Italy.
30 April	Russians take Berlin. Hitler commits suicide.
4 May	German surrender.
8 May	VE (Victory in Europe) Day.
2 August	Potsdam conference: Atlee, Truman and Stalin dismember Germany.
6 August	US atomic bomb destroys Hiroshima.
8 August	US atomic bomb destroys Nagasaki. Russia declares war on Japan.
14 August	Japan surrenders.

INTRODUCTION

•

A diary entry written on Monday, 13 January 1941, captures the flavour of the time: 'Curious news about Rudolph Hess, Hitler's right-hand man: he has landed in Scotland from a plane on Saturday night. Planted potatoes on tennis court . . . lettuce in drying ground.' So matter of fact are these two statements, merging to equal importance; they reflect the reality experienced by many, for the acts of the Second World War ran in tandem with everyone's life. As the U-boats sank cargo ships in the Atlantic, women worked out how many 'points' they had to spend in their food ration books and gardeners turned their lawns into potato patches. When bombs hit cities, sparks also flew in country kitchens, for not every hostess and evacuee mother found sharing a stove easy; and with their apprentices fighting Hitler, old-style headgardeners had to come to terms with women working in their gardens.

Lord Woolton, minister of food from 1940 to 1943, believed that housewives were war workers, and Mr Middleton, the wartime 'wireless gardener', stated that potatoes and onions were munitions of war 'as surely as shells and bullets'; and so they were, in both cases.

This book tells the story of the kitchen war workers and those that made vegetable ammunition. It accompanies a television series which features cook Ruth Mott and gardener Harry Dodson, known for their TV roles as 'Victorian' cook and gardener respectively. Both Ruth and Harry were amply qualified for their wartime roles. Ruth's war included being a cook in a Red Cross convalescent home, budgeting and coping with rations for her parents and daughter, and looking after the garden while her husband was in the forces. She also did premium-collecting rounds for an insurance company whose male worker had been called up, and in the latter years of the war catered for weddings, of which there were many!

Harry was called up at the age of nineteen, when he was employed as an undergardener in private service. He joined the Royal Sussex Regiment and fought in France. Discharged on medical grounds in 1941, he then worked for the Admiralty as a gardener at HMS *Vernon*, billeted in a large house called Leigh Park in Hampshire. Harry was 'second of six' gardeners who were on what was known as food production. In their case this was growing produce for HMS *Vernon*'s canteen. It was also Harry's job to make sure that the grounds around the mansion did not look anything like an Admiralty establishment, particularly from the air, but merely those of a private country house.

In 1945, anxious to get back to private service, Harry moved to Nuneham Park, the Oxfordshire estate of Lord Harcourt. However, like practically all big gardens at the time, this too was on food production, working very much as a market garden and supplying produce for Oxford shops. Harry left Nuneham in the autumn of 1947 to become headgardener at Chilton, where he still resides.

Facing page: Ruth Mott
and Harry Dodson.
Left: Anya, Harry and the
garden's broadbean crop.
Below: Tracey.

For the television series Ruth was given two 'evacuees' to billet, Tracey Godsmark and her little boy Paul. Tracey became 'Joyce' for the series as it was the general consensus of opinion that Tracey was not a wartime name. In fact research revealed that it only became popular after Grace Kelly's portrayal of 'Tracey Lord' in the 1956 film *High Society*. Harry was given a 'land girl', Anya Medlin, to help him 'Dig for Victory'. Anya, or 'Annie' as she was known, was pretty handy as she had done a stint of working for Harry before the filming. She merely changed her jeans for corduroy breeches and the rest of the Women's Land Army uniform.

In addition to the memories of Harry and Ruth this book also contains the stories, anecdotes, diary entries and thoughts of many men and women who were involved with kitchens and gardens during the war years. Some cooked or gardened for a living; others advised and taught, or as schoolchildren were taught, and many simply (not that wartime *was* simple) cooked for their family and tended their gardens and allotments.

It is hoped that this mixture will strike a chord in those who remember the war and perhaps kindle an interest in those who do not.

CHAPTER ONE
WAR BEGINS

The morning of Sunday, 3 September 1939, was bright and sunny. Both Harry Dodson and Ruth Mott remember the fine weather that day.

In the gardens' bothy at Ashburnham House in Sussex, where nineteen-year-old Harry was employed as a garden journeyman, the foreman had his wireless switched on and the gardeners sat expectantly round it. The voice from the speaker said:

Here is an announcement. At 11.15 – that is, in about two minutes – the prime minister will broadcast to the nation. Please stand by.

There was the sound of bells and then the announcer spoke again:

This is London. You will now hear a statement by the prime minister.

Neville Chamberlain began:

I am speaking to you from the Cabinet Room at 10 Downing Street. This morning the British ambassador in Berlin handed the German Government the final note stating that unless we heard from them by eleven o'clock that they were prepared, at once, to withdraw their troops from Poland, a state of war would exist between us. I have to tell you now that no such undertaking has been received and that consequently this country is at war with Germany . . .

When the prime minister had finished speaking there was another peal of bells and then the announcer read Government notices about places of entertainment closing until further notice; of what people should do in an air raid and how gas masks must always be carried.

Harry remembers that what he heard did not give him any feelings of anxiety, because although he had doubted that there would be a war, it was something that for the past twelve months everyone had been talking about. However, he knew that he would be called up, for from that day all men between the ages of eighteen and forty-one were liable for conscription.

Chamberlain's announcement did not have any immediate effect on Ruth either, because she did not hear it. At the time she was staying with her sister at Luton and at 11.15 am was out walking on nearby hills. When she returned she found her sister in tears over the sink. 'She remembered the 1914–18 war,' Ruth explains, 'and she wasn't very happy about things at all.' She goes on to recall: 'The first thing we wondered was whether we were going to be bombed, because there had been a lot of talk about

Facing page: War is declared, 1939.

11

it in the papers and that made you think it was going to happen straight away. It didn't, although there was a siren very soon afterwards, but whether that was to see what people's reactions would be I don't know, for nothing happened.'

Indeed that first siren after war was declared was a scary sound. Jean Neilson of Bath, then a London schoolteacher newly evacuated to Long Sutton, Lincolnshire, heard it penetrate the farm labourer's cottage where she was billeted. Looking back to that time, she remembers: 'The husband of the household said we had to put our gas masks on and we all did. Then his wife suddenly said, "The baby hasn't got one," and took *hers* off. So we all took *our* masks off too. It seems hilarious now, but really we were all frightened to death at the time.'

When Ruth left her sister's house everyone told her not to return home via London because it was sure to be bombed. 'So,' she says, 'I took a very devious route, hopping off one bus on to another all round through High Wycombe and then to Reading.' London was not bombed, but out in the Atlantic, just a few hours after war had been announced, a German U-boat sank an unarmed liner, the *Athena*: an action that heralded the ability of enemy submarines to blockade Britain from its overseas food supplies. However, measures were already in hand to counter U-boat starvation tactics, for the moment war was declared the British Government took over every chief food commodity – wheat, butter, bacon, cheese – whether it was in transit on the water from overseas, on the roads in Britain or stored in different parts of the country. By the end of Sunday, 3 September, officials were in charge of millions of pounds' worth of foodstuffs. The purpose was to stop it being hoarded and sold later at increased prices. Moreover, orders were made holding food prices at a standstill. (Later, after investigation, specific prices were fixed.)

Three years earlier the Government had taken the precaution of setting up the Food (Defence Plans) Department, under Henry Leon French, to enable it to exercise just such food control should war break out; for supplies had to be kept up and prices kept down. The department had divided Britain into fifteen divisions, within each of which every local authority had its food executive officer (usually the council clerk).

Now all food executive officers received a telegram which incorporated a code. To interpret the code they had to read the contents of a sealed envelope left in their care. The message was to take the necessary steps for opening a food control at any moment. At specially called council meetings Local Food Control Committee members were appointed – these consisted of five trade members (always including a grocer, a butcher and a Co-operative Society representative), one trade employee and ten to twelve consumers – and Food Executive Offices were opened.

On the same day telegrams also authorized the formal appointment of each county's War Agricultural Committee. Given power by the

> I was brought up in Rotherham. When war was declared I was ten years old and on holiday with my parents in the Isle of Man. We came back on the Isle of Man ferry, which had a line of flags flying. A young man on board said he could read what the flags said – it was: 'Submarine in vicinity.' People on board laughed about it. When we got to Liverpool docks I remember seeing the liner *Athena*, all white and gold, beside the quay getting ready to depart. Its route would be retracing ours, then it would continue past the Isle of Man towards southern Ireland and the Atlantic.
>
> *Sheila Gray, Langley, Berkshire.*

Cultivation of Lands Order 1939, the committees were to set about increasing home food production. Being largely industrial and metropolitan, Britain was heavily reliant on imported food. In fact, just prior to the Second World War we imported more than half the total of our meat supplies, 70 per cent of our cheese and sugar, nearly 80 per cent of our fruit and about 90 per cent of our cereals and fats. Only potatoes and fresh milk were produced entirely at home.

To advise them the War Agricultural Committees had specialist sub-committees and later, at parish level, district sub-committees. It was to be an uphill task. Under the influence of twenty years of peace and no encouragement of good prices – for foreign countries provided Britain with cheap food – many farms had become simply pasture. To make matters worse any livestock kept on the pasture was fed almost wholly on imported foodstuffs. The pasture needed to be turned into crops of corn, potatoes and cattle fodder.

To start the process a massive ploughing campaign began. Farmers were offered the incentive of £2 an acre if they ploughed up fields which had been grass for seven years provided that they did it before the end of December. Some men used horses to pull their ploughs, others had tractors. Tractors had the advantage that they needed no rest and by men working a shift system could be driven all day and all night. Ploughing at night in black-out conditions was not easy. In later years it was written that to keep a furrow straight these nocturnal ploughmen needed 'the instincts of both owl and acrobat'.

Harry in uniform.

On Monday, 4 September, the gardens at Ashburnham were fairly quiet. Four or five young gardeners who had gone off work on Saturday had not returned. They were members of the territorial army and had been required to report to the drill hall on Sunday morning. Harry found himself doing jobs around the gardens he had not done before and the foreman made plans for how things might be managed. However, within a week or two Harry's call-up papers came and on that day he told the foreman he wanted to leave so that he could have a few days at home before joining his regiment.

Home was Blackmoor in Hampshire, where his mother told him that Dick Lacy from next door had also had his papers. The two young men had not seen each other for years. Dick was older than Harry and had left home before him to go as an underkeeper at Petworth House in Sussex. In fact Dick went back to Petworth for a day or two to say goodbye to his young lady and told Harry that he would look out for him at Chichester barracks. They did meet up and shared the same hut.

Harry's regiment was the Royal Sussex. He found that most of the others there who had been called up were from country life. 'There was no end of gardeners, grooms, chauffeurs and footmen in my squad, and apart from two young schoolmasters we'd all come from the same sort of estate life and we had many a pleasant hour sitting on the beds in the evening polishing our boots and cleaning our equipment and talking of where we'd been and what we'd been doing.'

Harry settled well into army life. He puts this down to his upbringing for, he says, not only had his family kept good discipline but his work in private service had also accustomed him to it. 'After bothy life and the strictness of headgardeners and their foremen, the old sergeant shouting was no different.' Harry's training at Chichester was preparing him for service in France. He did go to France, but in 1941 was discharged from the Army on medical grounds. He went back to professional gardening but the big gardens he worked in no longer grew delicacies for the mansion owner; instead the gardeners 'Dug for Victory' to supply canteens or city shops.

Ruth, working in the kitchens of a large private house called Canfield Place, near Hatfield in Hertfordshire, also decided to do her bit and at the start of the war applied to join the Auxiliary Territorial Service (ATS). Ruefully she says, 'To this day they have never sent for me. They obviously thought I wasn't a very suitable candidate!' However, it turned out for the best, because her parents became ill and she had to return to Berkshire to look after them.

On 29 September, National Registration Day, each householder had to fill in a form giving the particulars of everyone living in the house. The following day the forms were collected and the person collecting wrote out an identity card for everyone on the return. Meanwhile Food Offices used the information from the forms to fill in names and addresses on ration books, which were then posted off to the public.

The question of food rationing had already been looked into by the Food Department, for Britain's experience during the First World War had shown the importance of planning ahead. It was 1918 before food control had been complete and rationing could begin. Up to that point housewives had queued for a few ounces of sugar or a scrap of meat or cheese. It did not matter whether a woman was shopping for herself or for her family: the minuteness of the portion she received was the same. If more were required she had to join another queue, and to add to her frustrations supplies sometimes ran out before she reached the counter. It got to the point where queuing began to cause grievance and unrest. However, rationing allocated food according to the size of the family and within a few weeks of its start date in 1918, when shoppers and shopkeepers became used to handling ration cards, queues dwindled.

At the beginning of November 1939 people were warned that butter and bacon would be rationed and they were told to register with a retailer for these by 23 November. They were also told to register for sugar – not because it was then thought it would be rationed, but merely to help with distribution.

On the land severe frost at the beginning of 1940 held up the ploughing campaign. The urgent need to continue as soon as possible was stressed by politicians. On 28 February, speaking at a luncheon in London, MP and former prime minister David Lloyd George said: 'We can double the yield of our soil, and no submarine or magnetic mine or aeroplane can get at it.' This message was repeated on the wireless. By 17 April 1,900,000

Facing page: Filling in names and addresses on ration books.
Inset: Ration book cover.

ON HIS MAJESTY'S SERVICE

Your
Ration Book
Issued to safeguard your food supply

OFFICIAL
PAID

HOLDER'S NAME AND REGISTERED ADDRESS

Surname_____THOMSON_____

Other Names_____Catherine_____

Address_____3 Rowan Rd_____

ACCRINGTON

NAT.
REG.
NO.   NTBR   283   2

Date of Issue 7 JUL 1941 Serial Number of Book

If found, please return to

ACCRINGTON NH 913440
FOOD OFFICE.

R.B.1 [General] 4

The first days of rationing.

acres of land had been newly brought under the plough. As ploughing was not due to finish until 30 April, hopes were high that the two million mark would be surpassed.

There was also good news on imported food. The first six months of the war had not turned out quite as expected. There were no bombings and the Germans had not got into their submarine campaign. In this lull before the storm the Ministry of Food (which had been officially set up on 8 September, with W. S. Morrison as minister) bought millions of pounds' worth of foodstuffs and shipped them to Britain. To cope with the influx, food storage depots sprang up all over the country. On the outbreak of war food had been sent away from vulnerable areas, but now it was gradually brought back.

However, behind the scenes a precautionary experiment was being carried out to discover just what would happen to normal men and women if food imports were severely restricted and everyone had to make do with very little fat, sugar and meat. For this experiment the Medical Research Council kept eight people for three and a half months on rations based on the experiences of the First World War, the 1938–9 agricultural position and the scientific knowledge of nutrition available in 1939. The human guinea pigs were allowed 4 oz of fat and 5 oz of sugar a week. Bread, potatoes and other vegetables were unrationed. (Interestingly, as it turned out, this experiment-diet was more austere than that which people during the war actually had to experience.) Despite the severity of their diet, it was found that once they had adjusted to it the men and women were healthy, satisfied and content.

A brief account of the experiment was circulated to various Government departments in March 1940. Over the next few months it must have made reassuring reading, for in April the Germans invaded Denmark and Norway and, in May, Holland, Belgium and Luxemburg. At the end of June, France surrendered. These happenings dealt a heavy blow to Britain's food supply. Between them these countries had provided Britain each year with over 1,750,000 tons of foodstuffs – in fact, over half our bacon and ham, shell (as opposed to dried) eggs, condensed milk and milk powder and 30 per cent of our butter.

In June, Italy entered the war and a lot of food which had formerly been transported through the Mediterranean had instead to take a longer route round the Cape.

At the same time enemy action at sea was beginning to bite. By the end of 1940, 728,000 tons of food and animal foodstuffs had been sunk. That year was also to have the highest loss of food in the shortest time (September to December) brought about by air attacks. During that time 159,000 tons were damaged. However, about a third of the food damaged by air raids was officially salvaged and went, depending on its state, for human consumption or animal feed.

Ruth can relate that a bit of unofficial salvaging also went on. Before he was called up her late husband Bill was in the auxiliary fire service at Pangbourne, Berkshire. His unit was often despatched to bombed factories in Bristol and Plymouth and Ruth recalls that he would come home to tell tales of having stood waist-deep in baked beans or having seen meat and bacon floating around a flooded factory floor. When the latter happened he used thoughtfully to bring home a piece to support his tale.

CHAPTER TWO

WARTIME SHOPPING

When Lord Woolton succeeded Mr Morrison as minister of food in April 1940, he realized that in order to give the public a balanced diet it was up to him to set out the basis of food supplies. That is, he had to work out how much to rely on what could be imported and how much to tell the minister of agriculture to grow. He decided that the safest course was to base the diet on home-grown foods. Woolton had the advantage of having studied science in his student days, but knew that since those times knowledge of nutritional values had increased significantly. He enlisted medical experts and his scientific adviser Professor Jack Drummond to help him.

Every cloud has a silver lining and the clouds of war provided the nutritionists with an ideal opportunity to reform the nation's diet and make it healthier. Sometimes, however, their recommendations were hard to take: for example, the 'Basal Diet'. Per person per day this was to consist of 12 oz of bread; 1 lb of potatoes; 2 oz of oatmeal; 1 oz of fat; 6 oz of vegetables and $^6/_{10}$ pint of milk; plus a small amount of sugar and a few other luxuries. The diet was not implemented for Winston Churchill took a dim view of such exigencies. On 14 July 1940 he wrote to Lord Woolton:

> . . . The British soldier is far more likely to be right than the scientists. All he cares about is beef . . . the way to lose the war is to try to force the British public into a diet of milk, oatmeal, potatoes etc. washed down on gala occasions with a little lime juice.

The 'British public' was at that time unaware of the dieticians' efforts: its chief concern with food was the rigmarole of simply getting it. Rationing had begun on 8 January 1940. On that day weekly allowances per person for butter became 4 oz, for sugar 12 oz and for bacon and ham 4 oz. In order to help the shopkeeper easily cut out the appropriate coupons everyone was advised to keep their ration book flat. 'You wouldn't like to be caught bending,' Government notices stated pithily.

There were three types of ration book. The general ration book (RB1) was for men, women and children over six years of age; the child's ration book (RB2) was for children under six; and the traveller's ration book was for people like lorry drivers and commercial travellers. There was also a special seaman's book.

On 11 March meat went on ration, but unlike the other rationed commodities it was rationed by price, not by weight. The weekly allowance

Facing page: One month after the introduction of rationing, this shop is keen to assure housewives that there are still plenty of unrationed foods.

Old Mrs Maltby at the shop said, 'Well, when the war's over they'll have to reckon that most of us what has had to do with the food trade will need places in the lunatic asylums!' But seriously, I think the food authorities have done a wonderful job. There's really no shortage anywhere of essentials.

From the diary of Miss C. M. Edwards, Binbrook, Lincolnshire. 28 September 1943.

Facing page: Fifty years on and for the benefit of the television camera, Ruth renews acquaintance with a ration book.

for an adult was 1s 10d (9p) and for a child below six 11d (4½p); restaurants were allowed 1d (½p) and colliers' canteens 2d (1p) worth per meal. On 7 July tea was restricted to 2 oz per week and on the 22nd cooking fats and margarine to 2 oz.

Allowances fluctuated during 1940 and by the end of the year the system of cutting coupons out of a ration book was dropped. The coupons were made smaller and the shopkeeper could cancel a week's worth with the stroke of a pen. This saved time and paper.

The period between July 1940 and June 1941 saw the worst losses of food through sinking at sea of the whole war. The scarcity of supplies brought more food on to ration. In the spring of 1941 people's diet dropped to its lowest average of the war. The meat allowance was reduced and milk, fish and minor foods like jam and onions were scarce. Cheese was in such short supply that it was rationed at just 1 oz per week. Many grocers grumbled that they could not cut 1 oz rations, so it was cut once a month!

It was at this time that America kindly provided a helping hand. On 11 March 1941 a Lend-Lease Bill was passed there. By this Bill America could let another country have articles of defence if it was considered that such defence was vital to the USA. No repayment was asked for, although the USA did expect certain trade concessions after the war. Thus it was that although Britain's dollar reserves were exhausted (so that in the normal course of events they could not have been paid for) consignments of cheese, lard and canned foods were shipped from the USA to Britain. Had this not happened, Britain would have been faced with the dangerous and chancy business of bringing food from further afield. The first consignment of Lend-Lease goods arrived on 31 May 1941.

Rationing was achieving its aim of equal distribution that enabled everyone to get their fair share. In fact shoppers wanted more articles put on ration. For example, a certain amount of discontent was felt if it was found that a neighbour had been able to get hold of unrationed items like tinned salmon or dried fruit and you had not. However, the Ministry of Food could not ration articles of which there were not sufficient in the country to guarantee supplies for everyone. It was a problem, and the arrival of Lend-Lease goods would make the situation worse.

By the late autumn of 1941 sufficient stock of Lend-Lease canned meat and fish had been accumulated to begin distribution to the public. On 1 December the Ministry of Food introduced another form of rationing. Known as 'points rationing', it used Lend-Lease foods as its base and was to be over and above the existing 'straight rationing' already in existence. It worked on the principle that each consumer would have so many points to 'spend' on any number of foods. It had the benefit of allowing people choice, for if they wanted to splash out and spend most of their points on one luxury item they could. Alternatively they could spread the points to buy a number of articles. Also consumers were not tied down to spending them in the shop with which they had registered but could use them in any shop.

A month before points rationing was due to start a 'stop sale' order was put on 'points' foods so that retailers could build up stocks. Forty-five million people had to have the new pink ration books, and in many Food Offices Women's Voluntary Service (WVS) members were called in to serve and cut the queues.

The scheme turned out to be highly successful, and soon points rationing was extended to other foods, including condensed milk, biscuits and golden syrup. The number of points a consumer had per four-week period fluctuated; sometimes it rose as high as 24. The number of points each article called for also changed; it depended on availability. For example, if there was a good supply of tinned sardines in the country, the points needed for sardines went down.

For all its merits the points rationing system did have drawbacks. For one thing the ration book was troublesome to shopkeepers. It had A-, B- and C-lettered coupons whose value varied every four-week period. Also the Ministry, worried about too great a demand, released only a certain tonnage of points goods per set period, and although it tried to equal the number of points with the goods released, sometimes, despite having the points to spend on a certain item, a shopper could not get it. This led to some scarce points goods being reserved for a shop's registered customers. This was a pity, for when the points scheme was introduced it had been hoped that it would see an end to under-the-counter sales and queuing. However, people had become inured to both these irritations, particularly the latter.

Ruth remembers that, as she lived in a village, there were some things like fish and little extras she could not get and so once a week she used to go into a nearby town – perhaps Newbury or Reading. On these occasions if she saw a queue she stood on the end of it until her turn came at the counter and then she knew what she had been queuing for! She has a nice apocryphal story about one war-time queue in Reading. Apparently an old man saw the queue and joined the end of it. After a while he said to the person in front, 'What are we queuing for?' and was told, '*The Tales of Hoffman*'. 'Ah', said the man philosophically, 'it's surprising what we eat these days.'

A third form of rationing, born off the back of points rationing, began on 26 July 1942. It was 'personal points' and covered just chocolate and other sweets.

Some foods did not fit into either straight or points rationing because they were too perishable or too seasonal (that is, sometimes there would be a glut and sometimes not enough). Eggs, milk and fish fell into this category. The Government organized special schemes which controlled their distribution.

Ruth recalls that the more there were in a family, the better rationing worked because, added together, every family member's bit of ration came to a reasonable amount of a particular food. This was a help when cooking. However, she concedes, 'If there were only a few in the family, or one, it hit you very hard.'

Single ration-book holders suffered another disadvantage, as Elizabeth Cornish of Canterbury explains. Her husband, a naval officer during the war, was catered for on board ship, so she had a ration book just for herself. When she went to the shop she did not receive any preferential treatment. Under-the-counter sales were carried out with people who had families and who had built up a rapport with the grocer. Yet there was one way in which a single person could 'work' the system – well, a little. Rachel Thorpe of Leicester remembers that when she went into digs her landlady did the cooking and asked her to register at a different shop from the family. She explained that different shops offered different things and Rachel might come home with something her shop did not have!

In some respects there certainly were *different* things in the shops. Lend-Lease had brought them. One was Mor, spiced, sugared ham; then there was Spam (minced pork shoulder) and pork sausage (pork with jelly and fat). Another American import was soya flour made from the soya bean. Its name was confusing for it was not flour as the British housewife knew it and contained no starch. In food value it closely resembled eggs,

A queue outside a shop in Lambeth, London.

"HAVE YOU BROUGHT YOUR FAT
RATION WITH YOU?"

Above: Mrs Whitham, mother of sixteen children, working out the family's weekly rations.
Above right: Rationing finds its way into holiday postcard humour.

being high in protein, carbohydrate and fat with a certain amount of iron and vitamins. For the adventurous it would have a number of uses (including that of laxative), but most women used it just to make mock marzipan. The recipe is on the facing page.

On the page of her diary which charted the first week in December 1941, Kate Vickers of Birmingham wrote: 'JAPAN war on BRITAIN AND AMERICA'. In smaller letters, though doubtless it was of equal if more domestic concern, she added: 'No wrapping paper for bought articles'. This development meant that as well as remembering to take her ration book when she went to buy the groceries, a housewife had to take her own wrapping paper. Shortage of paper also affected food packaging. When paper supplies fell to a quarter of what they had been pre-war, all attractive multiple wrappings had to go. Instead minimum amounts of paper and board were used and experiments were carried out to see how few thousandths of an inch would carry food safely from the shop to the kitchen.

In addition to changed packaging shoppers had to get used to finding different brand names on the shelves, not always their favourites. The reason for this was the difficulty with transport. Wartime conditions made petrol and manpower short; the military placed heavy demands on rail and, with the loss of major rubber-producing areas to the Japanese, tyres became scarce. To cope with the problem the Government limited delivery distances. For groceries and provisions the country was split into nine sectors and retailers had to draw their supplies from wholesalers solely within their particular sector.

Efforts to solve transport difficulties also changed the shape of certain foods. As some ships were lost in enemy action and others were taken over for carrying troops and munitions, fewer and fewer were available for transporting food. In order to keep up food supplies, drastic measures had to be implemented to save shipping space. Milk and eggs were shipped in powder form. Some meat was also dehydrated; other meat had the bones taken out – in fact in the latter case housewives sometimes found it difficult to identify the anonymous lump they were looking at. By 1944 this 'putting food into battle dress', as one food official termed it, had saved the carrying capacity of seventy-five 10,000-ton ships.

If meat had been compressed, then so too had variety on the grocer's shelves. Take, for example, biscuits. Before the war one firm had made 350 different sorts, but during the war it made only twenty. Loss of variety came about because the Government concentrated food production into a small number of factories: highly mechanized food factories had been taken over to make munitions. There was, however, one type of food on which the Government did not cut back – pickles, sauces and sweet and savoury spreads. It was realized that people needed these to relieve the monotony of bread and potatoes.

Women working in factories found shopping difficult, because there was no time to do it during the day and by the time they went home most shops had shut. The Hounslow branch of the Women's Voluntary Service offered a solution to this problem. The local leader, Mrs Brown, had a squad of thirty cycling volunteers who would do shopping – even find the ration books in the dresser drawer if necessary – and deliver it back. The service was free. By March 1941 over fifty housewife war workers were availing themselves of Mrs Brown's 'shoppers'.

For those who *could* go shopping it was wise, if the shop were in an area which had suffered a recent air raid, to be on the alert and not to judge some foods by their exterior appearance. Bomb blast addled eggs and it turned butter green and – much more dangerous – some shopkeepers, unwittingly or otherwise, sold goods which were impregnated with tiny splinters of glass.

When certain foods were not to be found in any shop, housewives had to resort to buying substitutes. Onion salt had to take the place of onions, and prunes (when finely chopped) could do instead of dried fruit.

Contemporary illustration showing how different ways of packaging meat could save shipping.

FROZEN BEEF, WITH BONE IN	🚢 🚢 🚢 🚢 🚢
FROZEN BEEF, BONELESS	🚢 🚢 🚢
CORNED BEEF	🚢 🚢
DEHYDRATED BEEF	🚢

🚢 SHIP WITH REFRIGERATED HOLDS
🚢 SHIP WITH ORDINARY HOLDS

MOCK MARZIPAN

Joan Veich of Earlswood, Warwickshire, still uses this recipe as 'it's so easy to apply'.

2 oz margarine
4 oz sugar
I tablespoon water
2 teaspoons almond essence
5 oz soya flour

Melt the fat and add the sugar, water and essence, and beat well together. Add the flour and beat into the mixture. Knead until the mixture stops cracking. While still warm, mould on to the cake: it will set firmly.

Business as usual despite the bomb damage.

The latter became scarce when Italy entered the war and the Mediterranean became out of bounds.

Ruth remembers that she and a workmate once bought a sugar substitute. They had seen it advertised in the paper, where the manufacturers stated that so much was equivalent to 7 lb of sugar. It proved to be a powdery substance, something like modern sugar substitutes. Disappointingly, however, it was 'not nice at all' and so they did not repeat the exercise.

Milk and egg substitutes also came on to the market and, although they looked like the real thing, many were worthless. To protect the public the Government issued a Food Substitutes (Control) Order. This prohibited the sale of any substitute foods other than those made under licence to the Ministry of Food. In 1944 a Defence Regulation also gave the Ministry control over the labelling and advertising of foods. In particular this covered claims that might be made about a food's vitamin or mineral content.

Shopping was not the only way of getting food during the war. Sometimes people obtained it through the black market. Ruth defines black-market goods as 'anything that shuffles along under cover'. She goes on:

> You'd probably hear that there'd be some sugar about some-where, if you could find your way to it, which had 'fallen' off the back of a lorry. Pheasants 'came' out of trees too. On the subject of these, I can remember my mother telling me that in Reading during the First World War police were going round looking in houses for black-market stuff and one old girl had some pheasants. When she heard the police were coming she slapped some pastry over them, feathers and all, and popped them into the oven!

It is not known what Ruth's pheasant lady would have been fined if she'd been rumbled, but certainly penalties for black marketeering in the Second World War were heavy. Punishment could be a £500 fine and two years' imprisonment plus also having to pay three times the capital involved in the transaction. Perhaps it was these measures and the efficiency of the Enforcement Intelligence Bureau, set up to cope with black-market problems, which led one official account of 1939–45 food control to state: 'There was never in the United Kingdom an organized black market of the dimensions reported from some other countries.'

Finally there was one way of getting your groceries which did not involve money at all: bartering. This took many forms. Margaret Clark of Burnham, Buckinghamshire, recalls that when she lived in Lincolnshire her family's fish merchant gave them fish when it was plentiful in return for apples and vegetables from their garden. Jean Howard of Bath, whose father was a doctor, says that he accepted fruit and eggs in exchange for visits. In-family bartering also went on. Dolly Wall of Winford, Bristol, had an aunt next door who made butter, 'so she'd let me have her fat and I let her have sugar'. Dolly's mother-in-law kept a pub and she preferred a drink of beer to tea, so her tea came Dolly's way too. Mother-in-law also did a swap with whisky for meat.

Swapping could sometimes have unexpected results. Viola Williams of Salisbury recalls the buses which used to bring country people into the town to shop:

> They were hilarious going back, because everybody would be swapping everything. It was sort of 'I'll give you a couple of pounds of potatoes if you'll give me a couple of eggs.' The trouble was you were quite likely to finish up with what you started with, after it had gone all the way round the bus being swapped for something else!

If possible, buy the rations at the end of the week and use them during the following week, so that you always have a week's rations in hand on which to draw in case of emergency. If they are bought at the beginning of the week and used up before the weekend, you may find yourself very awkwardly placed if a guest arrives unexpectedly.

From Cooking for Two, published by Good Housekeeping.

Food must be chosen carefully in relation to needs, and what the market offers. Day-to-day information about prices, bargains and gluts will be found in newspapers and given on the radio. It is important to buy the right amount of food and so avoid 'left-overs'. Over-cooking, which is wasteful, should be avoided.

From the School in Wartime, memorandum no. 19, published by the Board of Education, 1940.

DIG FOR VICTORY

CHAPTER THREE

ADVICE AND PROPAGANDA

It seems that everyone who cooked or gardened or who wanted to do either during the war years had the benefit of advice *ad nauseam*. This came not only in the form of the printed word – leaflets, pamphlets and books – but also from the wireless and from films.

PAMPHLETS AND PEOPLE
GARDENING

The famous slogan 'Dig for Victory' was not on people's lips until 1940 when it was coined by a London evening paper. Prior to that the Government had promoted food production under the less catchy 'Grow More Food Campaign'. This campaign had been launched in the previous year by the then minister of agriculture, Sir Reginald Dorman-Smith. For some gardeners it got off to a less than auspicious start. The problem lay with an advice leaflet called 'Growmore Bulletin No. 1', the result of collaboration between the Ministry of Agriculture, the Royal Horticultural Society and various research and advisory bodies. Its aim was to give amateurs simple instructions on how to grow vegetables in a private garden or allotment. The bulletin was prepared in July and August of 1939 when it was known that war was in the offing. However, at that time it was impossible to forecast the date that war would actually begin, and so the bulletin included a general cropping plan rather than one aimed at a specific time of year. The intention was that the document should be released to the public immediately upon the outbreak of war. In September the scramble to get it out led, unfortunately, to some printers' errors.

Professional gardeners (a breed notorious even to this day for differing over advice) were quick to criticize the bulletin. The printing error of 3 in. instead of 3 ft for the planting distance between marrows was ridiculed. They thought the method given for rotation was unclear and disagreed with the times advised for sowing, the choice of varieties and the space allocated between rows. The small amount of ground recommended for potatoes compared with the area given to leafy green vegetables was another bone of contention, particularly among northern gardeners. As one of their ilk remarked in a letter to the *Gardeners' Chronicle*, the northern working man was not interested in ½ in. of boiled spinach served with ½ oz of scrambled egg but wanted something that would 'take the wrinkles out of his tummy'.

The originators of the bulletin did their best to defend their work. They promised corrections to printing errors and argued that the high percentage of leafy green vegetables was to provide vitamins which in peacetime would come from imported fruit. It was a worthy aim, but unfortunately severe weather in the winter of 1940 made it disastrous for green vegetables.

Following more criticisms, 'Growmore Bulletin No. 1' appeared in a revised form in January 1941. One month later a further significant alteration was made: the leaflet changed its name to 'Dig for Victory Leaflet No. 1'. In the middle of the title of each leaflet was a round logo showing a booted foot pressing a spade blade into soil. The foot belonged to a Mr W. H. McKie of Acton, London, and a photographer had caught it at just the right moment. Rarely can a foot have had such publicity. Its image must have been reproduced millions of times, for the logo appeared on practically every one of the following twenty-five Ministry 'Dig for Victory' leaflets. Each leaflet advised on some aspect of gardening, whether it was coping with potato blight or saving seeds. Also available to amateurs and prefaced by Mr McKie's boot were pocket-sized pictorial instructions. These unfolded lengthways and showed, step by step, how to dig or sow.

For dwellers in cities and large towns, gardening advice could be had by joining allotment associations or gleaned from news-sheets issued by horticultural committees which were set up by local councils to promote food production. Usually the key mover in a horticultural committee's campaign was the local parks superintendent. Just such a person in Portsmouth was Mr F. Baker, who transferred his office from a park on the outskirts of the city into the main high street so that he could be more readily available to answer questions. Fred Daw, parks superintendent for Oldbury in Worcestershire during the war years, remembers how, as food production officer for the borough, he arranged for demonstration allotments to be dug in the parks. There were two kinds, one laid out to the Ministry's cropping plan and one to suit local conditions. Fred says that information bureaux were set up by the allotments and manned by park staff. On Saturday and Sunday evenings practical demonstrations were given or the public invited to discussions, perhaps on pest control, perhaps on the management of tomatoes. Forthcoming events were advertised on notice boards in front of the plots.

There were good attendances for, as Fred recalls wryly, 'People soon found out that if they didn't grow it themselves, they didn't get anything.' It was also part of his job to give gardening instruction to schools, to assist allotment and garden societies and to lecture to any group that wanted advice on food production.

For rural gardeners advice might come in the form of talks at the village hall, generally arranged by village produce associations. The Ministry of Agriculture supplied free lantern slides for speakers. Also in country districts private professional gardeners suddenly found themselves in demand. Many were unaccustomed to addressing public

Left: Fred Daw (extreme left) dispensing advice to wartime gardeners.

WILLS'S CIGARETTES

FREDERICK GRISEWOOD

meetings and to help them gardening periodicals ran columns of advice on the best way to plan and deliver talks. More experienced speakers could be had from the Royal Horticultural Society. The Society made it known that if a group could be gathered together, no matter in what county, it would supply a free lecturer.

However, perhaps more popular than straight lectures were 'brains trusts', which took place at both town and country venues. The format for a brains trust was a panel of horticultural experts, a quizmaster and an audience. In the town the experts might be the local parks superintendent, a seedsman and a chemist. The most sought-after quizmaster for such occasions was the radio personality Freddy Grisewood. Brains trust panellists had to be prepared to field a wide range of questions. At Urmston in Lancashire an allotment holder stood up and asked whether he should give up his allotment because his wife complained that his appetite had grown so big he ate more extra food than he grew. Back came the answer: 'Get an additional plot!'

Certain professional horticultural advisers received their pay directly from the Ministry and worked under the County War Agricultural Executive Committees – for example, Ministry inspectors. The main job of these busy men and women was to see that nurserymen abided by Ministry regulations. However, in the evenings they also gave talks to amateurs and allotment holders. This side of their work was unpaid and often undertaken in less-than-ideal conditions. Ron Sidwell, who, sadly, died shortly before the publication of this book, was an inspector in the Vale of Evesham and recalled talking to half a dozen people grouped round a pub table while the rest of the pub carried on noisily around them.

Also responsible to the 'War Ags.' were county horticultural advisers. Before the war many had worked for the county councils as horticultural officers. Their wartime role was to advise allotment societies, schools, service camps and any organizations wanting help with food production. Viola Williams of Salisbury was an assistant horticultural officer working under the Wiltshire War Agricultural Committee. Her tasks were various. As her visits and advice were free, she was much in demand. At one time she was responsible for all the allotments in the county. Grafting was another service she carried out and Viola says that in one particular village in Wiltshire she grafted practically every tree. Apparently the village had an orchard of old apple trees and wanted new varieties. She remembers that the job took weeks.

At one point she travelled round in a sort of bus-cum-caravan with three other advisers. 'There was a poultry lady, a cookery lady, another horticultural lady and me. We were known as 'the Circus' and we went around, and provided that the weather was all right we stood in the middle of the village and if people wanted to ask questions, or if they wanted something demonstrated, we were there to deal with it. We enjoyed it – we were lucky in that we were all compatible and we had a very good time.'

Another peripatetic adviser paid by the Ministry of Agriculture, but for a different task, was Elizabeth Hess. In 1939, when it was known that war was coming, she was appointed agricultural organizer to the National Federation of Women's Institutes. Her remit was to travel round the whole country and talk to large meetings (with at least a hundred in the audience) of Women's Institute members, advising them what to grow and how to harvest it. She dealt with queries on the depth of digging, on the distances at which seed should be sown – in fact the sort of things a trained gardener knew but the ordinary housewife, suddenly left to cope alone with a garden, did not. She also designed a pruning chart for soft fruit which was printed and sold to members for 1d (½p).

Elizabeth remembers that, on her forays around the country, hospitality was provided by WI members. On one evening she might be in a castle, on another in a fisherman's cottage. 'Sometimes I had to be dressed for dinner and sometimes I could go in my coat and skirt that I'd been wearing all day long.'

Petrol was short, so whenever she could she tried to travel by train. There were, however, some places accessible only by road and when visiting these she drove a Morris car supplied by the Ministry. The car was new but was very slow to start once it had got cold. Elizabeth recalls how this particular mechanical drawback manifested itself one memorable evening. On the occasion her hostess for the night swept out of the meeting blithely saying to her, 'George [the chauffeur] is outside with the car. Follow him and we'll get home.' However, George, car and hostess had disappeared from sight before Elizabeth could get her little Morris started. 'There I was, left at Bury St Edmunds, not knowing which way to go.' Black-out conditions, lack of signposts and unfamiliar roads did not help. She made her way 6 miles along the road to the nearest village,

Facing page: Cropping plan from a Ministry 'Dig for Victory' leaflet.

32

THIS PLAN WILL GIVE YOU YOUR OWN VEGETABLES ALL THE YEAR ROUND

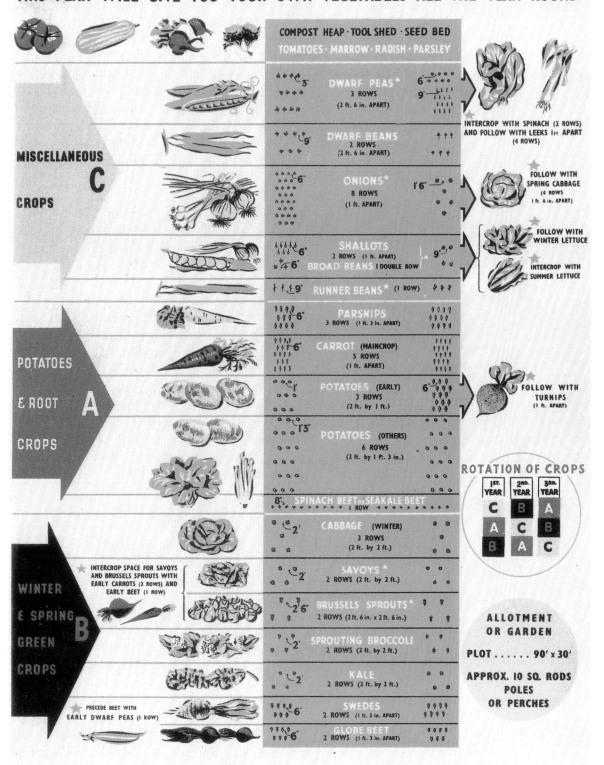

COMPOST HEAP · TOOL SHED · SEED BED
TOMATOES · MARROW · RADISH · PARSLEY

MISCELLANEOUS C CROPS

DWARF PEAS*
3 ROWS
(2 ft. 6 in. APART)

INTERCROP WITH SPINACH (2 ROWS)
AND FOLLOW WITH LEEKS 1ft APART
(4 ROWS)

DWARF BEANS
2 ROWS
(2 ft. 6 in. APART)

ONIONS*
8 ROWS
(1 ft. APART)

FOLLOW WITH
SPRING CABBAGE
(4 ROWS
1 ft. 6 in. APART)

SHALLOTS
2 ROWS (1 ft. APART)
BROAD BEANS 1 DOUBLE ROW

FOLLOW WITH
WINTER LETTUCE

INTERCROP WITH
SUMMER LETTUCE

RUNNER BEANS* (1 ROW)

POTATOES & ROOT A CROPS

PARSNIPS
3 ROWS (1 ft. 3 in. APART)

CARROT (MAINCROP)
5 ROWS
(1 ft. APART)

POTATOES (EARLY)
3 ROWS
(2 ft. by 1 ft.)

FOLLOW WITH
TURNIPS
(1 ft. APART)

POTATOES (OTHERS)
6 ROWS
(2 ft. by 1 ft. 3 in.)

SPINACH BEET OR SEAKALE BEET
1 ROW

ROTATION OF CROPS

1st. YEAR	2nd. YEAR	3rd. YEAR
C	B	A
A	C	B
B	A	C

CABBAGE (WINTER)
3 ROWS
(2 ft. by 2 ft.)

WINTER & SPRING GREEN CROPS B

INTERCROP SPACE FOR SAVOYS
AND BRUSSELS SPROUTS WITH
EARLY CARROTS (2 ROWS) AND
EARLY BEET (1 ROW)

SAVOYS *
2 ROWS (2 ft. by 2 ft.)

BRUSSELS SPROUTS*
2 ROWS (2 ft. 6 in. x 2 ft. 6 in.)

SPROUTING BROCCOLI
2 ROWS (2 ft. by 2 ft.)

KALE
2 ROWS (2 ft. by 2 ft.)

PRECEDE BEET WITH
EARLY DWARF PEAS (1 ROW)

SWEDES
2 ROWS (1 ft. 3 in. APART)

GLOBE BEET
2 ROWS (1 ft. 3 in. APART)

ALLOTMENT
OR GARDEN

PLOT ...... 90' x 30'

APPROX. 10 SQ. RODS
POLES
OR PERCHES

then sat and waited in faith. George and the Rolls eventually turned up. Even when the Morris was fairly bowling along, road travel was not easy. For example, in country districts where people were suspicious of strangers, Elizabeth remembers how her enquiries for directions generally led to instructions to go in the opposite direction. 'They were sure', she says, 'you'd dropped from the skies;' and adds, 'if you happened to have a German name like Hess, it didn't help.'

Travel apart, Elizabeth Hess cannot recall any other great problem in her advisory work. In fact she found it very helpful having the Women's Institute organization behind her. Also the members she spoke to were so appreciative and willing to learn that, she says rather modestly, 'It made life awfully easy for people like me, going around trying to be useful.'

COOKING

Frederick James Marquis became minister of food on 4 April 1940. He was fifty-eight years old and had been created Lord Woolton in 1939. His background amply qualified him for his new job, for it had given him an understanding of people, the knowledge of how a Government department ran in wartime and a head for business.

Marquis was educated at Manchester Grammar School and went on to Manchester University to study science and economics. At university he had become involved in the activities of Ancoat Hall, a centre for social work and charitable help for the poor of the area. At Ancoat he mixed with philanthropists, including a Manchester jeweller called J. J. Mallon. Mallon, influenced by the settlement, went on to dedicate his life to stamping out sweated labour. Marquis got to know Mallon well, for he married Miss Maud Smith, one of his voluntary helpers.

Minister of Food, Lord Woolton.

When Marquis graduated he went to work as a maths master at the Old Grammar School in Burnley. He taught in the day and in the evening lectured to cotton-mill workers. At the age of twenty-four he was invited to become warden of the David Lewis Club, part of a charitable trust, in Liverpool. Marquis accepted the job with the intention of using it to make a two-year study to discover why so many people were poor. When he wrote his memoirs he looked back and wondered if it was optimism or youthful arrogance which led him to believe he would find the reasons. It might, he thought, have been either, but these were two qualities he needed in full measure to balance the sordid conditions in which he lived and worked. 'It was,' he writes of the job, 'an experience that was to fashion much of my thought and action for the rest of my life.'

Marquis's experience of wartime Ministry work came with the outbreak of the First World War. He was asked by the Local Government Board to report on the effects of war on prices and consumer goods and on disturbance of business. This entailed him in sending nightly reports to Whitehall. Later, being unfit for military service, he found himself organizing the supply of blankets for the armies in France, Belgium and Italy and equipping the whole of the Romanian and Russian armies with everything except their weapons. Through being in charge of the distribution of boots he became secretary of the Leather Control Board in the War Office.

After the war Marquis worked for the Boot Manufacturers' Federation until, at the age of thirty-seven, he was asked to join the firm which ran a chain of big department stores called Lewis's. He had some misgivings about his move to their Liverpool premises, for he had no experience of business and felt that he might be too old to learn. However, he soon proved his worth. He foresaw a recession and persuaded the company to sell a large amount of its stock at a reduced price rather than keep it until the recession came and prices fell. His object was to enable the firm to be in a position to buy fresh stocks on its own terms. The strategy worked, making Lewis's £750,000 profit.

In 1939 Lewis's opened a new store in Glasgow. To some people's surprise it was not in the popular shopping area of Sauchiehall Street but in the lesser-known Argyle Street, yet despite its situation the new store proved successful. Choosing Argyle Street had been Marquis's doing. At a luncheon given by the lord provost of Glasgow he admitted having personally spent several hours in both streets walking up and down and watching the crowds before immediately entering into negotiations with the owners of the building in Argyle Street.

Such was the man who became the new food minister in 1940. On taking up his post Marquis, now Lord Woolton, made no bones of his retail background and even used it to further his cause. He said:

> I suppose I am going to run the greatest shop the world has ever known. I am not a trader any more, but I want to appeal to the people who are my fellow traders to play the game. I want to appeal to them to take the full and proper measure of their responsibility and when things go wrong not to make their alibi – not to say, 'Of course, these things are difficult, but it is the minister of food.' If the shopkeepers, distributors and wholesalers will help, there's no reason why the whole thing should not work smoothly.

It was not just shopkeepers whom Woolton wanted to play their part, it was shoppers too, and to reach them he decided to change existing Ministry propaganda posters. Of one which read 'Let your shopping save your shipping' he exclaimed, 'What could that mean to any ordinary housewife? She could not repeat it unless she had been very fortunate, or very wise, in the preservation of her teeth!' He set about instituting slogans which made direct statements such as 'Don't waste bread'. He also arranged for a press conference to be held every Tuesday morning and then used the occasion to conduct a two-way traffic. He gave the reporters food news and, when he had finished, submitted himself to interrogation based on letters of complaint about food that the newspapers had received from their readers. The number of journalists attending the press conferences grew from half a dozen to over eighty.

Lord Woolton takes advantage of the open space of a bomb site, to talk to the public.

Woolton also realized the importance of humour in getting a message across, and when food rationing seemed increasingly inevitable he enlisted the help of music-hall duo Elsie and Doris Waters. The sisters wrote their own material; fair-haired Elsie played a character called 'Gert' and dark-haired Doris was 'Daisy'. 'Gert and Daisy' used to appear before the microphone in their charlady clothes. Lord Woolton told them he wanted their help in making people see that food rationing was not a matter for perpetual gloom. So, in whichever town they appeared, the Ministry would arrange for the mayor to call a meeting to discuss food economy and 'Gert and Daisy' would join in. In fact, they did a lot to raise spirits during the war simply by their ordinary act. Ruth used to go to Reading to see them at the Palace Theatre. 'They always drew a large audience because they were so down to earth and humorous,' she says. 'They gave us lots of laughs in wartime when we really needed them.'

It was part of Woolton's mission to give the public facts, not to preach at them – for example, to state which foods were valuable and what recipes used them to best advantage. Mather and Crowther, the advertising agents for the Ministry of Food, held a meeting to decide the best way of tackling MoF advertising. No firm plan resulted from this meeting, but one of the young designers, Eric Ferguson, took home a layout pad that evening. An air-raid warning made it a difficult night for thinking, but when finally the 'all clear' came he took out his layout pad. He had been married only a few years and had two young children. In looking back to that night Eric recalls, 'I simply thought what I wanted to see, what I wanted to eat, what my wife and children would want . . .' The phrase 'Food Facts' came into his mind, and under that heading he designed a week's programme of what to buy and what to do in the garden and kitchen.

The next morning Mather and Crowther staff met again, but actual ideas were thin on the ground. When Eric was finally asked for his views

he could not get his words out and so instead pushed his layouts up the table. He recalls that his boss, Sir Francis Meynell, seized on them, saying, 'This is it!' Ministry approval was immediately sought and given and Eric set to work. 'Food Facts' appeared in all the daily papers and in the *Radio Times*. Eric designed twelve weeks of 'Food Facts' before being called up for army service, and he did another eighteen months' worth after being discharged. Then his wife found that they could not manage on the wage he was getting and so he left Mather and Crowther. He moved on and eventually in 1950 joined an advertising agency called J. Walter Thompson. By a twist of irony he found that this new agency was charged with designing 'Food Facts', and so he got to do the last ones which were published in the early 1950s.

The Ministry of Food also issued war cookery leaflets. These could be picked up in any Food Office. No. 1 promoted the use of oatmeal and

Gert and Daisy (Elsie and Doris Waters) share the microphone with their real-life brother, Jack Warner.

MINISTRY **OF FOOD**

THE WEEK'S
FOOD FACTS №3

Start now to collect these useful advertisements. Pin them up in your kitchen.

PLEASE make full use of the fruit and vegetables now so plentiful. It is important that we should eat home produce rather than food which has to come from overseas. *Never* waste anything, however small. *Never* eat more than enough. You'll be fitter, you'll save money, you'll make cargo space available for materials of war. *Every time you cook you can help or hinder Hitler!*

ON THE KITCHEN FRONT

HEALTH HINT. Among the protective foods, *salads* have a high place. Eat a salad every day while they are so plentiful.

BUTTER PAPER. Always scrape the paper in which butter or margarine has been wrapped. The papers themselves should be saved for greasing baking dishes or covering food while it is cooking in the oven.

REMEMBER that a plate of fresh home-grown fruit (plums for example) makes a refreshing dish. It will save fuel and will help to cut down the nation's consumption of imported food. *You can hear other useful time-and-fuel-saving hints on the wireless each morning at 8.15.*

RECIPE for Vegetable Hot-Pot
Prepare and cut into convenient pieces ¼ lb. potatoes, ¼ lb. carrots, ¼ lb. onions and ¼ lb. turnips. Put into a saucepan with a teacupful of hot water, put on the lid, bring to the boil and cook for 15 minutes. Then add a teacupful of shelled peas, ¼ lb. tomatoes and a few sprigs of mint, season with salt and pepper, put on the lid again and cook for 20 minutes more. Strain off the liquid which can be used in preparing a parsley sauce to serve with the vegetables.
Another way: If an ounce of dripping or margarine can be spared it should be melted in the saucepan and the vegetables tossed in it before the water is added to the pan. This much improves the flavour of the hot-pot.
Save food, spare cargo-space, save money!

THE MINISTRY OF FOOD, LONDON, S.W.1

Eric Fergusson's FOOD FACTS design appeared in newspapers during the war and continued until the early 1950s.

no. 2 extolled the virtues of cheaper cuts of meat. By June 1945 the Ministry was on no. 24, 'Drying and Salting'. More appeared during the austerity years which immediately followed the war. These leaflets were easy-to-read, sensible pieces of work. Ruth recalls that there was normally something she could use in them, and even if she did not follow the recipes word for word she could adapt them to whatever was in the cupboard, although she adds that in that place there 'wasn't a great deal in those days'.

As the Ministry of Agriculture had its county people advising on horticulture, so the Ministry of Food had home economics advisers. Their role was to encourage mainly country women to make full use of everything in the food line. They travelled round demonstrating how to make pieces of pig into sausages, black puddings and pork pies; how to paunch a rabbit, use its meat and cure its skin; and how to deal with poultry. They taught cookery and some also taught WI members how to make jam and bottle and can fruit. Jean McCredie Forster, who was a domestic adviser in Wiltshire, did the latter. For her 'fruit schools' there was usually a stove in a village hall but she always turned up with the fruit and utensils. Classes went well, although there was a minor difficulty, Jean remembers, with blackcurrants. Apparently some women made blackcurrant jam like they did at home – that is, they did not put in sufficient water, and the currants ended up like little hard buttons.

Cookery demonstrations in towns and cities were largely part of the National Food Education Campaign, launched in April 1940. This venture was the brainchild of the Ministries of Food, Agriculture and Health combined with the Board of Education. It had three objectives: to show how people could be fed by using mainly home-produced foods (dairy and garden); to demonstrate cooking and serving methods which eliminated waste; and to advise how to keep healthy on a wartime diet. Sugar and meat for classes and demonstrations could be had by means of permits from food executive officers.

In June 1940 cookery demonstrations and classes were arranged in many of the towns of Northern Ireland. Wireless announcements advised housewives to get details of the venues from their local Food Office. In Scotland the Women's Voluntary Service had a demonstration van which was taken to working-class districts.

Local authorities, gas boards and electricity boards also became involved. Gwyneth Silvanus of Salisbury recalls that her sister Mair Blundell was a wartime cookery demonstrator with the electricity board in South Wales. 'One memory I have was of my sister setting out to catch the bus to take her to various women's clubs dotted around South Wales – she would be armed with a bag containing the wherewithal to demonstrate a recipe or two and also a primus stove. The latter was essential, for most meeting places had no cooking facilities and even those that did could only boast a paraffin heater of doubtful efficiency.'

The Electric Power Co. of Shropshire, Worcestershire and Staffordshire had a Kitchen Front Club and its advertisement urged women to 'turn up at the first meeting prepared to help and be helped'. Throughout

FREE FOOD ADVICE *and recipes*

12 eggs a month for all

Women watch a Ministry of Food cookery demonstration given in a London store.

the war years Central London Electricity Ltd produced a series of coloured cards filled with tips and recipes, each card optimistically headed 'Cheerful Rationing'.

Margaret Weeks, who now lives on the Isle of Wight, recalls that during her wartime experiences as a teacher with Nottingham County Council she found herself being seconded for odd days to local collieries, her task being to demonstrate wartime cookery to the miners' wives. She used to take one or two of her schoolchildren with her to help with the washing up. The cooking took place in the colliers' canteen in the slack periods between meals. All ages came and she remembers that, with a family to feed, women were only too willing to come to classes to pick up new ideas.

Other teachers were called on to give lessons to parents in the schoolroom. They received official advice to rearrange the room to make it look less school-like. At this time Jean Neilson of Bath was teaching cookery at a school in Tottenham, London. One afternoon a week she was to have no children in her class but all mothers, and had to arrange a session teaching how to cook 'What we could get in the best way.' Basically she cooked what the Government wanted 'pushed' at the time, and in sufficient a quantity that the children who romped into the room at half-past three to join their mothers could taste it too.

Jean says that the lessons were as illuminating for her as they might have been for the recipients. One day one of the mothers said, 'I liked that oatmeal pastry you did last time.' Encouraged, Jean asked her what she had made with it during the week. The reply was a stony silence. Another mother came to the rescue with the explanation: 'We liked it, Miss, but 'e wouldn't eat it.' ''E', Jean explains, was the husband – and husbands, it seemed, would only eat what *their* mothers had cooked. However, the classes did work, for the women got together and swapped ideas and, not being short of conversation, turned the events into social occasions.

THE WIRELESS

GARDENING

Radio advice to gardeners took various forms. The Home Service included in its Scottish announcements seasonal advice for amateurs from the Scottish Gardens and Allotments Committee; and experts gave evening talks (for instance, Tom Hay, keeper of the royal parks, spoke on the importance of digging). In 1941 a midday programme designed to appeal to women was launched. It featured a Scotswoman and an Englishwoman discussing the problems of their gardens and how to cook the produce they grew. In 1940, when everyone was talking of 'Digging for Victory', the radio offered not so much advice as encouragement to amateur gardeners by broadcasting a play called *Digging for Victory*. The hero started off knowing nothing about gardening but ended up reading papers to the local horticultural society, and the play ended with the heartening quartet:

> *There's an obvious moral in Christopher Grigg*
> *If he can grow turnips, we also can dig*
> *So back to the land – and if you are able*
> *Contribute a sprout to the national table.*

Programme makers took their own advice when, in 1942, the outside broadcast staff adopted a 10-rod (90 × 30 ft) allotment in a London West End square. Listeners were treated to a running commentary as the likes of Wynford Vaughan Thomas and Raymond Glendenning began to get the plot into shape in their spare time. However, as a programme called *Radio Allotment* began, the site turned into a useful broadcasting location.

Most radio listeners of a certain generation remember the gardener-cum-broadcaster Mr Middleton with affection. Indeed it was a sad day on 18 September 1945 when the *Star* newspaper carried the following notice: 'By the sudden death today of Mr C. H. Middleton outside his unpretentious villa in Princes Avenue, Surbiton, radio has lost one of its most notable personalities.' Cecil Henry Middleton received, for his time, probably the largest fan mail of any radio speaker and, although he was only fifty-eight when he died, had achieved a longer broadcasting career than most. It began in 1931 when the Royal Horticultural Society recommended him to the BBC. In 1934 he started a series of talks called *In Your Garden*, each one broadcast at 2.15 on Sunday afternoon.

PRACTICAL GARDENING
As we are at war, almost everyone is either talking or writing about food production. Many of the talkers and writers are not practical men but employers listen to them on the wireless and read their contributions to the daily paper and consequently the practical gardener has no chance of doing his own job because his employer comes out and tells him what to do – he has seen it in the papers or heard it on the wireless. What hopes?

A Worried Gardener

From the Gardeners' Chronicle, *23 March 1940.*

Above right: Digging on the Radio Allotment. Left to right broadcasters Wynford Vaughan Thomas; Stewart MacPherson; Raymond Glendenning and Michael Standing.
Right: The *Radio Times* uses a cartoon to catch the eye of readers.

'RADIO ALLOTMENT' comes on the air again today at 1.15. Above is Ghilchik's impression of some of the O.B. team at work. In the centre Tom Hay is instructing Michael Standing, Director of Outside Broadcasting.

Mr Middleton, as he was known to listeners, was the son of a Northamptonshire headgardener. His quiet, low-pitched, easy voice betrayed his county of origin even though he had left Northamptonshire at the age of seventeen to work first in the seed trade in London and then as a student at Kew Gardens. As a broadcaster he was noted for his unflappable manner. It was a trait which, on one occasion in the early part of his broadcasting career, stood him in good stead. The studio clock was ticking round to the appointed hour but no announcer came into the studio. The clock hands reached 2.15 pm and the red light came on. Mr Middleton said quietly, 'This is the BBC national programme *In Your Garden* and here is Mr Middleton.'

Listeners liked Mr Middleton for his wry sense of humour and down-to-earth advice. It was a mutual exchange, for in the preface of one of his many books, he recounted the pleasure he received from listeners' letters. He cited a few examples: 'One lady tells me that since listening to me and following my advice, her garden has become "unrecognizable", while a gentleman writes to say that he likes my talks because there is nothing "brainy" about them.'

On the outbreak of war the Ministry of Agriculture was quick to see the value of Mr Middleton's talks and wrote to the BBC in some anxiety to make sure that *In Your Garden* would return after a natural break. The letter stated: 'It would be very helpful to us if he could get across the stuff we shall be putting out for the guidance of gardeners.' Even if Mr Middleton's talks had to include some Ministry propaganda, such was his skill at writing and delivering them that his popularity never waned. Three and half million listeners tuned in to him on Sunday afternoons.

During the war years he delivered his fifteen-minute talks from the BBC's studio at Evesham. He had to be at the studio every Sunday for

Above: Mr Middleton at the microphone.
Left: Wynford Vaughan Thomas interviews Mr Middleton at the Weston and Lois Weedon Horticultural Society's annual show.

with your radio dealer's help you can listen to

'IN YOUR GARDEN'

on your present set for a long time to come—consult him

A radio as good as Ferranti is worth holding on to at any time. And especially so in these days when the output of new sets is restricted.

make the most of your

FERRANTI radio

Above and facing page: Ferranti uses the programmes *In Your Garden* and *The Kitchen Front* to remind customers of the value of their radio sets.
Right: Burgeoning allotments on Clapham Common, London.

the purpose and in order to make travelling easier stayed in Northamptonshire with relatives. His niece, Sheila French, remembers him well as a jovial, smartly dressed man who became a founder member of the local horticultural society. In fact, she believes that he floated some of his ideas among local allotment holders before including them in his broadcasts. It was an onerous responsibility having Mr Middleton in their midst, and, Sheila says, the members of Weston and Lois Weedon Horticultural Society felt that they had to do better than his 3,500,000 listeners! Less impressed were Mr Middleton's brothers who regarded his status in the gardening world with some amusement. This was probably fuelled by the fact that Sheila cannot actually remember him doing a stroke of gardening but, as she rightly says, it was his ability to communicate that mattered!

Cecil Henry Middleton has several tangible memorials. One is a fine gate at the entrance to Lois Weedon allotments. Also fittingly the BBC has a garden incorporating some of Mr Middleton's favourite shrubs and ideas at its Written Archives Centre at Caversham near Reading. The gate to this garden was raised by public subscription and for years was set in the wall of the garden from which Mr Middleton had broadcast near the old Langham Hotel in London. When these premises were sold, Jackie Kavanagh of BBC Written Archives secured it for Caversham.

Lord Woolton realized that, in his attempt to devise publicity that would 'appeal to every individual woman in the country', he needed not only to use newspapers and leaflets but also to depend on the personal approach of the wireless. He knew that it would take his voice straight into people's homes and, once there, as he put it in later years, '. . . I could reason and explain, sometimes taking the public into confidence as to the reasons why they should take certain action, sometimes explaining government decisions.'

Professional broadcaster Howard Marshall, who was working at the Ministry of Food, taught Woolton how to use his voice and how to write his scripts. Woolton prepared with care, spending an average of eight hours working on what were twelve-and-a-half-minute talks. He admitted that, when broadcasting, he thought not of a mass audience but of an individual listening to him: 'In fact, I always kept a picture in front of my mind of the man in a cottage house, sitting without a collar, with slippers on, at the end of the day's work, with children playing on the rug, with his wife washing up in an adjoining room with the door open . . .'

It is to be hoped that the imaginary wife, relegated as she was to the kitchen, had keen ears. However, if she missed salient points she could always get facts and helpful food advice from *The Kitchen Front*, a radio programme specifically aimed at the working-class housewife. It first went out after the morning eight o'clock news on 25 June 1940 and was to continue on an almost daily basis throughout the war years. Programmes varied: one might be Ambrose Heath conducting an interview or giving out recipes and hints; in another Freddy Grisewood might talk about how to save fuel or make do and mend kitchen utensils. The Radio Doctor, Dr Charles Hill, spoke one morning a week, his topic promoting a healthy wartime diet. Humour was not neglected: some days the 'Buggins Family' or 'Gert and Daisy' did sketches which laced jokes with advice and recipes. At other times housewives from various parts of the British Isles were invited to give talks on their recipes; in fact, not only housewives – the Reverend Playfoot of Maisemore Vicarage, Gloucestershire, was invited on to *The Kitchen Front* to talk about his Vicarage Cake, which was apparently a 'wow'.

Speakers were paid 5 guineas (£5.25) and amateurs wrote down their recipes as they broadcast them. This stopped them reading too quickly.

Alas, many hopeful housewives who submitted recipes never got them on to the air. For example, a 1945 memorandum from the Ministry of Food to the BBC says of recipes for sugared almond fingers and plum trifle: 'I'm afraid that neither of these recipes is sufficiently out of the ordinary to warrant our putting them on *The Kitchen Front.*' This is significant, for it shows the involvement the Ministry had with the programme. All *Kitchen Front* recipes were tested in the Ministry's kitchens at Portman Square. For the first three years of the programme's existence the Ministry's hold was particularly strong and resulted in an uneasy

with proper care and attention your present radio will bring you

'KITCHEN FRONT'

for a long time to come —

Consult your dealer

A radio as good as Ferranti is worth holding on to at any time. And especially so in these days when the output of new sets is restricted.

make the most of your

FERRANTI radio

... Grandma Buggins on *The
Kitchen Front* remarked this
morning, 'Well, if you don't care
about the nice recipes I bring
you, I might as well go to Russia
and fish for surgeons in the
vodka!'

*From the diary of Miss C. M.
Edwards, Binbrook, Lincolnshire.
2 January, 1942.*

relationship between Ministry officials and the programme's producers. The Ministry was involved in the drafting of all scripts, and if given a script already prepared by a speaker could ask for alteration if it were not to its liking. It also wanted all mail received by *The Kitchen Front* to be posted on to Ministry headquarters. At one point the Ministry drew up a list of 'star' speakers, who included Lady Woolton and the Queen. The BBC was not particularly happy with the list and it caused a certain amount of embarrassment over who should issue the invitation to the Queen – Lord Woolton or the BBC. It is not known whether these 'star' talks took place.

Sometimes the Ministry's requests to the programme bordered on the ludicrous. In January 1943 Lord Woolton had said that he wanted the phrase 'Eat potatoes instead of bread' broadcast every day for a month. Ministry writers could get the phrase into *Kitchen Front* speakers' scripts on all days of the week but Wednesdays and Saturdays, and they therefore wrote to the BBC's director of talks asking him to instruct announcers to use the phrase on these days. The BBC agreed but wrote wearily that it hoped 'there was nothing sacrosanct about this phrase since it would be a little bare to say: "This is *The Kitchen Front*. Eat potatoes instead of bread. Here is Mrs Buggins."'

The Ministry's involvement did not stop there. In the same month it asked for a talk on swedes to be cancelled and to be replaced by a live talk on the use of green vegetables. Officials declared that they were acting on a 'policy directive' put out because of a glut of green vegetables caused by the mild weather. Similarly in the late spring a talk to be given about the 'kitchen front' in the USA was summarily cancelled as instead Lord Woolton wanted a food executive to talk about the hold-up in people getting their ration books. The USA talk was re-instated in July, ironically to replace a talk on milk cancelled by the Ministry 'on policy grounds' as it wanted no publicity about milk at that particular time.

Even such experienced *Kitchen Front* broadcasters as the Radio Doctor occasionally fell foul of the Ministry. On one occasion his script (entitled 'Spacing Meals') was delivered to the Ministry for approval at 11 am (it was due to be broadcast at 8.15 the following morning). At 5.30 it got the thumbs down because it mentioned that 'those who didn't have breakfast wouldn't work efficiently until lunchtime': the Ministry thought that this might cause trouble in canteens where men would demand snacks in the middle of the morning. The doctor, understandably fuming at this decision at such a late hour, had to write another talk for the morning.

Matters between the Ministry and the programme makers finally came to a head in July 1943. The first indication of this is a letter from the programme's producer, Winifred Holmes, to Ministry official Emily Blair. It begins:

Dear Emily,
I am so glad you have sheathed the hatpin, because I have really enjoyed working with you and am very sorry to hear that you have been hiding all kinds of grievances.

The missive ends tantalizingly:

> . . . what a joke if you had been staying with us for the weekend when your rage came upon you!

That was on a personal level; on a more formal footing Mrs Holmes wrote to her own superiors contrasting the agreed working arrangements made between the programme makers and the Ministry of Food with what had been actually happening. For example, in the original arrangement it was agreed that the programme should issue invitations to speakers and invite them to contact the Ministry for the preparation of the script. In reality the Ministry was approaching potential speakers and telling them that they would be receiving an invitation from the BBC. This, Mrs Holmes argued, led to speakers believing that they were working to Ministry orders and accepting subjects and scripts written for them, thus becoming 'the mouthpieces of the Ministry and its policy'.

In an attempt to build up listening figures Mrs Holmes had introduced items of general interest into *The Kitchen Front*: for example, what meals fighter pilots had before and after their raids. However, her continued efforts in this direction were being thwarted. Ministry officials wanted only recipes and policy talks.

The whole matter was a thorny problem. The BBC tried a diplomatic solution. It wrote to the Ministry saying that (not least thanks to the Ministry's efforts) people were in no doubt about the food situation, but where clothes, fuel and salvage were concerned it was the BBC's duty to give advice and information. This being so *The Kitchen Front* would change its name to *The Household Front*, and in future deal with food on only three mornings a week and with other household matters on the remaining days.

The Ministry of Food protested but finally accepted with the proviso that the title *The Kitchen Front* would still be kept whenever a food subject was discussed or when the Radio Doctor broadcast. In September 1943 the working arrangements between the Ministry and the BBC were reviewed and settled to mutual satisfaction. In fact, for the first time ever the programme producer was invited to the Ministry's weekly press conferences.

Its experience with the Ministry of Food had proved a salutary lesson to the BBC. Internal memoranda from that time reveal the Corporation's resolve never to let other official bodies such as the Ministry of Health or the Board of Trade gain such an editorial stranglehold as that secured by the Ministry of Food. However, when in January 1945 the Ministry of Food finally withdrew from its involvement with *The Kitchen Front* scriptwriting, the BBC's director of talks wrote a memo to his staff which contained grudging admiration for the men from the Ministry. He wrote that he hoped that *Kitchen Front* talks would be as good as if not better than before, although getting sufficient information over in five minutes was a highly skilled bit of work, 'of which the Ministry of Food scriptwriters have made themselves masters'.

At the outbreak of war all cinemas closed, but by December 1939 all had re-opened and people flocked to them. The make-believe world of Hollywood and Elstree helped to blot out the hardships of war and it was not unusual for film goers to come out of one cinema and go directly into another across the road.

However, war penetrated even the womb of the cinema. News-reels charted its progress and the Ministry of Information, combined with various other bodies, subjected the audience to propaganda. The Ministry of Food was responsible for fifteen-second 'food flashes', which might persuade people to try salt cod, or encourage them to eat certain vegetables. To drive its message home a 'flash' had to combine wit with brevity: for example, 'Winter means leeks. The kind you burst without heat. The kind which you eat until you burst.'

Gas and electricity boards sponsored films. One, called *What's for Dinner?*, featured a wife in a dilemma because her family was bored with repetitive meat dishes or lack of meat. The commentary directed her to buy a casserole dish because it 'cooks anything and cooks it well'. The film then shows how to prepare neck of mutton casserole with vegetables.

Moving pictures also played their part in the world outside the cinema. Working with the Ministry of Agriculture, Plant Protection Ltd made a series of five colour films under the title *A Garden Goes to War*. Linked together, these silent films showed a gardener carrying out garden techniques throughout the seasons, starting off with digging and ending with storing his crops. Showings were free. A typical audience for them was, according to the *Gardeners' Chronicle* of January 1941, 'one thousand two hundred people in an Ilford air-raid shelter at Christmas'.

BOOKS

Despite a paper shortage, a bewildering number of cookery and gardening books were published during and just after the war years. Newspapers did their bit, gardening correspondents such as Percy Izzard of the *Daily Mail* and E. T. Brown of the *Daily Mirror* putting their advice into volume form; and the *Daily Express*, quick off the mark, publishing its *Wartime Cookery Book* in 1939. Interestingly a number of people who bought that book admit to still using it occasionally today. The *Radio Times* published a collection of recipes sent in by readers and the wireless programme *The Kitchen Front* led to a string of books based on its talks, tips and recipes. The jolliest of these is *Gert and Daisy's Wartime Cookery Book*, written at the request, they admit, of those 'who didn't switch off when we did our "Feed the Brute" talks . . .'

Country Life magazine produced a series of books under the title *Home Front* and *Good Housekeeping* published books tackling such subjects as unusual vegetables and how a newly married wartime wife might budget and cook.

Facing page and page 51: Some of the many wartime books offering cookery and gardening advice.

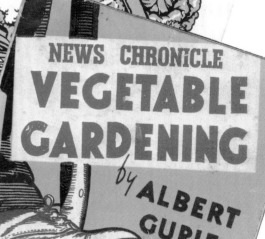

Fuel boards produced clear, sensible advice books on cookery, and food manufacturers like Stork Margarine, Brown & Polson (cornflour and custard) and Royal Baking Powder issued books of recipes which incorporated their products. Stork's book also helpfully included a page of tips on how to save your dinner if it was in the oven when an air-raid warning sounded.

In 1948 Lady Syonsby re-issued (with additions) her 1935 *Cookery Book*. At the time it must have made a tantalizing read, for it is filled with delicious-sounding dishes which incorporate ingredients such as fresh butter, thick cream and chicken breasts. Admittedly in a brief introduction the author advises the substitution of margarine for butter and top of the milk for cream, but even so the book must have seemed a touch over the top to 'austerity' housewives. A most eminently sensible book called *Easy Meals for Busy Days and Nights* was published by the director of education in Liverpool. It acknowledges that most women had shopping difficulties, ARP duties and other matters to occupy them and so concentrates on such useful topics as 'Saving time in the kitchen' and 'What to pack for the shelter'.

The publisher John Miles had the bright idea of getting over a hundred famous people to contribute to his *A Kitchen Goes to War*. Crime thriller writer Agatha Christie sent him a recipe called 'Mystery Potatoes': their mystery is deep, for superficially they appear to be just baked potatoes stuffed with anchovies. In 1944 Hutchinson published a similar book in *Fare-Ye-Well with Ladies of the Realm*, a collection of recipes from duchesses, wives of cabinet ministers and top-ranking women in the services. Each recipe is accompanied by a photograph and biography of the contributor. The book is more of an interesting social document than a practical cookery book, but it was produced for a good cause as all proceeds went to aid women and children suffering in war-torn Russia.

Well-illustrated gardening books were particularly valued by wartime gardeners and several have endured to present times. For example Mrs M. Batting of Salisbury inherited her father's copy of *How to Grow and Produce Your Own Food*, published by Odhams Press. She recalls that her father considered it to be his gardening bible and she too has felt the same about it over the years. Perhaps the most successful book of this type was *The Vegetable Garden Displayed*, published by the Royal Horticultural Society in 1941 and sold at 1s (5p) a copy. This contained three hundred photographs, taken at the Society's gardens at Wisley, which showed novices clearly and simply how to grow vegetables. In 1942 Royal Horticultural Society 'Proceedings' reported the book to be the best seller in the Society's whole history. By April of that year it had sold 125,000 copies and negotiations were under way to obtain sufficient paper (it was scarce during the war years) to publish a further 50,000. This was achieved the following month, but the rise in the price of paper plus 3d (1½p) for postage sent the book's price up to 1s 9d (8½p). The public were obviously not deterred, for by June steps were being taken for yet another edition, this time to be sold at 2s (10p), post-free.

Your own vegetables all the year round...

if y...

D
VIC...

fougasse

The KITCHEN FRONT

122 WARTIME RECIPES
broadcast by Frederick Grisewood, Mabel Constanduros and others, specially selected by the Ministry of Food.

6 D. NET

...ARDEN GOES TO WAR
BY STEPHEN CHEVELEY

Below: A cartoon from Peter Ender's *Up the Garden Path*.

"Another five minutes and it should be just right."

It is refreshing that, among all these well-intentioned books, one wartime author thought to bring out a volume consisting solely of spoof advice. He was Peter Ender and he called his book *Up the Garden Path*. Dedicated to 'the Government's Dig-for-Dear-Life Campaign', it is nicely laced with cartoons and contains such invaluable snippets as 'Devote a space in your garden to horseradish which, folded in half, makes an excellent stopper to gin bottles' and 'Never water peas in really hot weather. Fan them and unbutton their pods.'

COOKING STAPLES AND THEIR STORIES

MEAT

Pre-war food plans showed that the amount of meat eaten in Britain was 2½ lb per head per week. Roughly half of that amount was imported. The Government decided that in the event of war it would use mainly home-produced meat for civilians and imported meat for the services. Imported meat could also make up any deficiencies of civilian diet.

At the outbreak of war the Government bought all fatstock at fixed prices and slaughtered on the Ministry of Food's behalf in selected slaughterhouses. Following the rationing of meat in March 1940, its availability plunged during 1941–2, when it was 67 per cent of pre-war level. As regards imported meat, most of the supply which had formerly come from Australia and New Zealand was halted: it was needed on the spot to feed armed forces involved in the war in the Pacific. To make matters worse, refrigeration ships, because of their speed, were transferred to naval duties. It was at this time that ingenious methods had to be adopted to make meat smaller to save on shipping space: dehydrating it; taking the bones out and 'telescoping' carcasses.

Meanwhile the quantity of home-produced meat also fell. Numbers of livestock had become less, and because of a shortage of imported animal feeds, cattle were taking longer to fatten. Lend-Lease provided canned meats but the weekly adult meat ration fell from 1s 10d (9p) to 1s (5p) in March 1941. In July it rose slightly to 1s 2d (6p). By the late 1940s, when there was a world shortage of meat, the ration had come down to 10d (4p) for carcass meat plus 2d (1p) for canned corned meat.

Meat fell into two categories, grade A and grade B. Grade A was higher in price than B, and as meat was rationed by money, you got more if you bought cheaper cuts. There were, however, problems with these cheaper cuts. One was that young housewives simply did not know the names of them, let alone how to cook them. The Ministry of Food helpfully published a leaflet explaining the likes of silverside, brisket, salt aitchbone, flank, clod sticking, and hand with foot. Another drawback with cheaper cuts was that the flesh was coarse and some cuts contained a lot of gristle. There was also meat that was unduly tough, the result of the

Facing page: Unrationed meat might come your way more easily if you were charming to your butcher.
Below: Meat shortages provide a witty pun on this greetings card.

We very seldom "meat" now-a-days!

Government's policy of encouraging farmers to slaughter old, unthrifty cattle. Wartime recipe leaflets suggested various ways of coping with these problems, including pounding the meat to break the fibres, putting it through a mincer or steeping it in a 'marinade' of oil and vinegar before cooking. As to the actual cooking, most agreed that cheaper cuts should be done slowly. However, as Ruth pointed out, this meant that, although you might have saved by buying a cheaper joint, you used more fuel to cook it! The Ministry of Food, probably faced with such a criticism at the time, used one of its newspaper 'Food Facts' columns to explain methods of making tough meat tender without using the oven. One was to pot roast (cooking the meat slowly with a little fat in a heavy saucepan) and the other was to braise (a combination of pot roasting and stewing).

Cooking methods aside, the other main problem of the meat ration was how to make substantial, tasty dishes all through the week on such a limited amount. Again recipe books and leaflets of the time came up with helpful suggestions. For instance, it was recommended that dumplings or oatmeal pudding be served with stewed steak; that meat be minced and made into a savoury rolypoly; that the butcher be asked to bone a small joint so that it could be stuffed to make it go further. On the latter course the Ministry of Food coined the phrase 'Stretching by Stuffing' and came up with recipes that not only added bulk but also included body-building foods like eggs and soya flour.

Ruth's favourite way of making meat go further was to combine it with rice and onions. She explains: 'We used to do rice, boiled rice. Then a layer of fried onions and a little bit of meat. Then another layer of rice and so on, building it up to the top of the dish. It was a nice, tasty method to use.'

Not *all* meat was rationed. Unrationed meats were heart, liver, kidney, tripe, sausages, bones, trotters, heels, ox and pigs' tails, sheep's and calves' heads, ox cheek and plucks, and rabbit. Wartime recipes for these may have been nutritional but they have a rather gruesome ring – for example, sheep's head soup, brain fritters and cow heel pie. As to the offal items, sometimes these disappeared completely from butchers' shops. Ruth says that to try to get round this problem she had two of the family ration books registered with the village butcher and the other two registered with the Co-op. When the Co-op van came round it used to have a little fish and fruit and often a bit of offal which the butcher did not have. When the butcher did have liver he sold it to his customers according to the initial letter of their name and would work through so many letters of the alphabet each week. When there was no liver, the system stopped. When there was, he took it up where he had left off. He marked ration books to help him remember who had had their quota.

What Ruth's butcher did was simple and fair and perhaps others followed it. However, generally it seems that butchers enjoyed the power they held, for with some unrationed meats so sought after, women tried to ingratiate themselves with their butcher in the hope of preferential treatment. Mike Benson, a boy in Liverpool during the war years,

There's no wether on
  the tether
Where the wether used
  to be,
But there's chops upon
  the rafters
That Lord Woolton
  mustn't see.

They say it was the
  weather
That the wether couldn't
  stand.
It died of influenza,
But the smell of it
  was grand.

From the Stornoway Gazette, 1943, relating to the successful prosecution of a Lewis farmer who had killed a sheep for himself.

particularly hated his mother making up to the butcher when they went shopping. 'He was a miserable old b******,' Mike remembers.

Sausages sold quickly despite their uncertain composition. In the book *Nutrition and War*, published in 1940, there is the following witty observation on beef ones: 'It has been remarked of them with some truth that they are like life; for you never know what is in them till you have been through them.' The usual make-up of sausages was bread, meat, seasoning and colouring with some having more bread than others. Dolly Wall remembers that one day, when her cousin visited, she fried some sausages. She was very pleased with them because they were so plump. However, when they started to fry Dolly says they 'just went tiny'. Her cousin, looking over her shoulder said, 'Take 'em out before they disappear.' They had a laugh over it.

One sausage product that was dependable was American tinned sausage meat. Ruth remembers it as being about 2s 6d (12½p) a tin. She used to use it to make sausage rolls. The meat had the bonus that it was surrounded by a lovely layer of fat, 'so that you could make the pastry with the fat and then use the sausage from the middle'.

Ruth was also keen on Lend-Lease Spam: 'It was quite different from the Spam you buy today.' It was, other women recall, also 'different' from most other wartime foods and welcomed for that. Its versatility was also endearing. Spam could be used cold in sandwiches, fried for breakfast, and mashed up for shepherd's pie or brought out for special occasions. Elizabeth Cross of How Caple, Herefordshire, recalls that when, as a wartime WAAF (member of the Women's Auxiliary Air Force), she came home on leave, her parents produced a tin of Spam that they had lovingly saved for the event. She never had the heart to tell them that Spam was regularly on the menu in her Navy, Army and Air Forces Institute (NAAFI).

Before the war, conjecturing on what foods might be utilized should Britain be reduced to starvation level by enemy blockade, a nutritionist suggested eating hedgehogs, badgers, musk rats and snakes. A fellow professor, obviously believing that you should practise what you preach, had a foot of zoo python boiled for himself when it was killed at the outbreak of war. He ate it for lunch with potato chips, but came to the considered opinion that it was indistinguishable from boiled string. Meat from the zoo is not quite as far-fetched an idea as it might seem. Richard Bagshawe of Berkhamsted, Hertfordshire, remembers often being taken to Whipsnade Zoo for his wartime lunches. Apparently the zoo restaurant, which he says had a very good head chef and head waiter, used to serve venison from deer culled from the zoo's herd.

For those not able to partake of real venison, wartime recipe books provided instructions on how to make mock venison. It needed a combination of cold mutton, mushroom ketchup, red jam, onion, cloves and brown sauce. There are also recipes for mock goose (with breast of mutton) and mock duck. Peggy Stedman of Dorchester in Dorset used to make the latter. In 1943 she evacuated herself and her young son from Putney to Daventry and found herself a job in the canteen at the radio

MINT STUFFING

6 oz breadcrumbs
4 tablespoons chopped onion
6–8 tablespoons chopped mint
2 tablespoons vinegar
1 tablespoon sugar
2 teaspoons salt
2 teaspoons bacon fat
2 dried eggs, reconstituted

Mix all the ingredients together and use to stuff lamb or mutton.

MOCK VENISON

2 lbs cold mutton
1 teacup stock
½ wine glass mushroom ketchup
2 tablespoons redcurrant jelly or any red jam
1 tablespoon lemon juice
3 cloves
1 onion, finely sliced
seasoning
brown sauce, or any good brown stock

Slice the meat, removing all skin, gristle, etc. Mix all ingredients except the sauce and pour over the meat. Leave for 1 hour. Add brown sauce, boil for 10 minutes and transfer to haybox for 3–4 hours. Serve with potato on snippets of fried bread.

To make the brown sauce
Fry an onion and a carrot (both sliced) in some margarine, add ½ oz flour and stir well until brown. Add stock slowly, and seasoning. Simmer for half an hour. Strain off.

MOCK DUCK

1 lb sausage meat (pork if possible)
8 oz par-boiled chopped onions
1 heaped teaspoon chopped sage
8 oz white breadcrumbs
salt and pepper

Mix all the ingredients thoroughly and bake in a greased loaf tin for 1 hour at 375°F or gas mark 5. Serves 8.

MEAT RISSOLES

Margaret Clark of Burnham, Slough, Buckinghamshire, still uses this method which was enjoyed by her family during the war.

Take a cup of left-over cooked meat, mince it and add a cup of soft white breadcrumbs. With dripping from the joint, mix a roux: that is, melt the fat, put in the flour and stir briskly, then add about ¼ pint of appropriately flavoured stock (Oxo for beef, Marmite for lamb), gradually beating it in bit by bit until the mixture is the consistency of a very smooth but thick sauce. Add to the meat and the breadcrumbs, then spread the thick mixture onto a buttered plate and chill until set.
Cut into wedges and fry.

This recipe was used when you didn't have eggs to bind things together; but, of course, when well-flavoured and well-made, it is better than most rissoles because of the flavour from the dripping and the smooth mixture.

Pre-war, horsemeat was sold purely as dog food but the dogs in this queue probably only got the scraps!

transmitting station. She says that she used to make mock duck at the canteen, often in the middle of the night! It was served with apple sauce, roast potatoes, green vegetables and gravy.

Also in 1943 magazines make reference to horsemeat being very tasty, especially in steak and kidney pie. If that needed a strong stomach, worse was to come. In 1945 whalemeat reached the shops. One recipe book of the time, hoping no doubt to tempt readers to try its recipes, states:

> When we read of Jonah being swallowed by the whale, we never thought the day would come when we should be swallowing parts of the whale. We did not realize how tasty and appetizing dishes from whalemeat could be.

That may have been so, but I can find no one who has anything good to say about whalemeat. Ruth recalls it with adjectives that vary from 'awful' to 'terrible' and says that she used to soak it in milk to try to get rid of the fishy taste. Muriel Smith of Cirencester remembers that her family had it once a week to supplement the meat ration, but that it needed a good helping of onions with mashed potatoes to make it bearable. It seems that frozen whalemeat grew more fishy in taste if you thawed it slowly and it also became pulpy too. The secret was to use it at once. Ruth recalls it as being dark, solid meat – the nearest thing she can compare it to today is ox heart. Whalemeat was also tinned in various guises that included whale steak casserole, whale steak and kidney pudding and whalemeat roll, the last of which could be used in the same way as corned beef. If no-one liked whalemeat they enjoyed a joke about it. This went: 'A woman asked her butcher for "a whale steak, please, and the head for the cat".'

In the summer of 1943 representatives of forty-four nations met at a conference in Hot Springs, USA. They reached the conclusion that immediately after the war there would be a world shortage of food, particularly meat. By 1945 this was proving to be the case, and the only partial remedy was to decrease consumption, but America and Canada (including their troops abroad) were the sole nations capable of providing effective results by doing this. In 1945 the British ministers of food and agriculture went to Washington to ask if it could be done. Even so, and despite increases in British home production, meat stayed on ration until June 1954. In fact, it was the last food to come off ration.

A cheap cut of meat Ruth remembers buying during the war years was breast of lamb. Here she demonstrates preparing it, but says that years ago it would have been meatier.

FISH

Town dwellers might have thought that country folk, with their access to rabbits, eggs and the like, fared better than themselves during the war years. But Ruth remembers the benefit of town shopping. Not only was there saccharin in the shops to use as a sugar substitute but, she says, townspeople 'knew the minute that fish was in the fish shop and would go and get it'. Country folk, on the other hand, had to shop when the bus brought them to town, and if that time coincided with a delivery of fish they were lucky. However, even townsfolk had difficulties over fish. In Louth, a market town in Lincolnshire, the price of best cod in January 1941 was 2s 4d (11½p) a pound, whereas before the war it had been 6d (2½p) a pound. Because it was just below the fishing port of Grimsby, it would be logical to expect the fish in Louth to have been cheap and plentiful, but the fishing industry was not what it had been. Many fishing boats had been requisitioned by the Admiralty and some fishing grounds had been closed. Shop prices reflected the scarcity of fish. It was at this time, in 1941, that meat and other supplies were also scarce. By the spring the Government was compelled to step in and control the price of fish.

Moreover, in an attempt to cut the cost of its transport and spread the supply evenly, the Government set up the White Fish Zoning Scheme. There were five main zones based on the ports of Fleetwood, Milford Haven, Grimsby, Hull and Aberdeen. At each of these an allocation committee divided the white fish out among the primary buyers, who then had to distribute the fish within their zone. To stop them cutting costs by selling it at the nearest town, the Ministry paid all the transport charges and got the costs back by a levy on the primary buyers.

Although the zoning scheme saved on transport, it did not work so well in its other aim of making fish more available to shoppers. This was because fish catches could not be guaranteed and the number of people on which an allocation had been originally based was apt to change.

When fish did get into the shops it was not always what a housewife had been used to buying. The Ministry of Food devised the following cinema 'food flash' to reassure shoppers:

> Flat fish and round fish. Never mind the odd names, megrim and witch. If they are new to you it's because the new zoning scheme takes them to your town instead of another. Fish is now close to where it's landed. That saves transport.

There were other assurances. One of Central London Electricity Ltd's 'Cheerful Rationing' cards was cheerful about saithe or coley: "You can't tell a sausage by its skin", so don't be put off by the black skin of the saithe …' It advised steaming this fish, taking off its 'offending' coat and serving it with parsley and tinned shrimps.

Among canned fish pilchards, rather surprisingly, were new to many wartime cooks. Before the war they had been eaten more in other countries than in Britain. People were advised to eat them cold with a

---

SCRAMBLED EGGS WITH SMOKED FLAKED HADDOCK

2 eggs
salt and pepper
2 tablespoons milk
2 tablespoons cooked smoked haddock, flaked
1 oz margarine
2 slices hot buttered (or margarined) toast

Beat the eggs and add seasoning, milk and smoked haddock. Melt the margarine, add the beaten eggs, etc., and cook gently, stirring all the time, over a low heat until the mixture has thickened. Serve piled on hot buttered (or margarined) toast.

Submitted to A Kitchen Goes to War, 1940, by theatrical impresario Lupino Lane, famous for creating the dance, 'The Lambeth Walk'.

Lupino Lane

green salad or serve them hot, perhaps in a 'pilchard pancake'. Pilchards, like herrings, sardines and kippers, fell into the category 'fat fish'. The Ministry of Food produced leaflets promoting the health value of this kind of fish, particularly herrings which it lauded for containing vitamins A and D. The Yorkshire Council for Further Education was more down to earth:

on its 'Kitchen Front' fish recipe card it explained that fat fish protected you from colds and improved your eyesight, 'especially in the black-out'.

As to the other benefits of fish, 'Gert and Daisy' prefaced a chapter of fish recipes in their wartime cookery book by telling their readers it made brains. They said logically, 'It must do – look at the brains you want to open a tin of sardines'!

During the war years there were two kinds of fish which, despite Ministry of Food persuasive propaganda, never did become popular – in fact, it is probably true to state that they were quite hated. One was introduced round about 1944 and the other in the austerity years immediately following the war. The first was salt cod from Iceland, which was *very* salty. When buying it you had to remember to ask the fishmonger how long he had soaked it as it needed at least twenty-four hours. Even if he replied that he had soaked it well, to be safe it was advisable to soak it yourself for another twelve hours in cold water, skin side up. Elizabeth Cornish of Canterbury recalls buying salt cod *once* and adds that she never found anyone who could make it edible.

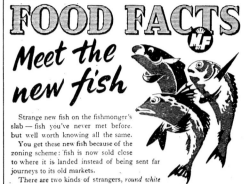

FOOD FACTS
Meet the new fish

Strange new fish on the fishmonger's slab — fish you've never met before, but well worth knowing all the same.

You get these new fish because of the zoning scheme: fish is now sold close to where it is landed instead of being sent far journeys to its old markets.

There are two kinds of strangers, *round white fish* (cousins of the cod), and *flat fish*. It is well worth while to look out for them in case they come your way. And don't judge them by their outlandish names or unfamiliar looks — beauty in a fish isn't skin deep! These newcomers have a fine flavour, are an economical food and are quick and easy to cook. Just follow the instructions given here:

CLEANING FISH
1 Wash fish thoroughly, under running water if possible.
2 Never skin fish before cooking, you lose so much goodness. After cooking remove skin only if very tough.
3 Cut off heads and tails before boiling or frying, but leave on for baking. Use head and bones for stock.

FILLETING FLAT FISH
When fish has been cleaned and dried, place flat on a table, and with the point of a *sharp* knife cut from head to tail down the backbone. Then insert knife in this slit and carefully separate the fish from the bone. Remove fillets, trim and cut into pieces convenient for serving. Use bones for stock.

BOILING FISH Steam whenever possible but if you must boil, place fish in warm salted water. Bring to boiling point and then simmer gently. Never boil fast or the fish will come away from its bones before it is properly cooked, and may be tough. Drain fish well before serving and use liquid for sauce.

LISTEN TO THE KITCHEN FRONT EVERY MORNING AT 8.15

THE MINISTRY OF FOOD, LONDON, W.1. FOOD FACTS No. 137

The other fish failure was snoek or barracouta, an Australian species. The Ministry of Food bent over backwards to promote it, appealing to a housewife's loyalty by saying that fish from Australia saved dollars; to her maternal instincts by saying barracouta was tasty and nourishing; and to her purse by making it cheap. It cost 1s (5p) for an 8 oz can and was not 'on' points: in vain. People joked that it came from Nuneaton and Ruth says, 'I think they gave it up as a bad job. I don't think they could educate anybody into eating *that*.'

EGGS

At the beginning of January 1943 the actress Hermione Gingold rang the BBC to say that she had found very amusing a book called *Take Forty Eggs* and she offered to do one or two readings from it. Staff of *The Kitchen Front* radio programme consulted with the Ministry of Food but were given the thumbs down – the idea was too jokey.

In fact, Lord Woolton, the minister of food, did have cause to take eggs seriously. At the beginning of the war they had not been rationed. This was because their supplies fluctuated and also the Ministry found it difficult to control their source. However, by 1941 the shortage of eggs

HOBART PIE

I can barracouta
8 oz tomatoes
4 oz cooked macaroni
I dessertspoon vinegar
I level tablespoon chopped parsley
½ oz melted margarine
seasoning
I tablespoon water
I lb cooked, mashed potatoes

Flake the barracouta, removing any skin and bone, and skin and slice the tomatoes. Arrange the fish, tomatoes and macaroni in a pie dish, with the vinegar, parsley, margarine and seasoning sprinkled between the layers. Add the water. Cover with mashed potato and bake for 30 minutes in a moderate oven.
Serves 4.

From the Ministry of Food Cookery Calendar, 1950.

WARTIME EGGLESS SPONGE

8 oz self-raising flour
2 level teaspoons baking powder
3 rounded teaspoons custard powder
pinch of salt
3 oz lard or margarine
2 rounded tablespoons castor sugar
milk to mix

Mix the flour, baking powder, custard powder and salt together. Rub in the fat and sugar and add enough milk to mix. Spread into two sandwich tins. Bake in the oven at 350°F or gas mark 4 for 10–15 minutes.

From Alice French of Oakley, Bedfordshire, who says it was her mother-in-law's recipe.

Facing page, top: Ruth carefully puts fresh eggs into a bucket of waterglass.
Facing page, bottom: A wartime tin of dried egg.

PARADISE PUDDING

3 level tablespoons dried egg
6 oz flour
pinch of salt
5 level teaspoons baking powder
2 oz fat
2 oz sugar
a little milk
6 tablespoons water
vanilla essence

Mix the egg *dry* with the flour, salt and baking powder. Cream the fat and sugar. Add the dry ingredients to the creamed fat and sugar alternately with the milk and water to make a soft consistency. Add the vanilla essence. Pour into a greased basin, cover and steam for 1 hour. Serve with jam or chocolate sauce. Serves 4–6.

From Dorothy Tanner of Hastings, Sussex, who says that this wartime recipe was quite nice and eatable.

was acute. Pre-war sources like Poland and China had been blocked; and home supplies had plummeted because the limited supplies of imported animal foodstuffs were channelled to cows to keep up the milk yield, resulting in a rapid fall in the number of hens on agricultural holdings.

Lord Woolton's 'spies' in food queues reported back to him that political agitators were using the egg shortage to create unrest. He was forced to put into action a plan for gaining control over domestic supplies. This entailed egg producers being paid more if they sold their eggs to packing stations than they would get if they sold them to the public. By June 1941 ordinary ration-book holders were allocated one egg as often as supplies permitted. Sometimes this meant one egg a month in winter, or in spring, when eggs were more plentiful, one or two a week. There was also a 'priority scheme' which entitled children, expectant mothers and invalids to a higher allocation. Small poultry keepers gave up their egg entitlement in return for poultry meal.

By 1944 the supply of home-produced eggs was roughly half its pre-war level and each person not under the priority scheme was getting about thirty eggs a year. One woman remembers receiving twenty-nine: she dropped one in the shop just after the grocer handed it to her and that was when the ration was one a month! To be given a dozen eggs at this time was riches beyond belief, although it did happen to Viola Williams. On her rounds as a War Ag. adviser a farmer asked her to get him a tractor, then, as she was getting back into the car, gave her the eggs. She could not obtain the tractor and blushes to this day when she goes by the farm.

To help ease the egg situation some were imported from the USA. Unfortunately, because it was unusual to get eggs from there, procedures over the first lot went a bit awry. In New York a huge number of eggs were taken out of cold storage, but because no shipping space was available they were left on the side of the dock. Eventually they were loaded into cold storage on a ship and brought to Britain. When they arrived, rotting in their millions, the smell was unbearable and dockers had to be paid extra to unload them. In some embarrassment the Ministry of Food secretly arranged for the entire consignment to be dropped down a disused mine at Skelmersdale!

Further consignments were not so unfortunate, but some women learned never to boil an egg (unless it had come straight from a farm). The procedure was always to open it to see if it was all right. Ruth was lucky because she got her eggs from a local farm, but when she worked for the Red Cross in the kitchens at Frilsham House, near Yattendon, Berkshire (the house had been turned into a forces convalescent home), she remembers a big crate of Lend-Lease eggs arriving. Most, when cracked, went off with a bang.

Not all wartime deliveries of eggs were disastrous. John Bubb, who was stationed in the Shetlands for the last two years of the war, often used to send his wife, Betty, a box containing either thirty or fifty eggs. 'The more there were, the more survived the journey to London,' she says, adding, 'unpacking them was quite something!'

PRESERVING FRESH EGGS

Shell eggs were preserved in the months from March to May when hens laid their most and supplies of fresh eggs were most easily obtainable. Ruth recalls that her mother used to call this time 'when eggs are fourteens' (that is, you got fourteen to the dozen!).

To store reliably an egg had to be newly laid or one day old at the most. There were several wartime methods of preserving. One was to use OTEG, which you bought from the chemist; it came with a pair of tongs. You used these to dip the eggs into the OTEG, a special solution which dried to form a coat of varnish on the shell, so sealing it.

The most popular way of preserving fresh eggs was to put them into a bucket or earthenware container and cover them with waterglass (sodium silicate). The alkali retarded the growth of micro-organisms and the silicate formed a protective coating on the shell.

'Shell eggs' was a new wartime word, coined so that housewives would know that these were eggs in their shells rather than dried or powdered eggs. They were to come into contact with dried eggs a lot, for imported dried eggs took up a quarter of the space of shell eggs and did not need refrigeration ships. The first distribution of dried eggs on a ration-book basis was in June 1942. For 1s 9d (8½p) you could buy a packet or tin which was equivalent to twelve shell eggs. Generally the allowance was one packet every eight weeks for an adult and two packets every eight weeks for children under six. Sometimes this allowance went up, and from July 1943 expectant mothers were entitled to three packets.

Dried egg had a mixed reception. Those who remembered 'Eggall', the powdered form of egg available during the First World War, were prepared to be unimpressed. Others, like Ruth, grabbed it with glee, pleased that it would help to eke out the egg ration. The new powdered egg was said to be 'a great departure' from the old sort and the Ministry of Food organized demonstrations showing how to use it to make

"DRIED EGGS
are <u>my</u> eggs –
my <u>whole</u> eggs
and
<u>nothing but my eggs</u>"

Dried eggs are the complete hen's eggs, both the white and the yolk, dried to a powder. Nothing is added. Nothing but moisture and the shell taken away, leaving the eggs themselves as wholesome, as digestible and as full of nourishment and health-protecting value as if you had just taken the eggs new laid from the nest. So put the eggs back into your breakfast menus. And what about a big, creamy omelette for supper? You can have it savoury; or sweet, now that you get extra jam.

DRIED EGGS build you up!

In war-time, the most difficult foods for us to get are the body-builders. Dried eggs build muscle and repair tissue in just the same way as do chops and steaks; and are better for health-protection. So we are particularly lucky to be able to get dried eggs to make up for any shortage of other body-builders such as meat, fish, cheese, milk.

Your allowance of DRIED EGG is equal to 3 eggs a week

You can now get one 12-egg packet (price 1 3) per 4-week rationing period — three fine fresh eggs a week, at the astonishingly low price of

1¼d. each. Children (holders of green ration books) get two packets each rationing period. You buy your dried eggs at the shop where you are registered for shell eggs; poultry keepers can buy anywhere.

Don't hoard your dried eggs; use them up — there are plenty more coming!

Note. *Don't make up dried eggs until you are ready to use them; they should not be allowed to stand after they've been mixed with water or other liquid. Use dry when making cakes and so on, and add a little more moisture when mixing.*

FREE — DRIED EGG LEAFLET containing many interesting recipes, will be sent on receipt of a postcard addressed to Dept. 627E, Food Advice Service, Ministry of Food, London, W.1.

ISSUED BY THE MINISTRY OF FOOD (S.74)

62

omelettes, savouries, fritters and so on. Gradually it found acceptance, so much so that Mr J. A. Peacock, director of egg supplies, was gratified to see one morning a newspaper headline with the interesting wording: 'Peacock's eggs make a luscious omelette.'

The general formula for reconstituting dried egg was: 1 level tablespoon of egg powder + 2 level tablespoons of water = 1 egg. *Good Eating*, a wartime cookery book which considered the 'dried egg cult . . . a fascinating and progressive branch of catering', attempted to answer the burning question 'To reconstitute or not?' The advice it gives is that in cakes, puddings and other dishes where dry ingredients are mixed together, the dried egg should be sieved in with the dry ingredients before liquid is added. Following this method made puddings lighter and cakes rise better and saved on washing up. In cases where dried egg *was* reconstituted, the advice was to mix it very smoothly and perhaps add a pinch of bicarbonate of soda or baking powder.

On the whole, dried egg seems to have been regarded by most as a godsend for cakes. Youngsters liked it for making scrambled egg and when eventually confronted with shell eggs were a bit nonplussed. One woman remembers that she had to re-learn how to make scrambled egg when shell eggs again became widely available.

In September 1945 Lend-Lease consignments stopped and in 1946 the Ministry of Food made a decision to cease supplies of dried egg. In March the Stork Cookery Service printed an 'Eggless Cookery' recipe leaflet, prefacing it with the words: 'It appears that we must be prepared to cope with being without dried egg, and also with not having enough shell eggs to spare for cake and pudding making.' However, the Ministry had not bargained for the ire of housewives who, seeing their dried egg threatened, held a demonstration and got the decision reversed.

There are some women who still prefer dried egg for cake making, although not of course using wartime issue. However, there is more than one kitchen store-cupboard which still holds the odd tin of wartime dried egg. The tins might be a little rusty round the edges and the state of their contents is unknown, but it would be unthinkable, after their fifty-odd years of tenure, to despatch them to the dustbin.

MARGARINE, BUTTER AND COOKING FATS

Lillian Harbard of Gloucestershire is very good on wartime reminiscences. 'At one time during the war I stayed for a while with a family who used to pass their chip pan over the fence,' she recalls. 'The neighbours would then top it up with a bit of fat, use it, then pass it back. It was a way of keeping a depth of fat in the pan. Everyone was so short of fat in those days.'

Dorothy Hinchcliffe of Murton, Cumbria, recalls wartime 'guleging':

I used to stay with a head gardener and his wife at a house near Kendal. One morning he said (he wasn't local, so his pronunciation had me foxed sometimes), 'Would you like to go guleging today?' I said, 'Fine.' So we put on wellies and we got togged up for outdoors. Then we took a couple of buckets and drove off. We called on a local gamekeeper who said, 'Yes, fine, all right, we're not shooting today,' then we went right out on what they call the Mosses, which is peaty land which spreads out into Morecambe Bay. It turned out we were going to collect gulls' eggs – 'gull-egging'! We got a big bucketful each, and they were as big as ducks' eggs. You'd think they'd be fishy, but they're not. I put them down in waterglass and had eggs for quite a long time. It was absolutely legal then, but you wouldn't be allowed to take the eggs today.

The reason for the dearth of fat was that, before the war, Britain had relied heavily on imported butter, lard and margarine. Foreseeing the difficulties war would wreak on fat supplies, the Government did take an emergency measure. Just before the war it bought a consignment of whale oil from Norway, incidentally pipping to the post Germany, which was also negotiating to buy it.

Whale oil, with other fish oils, was largely used to make margarine; the other essential commodity in its manufacture was groundnuts (peanuts). When Lord Woolton became minister of food he instructed ambassador Lord Swinton to act on his behalf and ask Nigeria to send groundnuts. The amount needed was formidable – 400,000 tons in a year. Despite this, the message came back: 'The people of Nigeria would see that the King's people at home did not go short of fat for the want of groundnuts.' True to their word, the Nigerians sent 400,000 tons.

Margarine and cooking fats were produced by Marcom, an association of manufacturers employed to manufacture and sell on behalf of the Ministry of Food. Margarine had the same fat value as butter but some sorts had not been 'vitaminized': that is, they lacked the 'sunshine' vitamins of A and D which grass-fed cows gave to butter. In February 1940 the Government directed all manufacturers to vitaminize margarine produced for domestic use. It then launched the encouraging phrase: 'Remember an ounce of margarine contains as much vitamin D as one egg.'

Although the output of margarine more than doubled during the war years, supplies certainly were not *ad lib*. Ruth remembers spreading it on bread *very* thinly. In fact, if there were a number of sandwiches to be made, she put it on with a shaving brush, brushing from one slice to the other so that there was 'just enough to keep the jam from soaking in'.

Despite the strides made in perfecting margarine, the Ministry of Food was aware of people's preference for butter and small amounts were kept on ration. Some of it came from British manufacturers and some from overseas, particularly New Zealand.

After butter was put on ration on 8 January 1940, all packets were marked 'National Butter'. The first allowance was 4 oz per person per week, but in the coming years the ration was to rise and dip, sometimes falling as low as 1 oz. Dorothy Hinchcliffe remembers that when rations were at their most stringent she had the galling experience of seeing tons of butter blocking the drains at King George's Dock, Liverpool. It had liquefied in the heat of a night bombing raid and run into the drain, where by morning it had solidified.

To help boost their rations many women saved the top of the milk: 8 pints could yield enough for 4 oz of butter. Ruth explains the method she used:

We had a very nice Jersey and Guernsey herd round here and the milk, in the old-fashioned bottle, had cream more than quarter way down. So we used to stand the milk and take that off and put it in a little jar – over about two or three days – then you just sort

Half-a-dozen young nasturtium leaves placed between two slices of bread and margarine make a tasty sandwich, especially for those who find margarine unpalatable. By this means improved flavour, vitamin C and other food values are supplied at no cost.

From Garden Work, August 1941.

WARTIME CHOCOLATE PUDDING

2 oz margarine
1 oz sugar
1 cup carrot, grated
2 tablespoons golden syrup
2 cups flour
1 teaspoon bicarbonate of soda
1 teaspoon baking powder
1 heaped tablespoon cocoa
pinch of salt
½ pint milk
A little vanilla essence

Cream the margarine and sugar together and stir in the grated carrot, syrup and the rest of the dry ingredients. Add milk and a few drops of vanilla essence to mix to a fairly stiff consistency. Put into a greased basin and steam for 2 hours.

of shook that until it became butter. Wash it out and put some salt with it and you'd got an extra little pat of butter for tea.

There were also ways to help eke out the fat ration for cooking. One wartime sponge recipe incorporates 3 tablespoons of liquid paraffin, and Violet Plimmer's book *Food Values in Wartime* (1942 edition) suggests soya flour as a fat-extender in cake making.

Suet was difficult to get. When making boiled puddings you could substitute very hard lard, 6 or 7 oz to 1 lb of flour. For pastry recipes which involved suet you could use half the recommended amount and substitute grated raw potato for the rest. Incorporating potato did have its drawbacks. You had to work fast when preparing the pastry because it quickly turned to a grey-brown colour. It was also advisable to eat the pastry straight after cooking because, if left, it became hard.

Mary Rankin of Salisbury was more lucky than most when it came to suet:

> As well as farming, my husband worked for the Milk Marketing Board and therefore visited all the local farmers, who knew him well. Now and again an animal died and the farmer would dress the carcass to be fed to sheepdogs and the like – there were no tins of dog food in those days. Any large lumps of suet would come my way in exchange for some of our fruit or butter or whatever.

Mary also put to good use the free cod liver oil issued to children at the time. Her children would not take it, so 'with all the windows open to let out the smell, I used to fry fish and chips. It was excellent for that. The smell did hang about a bit, but we didn't really care.'

This was not quite what the Ministry hoped to achieve with its cod liver oil. Its recommended methods of fat saving were set out in a leaflet called 'Making the Most of the Fat Ration.' This gives simple directions on how to render down bits of fat cut from cooked or uncooked meat and how to clean fat collected from the tops of stews and gravy. There is also a tip which advises against using fat for frying herrings or sprats, but suggests simply warming the pan and sprinkling salt in it before adding the fish. Ruth's comment on this last piece of optimism is: 'It didn't quite work out like that.'

Some American goods helped extend the fat ration. Their bacon, fattier and saltier than British, was valued for the dripping it produced. Nutritionists recommended using it to fry bread for children to give them extra nourishment. Mrs L. Roberts of Chale, Isle of Wight, also recalls the fat which was round tinned Spam being used for the same purpose. American lard was used by the food trade. Elizabeth Hess has reason to recall American lard, for six huge tins of it arrived in a consignment she was handling when she was organizer to the National Federation of Women's Institutes. It was a bit perplexing knowing what to do with such a large amount: 'I had to take it to the office and said, "Look, you must

Please Leave me Butter Alone

Everybody pinches me butter,
They won't leave me butter alone,
Nothing is better than butter,
For keeping the old man at home.
Everybody says I'm old-fashioned,
For keeping the things that are rationed.
You can have all me ham and me plum an' apple jam,
But please leave me butter alone!
Please leave me butter alone!

Written by F. D. R. Jones, sung by Gracie Fields and recorded on 'Our Gracie with the Air Force'.

Gracie Fields entertaining the troops in France, 1940.

find institutes that will take a tin of fat like that."' Eventually the lard went to people who could use it. If the recipient was a fish frier, it was probably gratefully received, for the fat supply to this type of business had been cut back by a quarter.

As the raw materials used for soap making were much the same as those used in making margarine and compound fats, soap went on ration in February 1942. The allocation was 16 oz of hard soap per four-week period, or equivalent quantities of other kinds. In July 1945 the ration was cut to 14 oz. Men's shaving soap was not on ration and Ruth says that she used to buy a stick to use as toilet soap. As to washing up, she recalls that at first you could not get anything to help with that.

> Soap rationed. Nora Cooper's nephew John Lloyd killed by bomb he was playing with.
>
> *From the diary of Kate Vickers, Birmingham, February 1942.*

We used to keep all the scraps of soap and put them into a swisher-thing that mixed them up. Then a product came from Australia – I think it was called Roo. It had a kangaroo on a little white lineny bag. It was washing-up powder. Although on ration, it was very popular. I suppose all today's washing powders stem from that, because it was the first powder I can remember.

MILK

> Instead of warm water [for reconstituting], mix dried milk with the same quantity of lukewarm coffee. This makes delicious boiled custard, using custard powder. Rice, sago, semolina and queen pudding are also delicious made with 'coffee milk' instead of with plain milk. Made rather thick, whipped with an egg whisk and put in the refrigerator, 'coffee milk' resembles a cold soufflé or is a good filling for a flan.
>
> *From Mrs R. S. Walford of Tunbridge Wells, quoted in the book Good Eating.*

From July 1942 onwards you had to stay with the milkman with whom you had registered, and in towns, to save on time and transport, the practice of several milkmen serving a single street was stopped. Instead a block of streets was allocated to a single dairy firm. If your block was not allocated to your usual milkman, you had to become the customer of the firm whose patch it now was.

The Milk Marketing Board bought milk from farmers and the Ministry of Food bought it from the Board. Once the milk was in its control, and before selling it on, the Ministry could say how much was to be supplied to manufacturers and how much was to go to the public. In fact, manufacturers received only 12½ per cent. The making of cream and ice cream with cow's milk ceased; chocolate production decreased and that which was made was of poorer quality. The remainder of the milk was divided up so that expectant and nursing mothers, children and invalids got almost half and the rest went to ordinary consumers.

There were several schemes for seeing that the 'priority' groups got their allocation. One was the national milk scheme of July 1940, which granted every child under five and every expectant mother 1 pint of cut-price milk a day. For some poor families the milk was free. To obtain the appropriate permits, women had to write to an area milk officer. Some of the reasons they gave for eligibility were so surprising that the recipients preserved the letters. One reads: 'Will you please send me a form for cheap milk. I have a baby two months old and didn't know anything about it till a friend told me.' Another, more brief, states: 'I had intended coming to the Milk Office today, but had fifteen children this morning.'

An unexploded bomb brings a milkfloat to a halt.

In April 1941 supplies of milk were guaranteed to expectant and nursing mothers and from October, under the milk supply scheme, this guarantee was extended to adolescents, invalids and institutions like schools. Mrs E. Robertson of Hampshire remembers that, having had tuberculosis, she was allowed ½ pint daily. She says that this extra ration helped with the family catering; it obviously helped Mrs Robertson too, for at the time of recalling this she was ninety-three!

Certainly in families with a number of children there was no shortage of milk, for a child's allowance was 7 pints a week up to the age of five years and 3½ pints a week from five to eighteen years. For those not able to claim 'priority', the situation was less happy, particularly in winter when milk was scarce. The Ministry of Agriculture tried to get farmers to produce more milk in winter by issuing notices in November and December which said 'BULL all heifers NOW'. Autumn-calving cows gave more milk in winter, and for this 'victory milk' the farmers could get high prices.

Ruth remembers a wartime encounter with milk on the move.

I was coming from the Newbury direction one day and there was a whole herd of cows out in the road. I thought it was rather dangerous, so I ought to call at the local police station. I knocked on the door of the police house and the special constables, who were there as well, came to the door. 'Oh, the cows are out down along the Newbury road,' I said, adding, 'there's about twenty or thirty of them, I would think.' 'Ah,' they said, 'well, do you know where they're going?' I answered, 'No, I didn't ask 'em!'

FRUIT SNOW

3 level tablespoons National
Household Milk (dry)
1½–2 oz sugar
4 tablespoons water
10 fl oz fruit pulp
a little flavouring
colouring (optional)

Whisk the milk, sugar and water together until smooth. Add the fruit pulp and continue to whisk for 10–15 minutes until light and frothy. Add the flavouring and serve. Half the mixture may be coloured if liked and served in individual glasses. If apple pulp is used, add lemon essence. If plum pulp is used, add almond essence.

From a Ministry of Food leaflet, September 1945.

When 'victory milk' was not plentiful, ordinary consumers could turn to a dried equivalent known as National Household Milk and to tins of condensed milk. The first consignments of these two commodities were distributed by milkmen during the winter of 1941. The following winter National Household Milk was continued at one tin per family per month. From April 1942 condensed milk was transferred to the points system.

National Household Milk was fresh milk from which fat and water had been removed. Apart from that it had as much body-building material and calcium as fresh milk. Despite these qualities it did not receive the acclaim eventually afforded to dried eggs. One wartime user remembers it as 'vile'. You made a pint of milk from it by putting a pint of lukewarm water in a wide-necked jug and then sprinkling and whisking in at the same time 5 level tablespoons of powder. Reconstituted milk could be used for making drinks. In its powder form it could be mixed dry with other ingredients to make cakes; steamed and baked puddings; sauces and custards.

Condensed milk was useful for making sweets, cake fillings and mock cream. The Ministry of Food recommended whipping it up with gelatine and fruit juice, coffee or chocolate flavouring to create 'simple "snow" type dishes with a party air'.

Ways of stretching your milk allocation were various. Soya flour whisked into a pint of water could take the place of milk in cakes and puddings. Milk in sauces could be just a dash added shortly before serving, its creamy taste kept by heating the sauce quickly and not boiling it. Welgar, which makes the breakfast cereal Shredded Wheat, advised saving milk by eating its product with hot or cold fruits. Another firm quick to see milk shortage as an advertising advantage was Bird's Custard, whose artists drew its logo bird leading a cow and captioned it: 'Bird's Custard makes milk go further!'

For those really intent on keeping up their intake of milk, the answer, if you had the right surroundings, was to buy a goat. Elizabeth Banks of Kington, Herefordshire, recalls that her mother took this step and learned to milk it by practising on a rubber glove in the bath!

CHEESE

Pre-war just over three-quarters of the amount of cheese eaten in Britain came from overseas. When the war cut off supplies from Europe, Britain had to rely on getting cheese from further afield, mainly New Zealand. An additional difficulty was that, with most milk being allocated for liquid consumption, supplies of home-produced cheese diminished. By 1944 all but 7 per cent of cheese was imported.

On 5 May 1941 when cheese was first rationed, the allowance was 1 oz per person per week. It rose to 2 oz in June, and in July 1942 actually reached 8 oz before tumbling again. The Ministry of Food tried to offset reductions in ration by decreasing the points needed on some tinned protein foods.

People doing hard manual labour and whose work debarred them from a works' canteen, such as underground miners and farm labourers, were granted an extra ration of cheese – although in later years it was learned that many miners disliked cheese and would rather have had jam! Rachel Thorpe, who worked for a time during the war on a fruit farm at Wisbech in Cambridgeshire, recalls how, although she used to pool her rations with those of her landlady's family, when her landlady made up Rachel's sandwiches she used to put in her 8 oz of cheese, saying: 'It's yours, so you might as well eat it.'

For those on ordinary rations, particularly when the amount was small, cookery experts warned that it was unwise to serve cheese with bread or biscuits. Instead the advice was to make tasty dishes from it. Not only would this make the ration go further, but because cheese increased the nutritive value of other foods with which it was used, it was also better health-wise. Ruth has a favourite wartime recipe which falls into this category: Cheese Pudding. She reckons that it is one of the few good things to have come out of the war. She remembers usually making it as a supper dish, but says that if it was made in the middle of the day it was useful because you could cut a cold slice when you came home or put it into a lunch box.

SUGAR

Although the Government bought large quantities of sugar from overseas – 1,250,000 tons in May 1940, the product of several countries, and 1,000,000 tons from an Egyptian entrepreneur – sugar in wartime Britain was not plentiful. Part of the reason for this, and certainly so in the case of the 1,250,000 tons, was that its arrival was spread over a long period. The output of sugar refiners Tate and Lyle dropped dramatically. Much of the plant at their Thames refinery was converted so that it would dehydrate vegetables for the Ministry of Food, and its fitting shops had to produce parts for guns. Their other refinery at Plaistow was kept going because it manufactured golden syrup, a product much in demand, particularly as it did not go on to the points system until July 1942.

When sugar was first rationed in January 1940, the allowance was 12 oz per person per week, but by May it had dropped to 8 oz. Manufacturers found these small amounts difficult and expensive to pack, and the shortage of paper did not help. Eventually only 1 lb and 2 lb packets were produced and the ration was made fortnightly.

There were two ways of boosting your sugar ration. At intervals the Ministry allowed a bonus for preserving fruit, or you could have extra sugar if you gave up your entitlement to preserves. For the latter 1 lb of sugar was equal to 1 lb of forgone preserves; later you could get only 8 oz of sugar for 1 lb of preserves. Ruth had charge of four ration books: her father's, her mother's, her daughter Bertha' and her own. She got extra sugar on two and jam on the other two. She remembers that her father hated going without sugar in his tea: 'That was really his worst sufferance

RUTH'S CHEESE PUDDING

10 fl oz milk
4 oz fresh breadcrumbs
½ teaspoon mustard
salt and pepper to taste
¾ oz Cheddar cheese, grated
1 egg, beaten
1 oz margarine or butter

Heat the milk and pour over the breadcrumbs and seasonings. Leave to soak for 30 minutes. Add the cheese, beaten egg and margarine and beat well. Put into a greased dish and bake in the oven at 375°F or gas mark 5 for 35–45 minutes until set and brown.

Ruth's Cheese Pudding.

CHEESE FRIZZLES

2 tablespoons medium or coarse oatmeal
1 tablespoon flour
2 tablespoons grated cheese
1 teaspoon baking powder
salt and pepper
water to mix

Put the dry ingredients into a basin. Mix well with enough water to make a fairly stiff batter. Heat a little fat in a frying-pan and, when smoking, drop in spoonfuls of the batter. Fry until golden-brown, then turn and cook the other side.

From Joan Pickering, Sudbury, Suffolk.

during the war, so everyone gave Dad sugar to keep him quiet.'

Managing to do without sugar in tea was a country-wide problem. Any number of people admit that they do not take sugar in their tea today because they gave up during the war and never went back to the practice. Gwyneth Silvanus of Salisbury is one of these and has even converted her husband. She stopped during the war when all her family gave it up so that they could accumulate enough to preserve their garden raspberries. Eileen Petts of Rochester, Kent, sacrificed hers for a more cosmetic reason: a teenager at the time, she dissolved her sugar ration in warm water and used it as setting lotion for her 'sausage' curls!

Wartime sugar supplies came not just from imported cane sugar but also from home-grown crops of sugar beet. In November 1939 the Government eased restrictions on the amount of acreage that could be used for growing sugar beet and many a land worker found themselves cultivating a crop. The beet was processed at large factories, usually in Norfolk. A Women's Land Army member from Huntingdonshire wrote the following heartfelt paragraph after a visit to Peterborough Beet Factory in 1943:

> As one tours the factory the atmosphere gets hotter and hotter and one cannot but admire the people who work under such conditions. As a member of the Land Army, I am quite content to help grow the sugar beet, although it means backaches, hoeing, singling and, later, pulling, knocking and carting.

Even some gardeners took to growing sugar beet. Seeds and advice on how to produce the syrup could be had from the Home Sugar Beet Growers' Association. Cookery and garden writer Eleanor Sinclair Rohde also supplied seed. She told readers to cook sugar beet in the same way as ordinary beet and recommended that they make sugar beet soup (see p. 159).

There were several wartime tips for saving sugar when cooking. Muriel Smith of Cirencester remembers cutting rhubarb into 1-in. pieces, putting it in a bowl with a liberal sprinkling of salt and then pouring hot water on it. When it was cool she strained it and cooked the rhubarb in the usual way, but it needed less sugar than usual. Muriel says that she kept the strained-off liquid which, when boiled in a stained aluminium vessel, would clean it beautifully. She also recalls using bicarbonate of soda to reduce acidity and so lessen the sugar needed for sweetening.

The bicarbonate-of-soda method was tried and tested by Long Ashton Research Station in Bristol. Writing up their wartime report, the Station's experts confessed to being mystified that more women did not adopt it. The method was to add only two-thirds of the sugar normally used when stewing such fruits as rhubarb, gooseberries, blackcurrants, redcurrants, raspberries, loganberries and plums. Then, when cooking was finished, bicarbonate of soda was sprinkled slowly into the fruit, which was stirred gently to avoid frothing. The ration was ½ level teaspoon of bicarb. to 1 lb of raw fruit. If the flavour was not affected too much, next

Saving Sugar in Tea
However well you believe you have stirred granulated or lump sugar in your cup of tea, there is always some of it which sets at the bottom of the cup and is only going to be washed up later. You will find that you can enjoy sweet tea and at the same time get remarkably further with your sugar ration if you do the following: when you have finished with your teapot, pour a little boiling water on the leaves and pour this at once into a little jar or bottle with granulated sugar. About twice as much hot tea as sugar. Cover when storing it. Shake or stir before use.

From Food without Fuss by Josephine Terry.

time you could try a bit more bicarb. Redcurrants and raspberries were apt to turn blue at their first contact with the bicarb. but regained their normal colour once stirred. For pie making, when the fruit went in uncooked, you dissolved the bicarbonate of soda in water and then added it when the fruit was put into the dish.

Other methods of sugar saving involved using substitutes like dates, syrup, treacle, small quantities of glucose, malt, molasses (supplied for agricultural purposes and, according to Mary Rankin of Salisbury, a bit off-putting to look at, being thick and greenish-brown, but nevertheless useful) and honey.

For those who could not obtain honey a recipe called Parsley Honey went the rounds. It involved sugar, water, parsley and a bit of vinegar. The *Daily Telegraph* carried a letter describing it as 'really good' and *Wartime Recipes* (Radio Times) noted that it tasted 'remarkably like honey'. However, Mrs E. Robertson, using a recipe which recommended 2 lb – 'an enormous bunch', she recalls – of parsley, 'boiled and boiled it', waiting in vain for the expected honey taste to develop. Unfortunately the result was so awful that no one could eat it.

BREAD

Lord Woolton would have approved of Ruth's Cheese Pudding (see p. 69), which used up stale bread, for wasting bread was something he aimed to stop. The spur to his campaign was the heavy loss of merchant ships suffered in 1942. In March alone, U-boat action sank 275 merchant ships *en route* for Britain.

Wheat took up the lion's share of shipping space, and to save space for munitions and also to save money, ways had to be found of cutting down on the import of wheat. As wheat was milled to make bread, that commodity became the obvious target for propaganda. Cinema 'food flashes' showed sinking grain ships and urged people to use potatoes to save flour. One flash commanded: 'Don't start cutting bread while there are potatoes on the table. That's it, my boy, help yourself and you're helping to save ships too.' Another relied on the single phrase: 'Don't waste bread – money and bread are both worth dough.' At special 'Save Bread and Save Convoys' exhibitions, diagrams explained that if every person in the country wasted ½ oz of bread a day it amounted to a ship-load of wheat every twelve days which equalled a convoy (thirty ships) per year.

Many magazines gave prizes to their readers for the best recipes using stale bread and the Ministry of Food issued leaflets with contents divided under such arresting headings as: 'Ways with Baked Crumbs', 'Ways with Soaked Bread', 'Ways with Grated Crumbs' and 'How to Use Left-over Toast'.

At about the same time housewives found that they had to get used to the 'national loaf'. Ruth recalls this loaf with little affection: 'The first day it was so moist you couldn't get it to cut any sense, and the second

To Keep Bread

Bread will not become mouldy in humid weather if its box is lined with kitchen paper and sprinkled with cornflour. This is especially applicable to brown bread.

From a wartime edition of the Manchester Weekly News *which awarded Mrs Bowman of Haltwhistle, Northumberland, 5s (25p) for this tip.*

How to Use Left-over Toast

If there is a slice of cold toast left, use it to thicken soup. When the soup is quite hot, put in the slice of toast and boil up together. If there are small unbroken pieces of toast left after the boiling, beat with a fork and blend with the rest of the ingredients.

From a Ministry of Food leaflet, January 1944.

Ask for NATIONAL WHEATMEAL BREAD *it saves shipping!*

A poster promoting wheatmeal bread.

A case in the paper today of a baker who had a permit for a hundredweight of flour for making rusks for greyhounds and he had intentionally baked too much bread every week and sold it to the greyhound owners as (stale bread). He had supplied them with 11 tons!! May he be suitably punished! He ought to be sent to sea with the ships that fetch the wheat and if he got shipwrecked so much the better! Six weeks on a raft in the cold Arctic sea wouldn't be too much punishment and here are we looking at every slice of bread and making do with potatoes wherever we can!

A case in the paper of a man who was buying (from two or three different bakers) eighty-nine 2 lb loaves a week! That's more than twelve loaves a day! (Four in the family!) He was well fined but no one seems to know what he *did* with it!

Two extracts from the diary of Miss C. M. Edwards, Binbrook, Lincolnshire. 22 January and 25 November 1943.

day so dry it cut your throat when you ate it.' Muriel Lee of the Isle of Wight, however, is kinder about it, remembering it as quite nice, darker than normal white bread but not as dark as wholemeal. Muriel's father was a baker on the Island and she recalls that, because of economies on fuel and deliveries, he was allowed to bake on only three days a week. Also for reasons of economy the national loaf was mostly tinned with a raised top: a cottage-loaf version would have taken twice the time and labour.

The national loaf was not invented suddenly; it evolved. Realizing that Britain imported nine-tenths of its cereal and flour, in 1937 the Food (Defence Plans) Department liaised with millers and nutritionists regarding how to economize on cereal and yet still produce a loaf which was palatable and nutritious. When war broke out millers were ordered to produce a grade of flour called 'national straight run'. This flour had an extraction rate of 70 per cent: that is, 70 per cent of each wheat berry which was milled to make it passed into the flour. In April 1941 the extraction rate was raised to 75 per cent. Synthetic vitamin B1 (aneurin) was added to the flour to help remedy the vitamin's deficiency in the wartime diet.

At the end of January 1941 millers had been told that the Ministry of Food was about to start a campaign encouraging the public to eat wheatmeal bread and that millers should get ready to supply the nation's bakers with flour with not less than 85 per cent of the wheat berry. The flour was to be called 'national wheatmeal'. People were not forced to buy bread made out of national wheatmeal and many did not, preferring white bread. A contemporary article reckoned that only one family in ten did buy it and that sales of the flour did not exceed 9 per cent of millers' total sales.

In March 1942 when the acute shortage of shipping forced a reduction in wheat imports, the Ministry told millers to mill *only* national wheatmeal and include in it the maximum amount of wheat germ. Another stipulation was that flour for bread was to be mixed at the mills and not by bakers themselves. Instead of being called 'national wheatmeal' flour was now to be known as 'national flour', and as it was all at 85 per cent extraction there was no need to add synthetic vitamin B1. However, from April 1942 calcium was added on a voluntary basis and its addition became

Above left: Display of National
Bread at Caxton Hall,
Westminster, November 1942.
Loaves were cut in half and
examined for their keeping
qualities.
Left: National bread was usually
tinned. Making cottage loaves
would have taken too much time
and labour.

DRIPPING SPREAD

Beat up 2 boiled potatoes with 1 oz of margarine. Crumble a meat cube and beat this in with the mixture. When spread on bread it tastes like delicious dripping.

Mrs. F. Owen, Cardiff.

From a wartime newspaper supplied by Viva Dewey of High Wycombe.

GARRION 'ROYAL' APPLE PIE

1½ oz margarine
1 teaspoon sugar
1 preserved egg
1 oz white flour
1 oz Garrion medium-cut oatmeal
½ teaspoon almond essence
2–3 large cooking apples
apricot or plum jam

Cream the margarine and sugar; add the whipped egg; gradually cream in the flour and oatmeal mixed; lastly add the almond essence. The result should be a soft mixture (too soft to roll out). Now take a small Pyrex dish – a shallow one – or the lid of a casserole and put spoonfuls of the paste into it. Spread it evenly over the base and a little up the sides. Have 2 or 3 large apples peeled, cored and quartered. Slice in sections like an orange and put a row overlapping on top of the paste; reverse the next row of apples, and continue thus until the paste is completely covered. Then spread with the apricot or plum jam and bake for 30 minutes in a moderately hot oven. Serve immediately. Most delicious and satisfying. Serves 4.

From the 'Garrion' Book of Recipes published by oatmeal and barley millers James MacGregor Ltd, of Garrion Mills, Wishaw, Lanarkshire, in 1944. This oatmeal recipe is the only one on its particular page, for MacGregors proclaim that it is 'worth a page to itself'.

compulsory on 1 August 1943. More calcium was put in than was needed to replace the nutrients lost in milling. The reason for this was two-fold: to counter the adverse effects of phytic acid in high-extraction flour and other foods (the acid forms insoluble compounds with calcium and iron thus decreasing their absorption into the body e.g. 10% of bran decreases iron absorption by half); and to raise the calcium level of everyone's diet.

Although it was vaguely known that bread was still palatable at an extraction rate of between 80 and 85 per cent, no real research work had been done on nutrients in wheat, particularly vitamins, and what happened to them during milling. By 31 December 1944 research work had made it possible for wheat to be milled at 80 per cent extraction rate without it losing goodness. Basically, as Jean Neilson recalls, this meant that you got the same amount of nutrients without meeting things in the bread you did not like and having them stick in your teeth!

Ruth had countered the above problem by sometimes rubbing her flour through a fine sieve. She says that the husks left in the sieve were welcomed by hens. In fact the bits left in national flour had in former times been taken out in milling and sold as animal feed.

One bit left in national flour caused some of the public consternation. It was the wheat germ. The Ministry of Food made much of its health-giving properties, but to most people germs were things which made you ill. It was explained in a radio broadcast that there were two sorts of germs and the one in the national loaf was the part of the wheat grain which in normal circumstances would germinate to grow a new plant. In short, the germ in the loaf was 'a bud, not a bug'.

There was one other health factor which weighed in the bread's favour. Some medical officers of the time took a stand that white bread eliminated vitamin E and affected fertility in both men and women. In fact they believed that this was what had caused the decline in Britain's birthrate from the 1870s onwards. However, it was not so much the bread's powers of fertility as its actual palatability which concerned most people. Ruth admits to putting plenty of jam on her slices of national loaf. There was not too great a shortage of jam, for the more bread was introduced into people's diets, the more the Government encouraged the production of jam and marmalade.

Bread was not rationed until after the war when there was a severe shortage of cereals. At the time Eric Ferguson was designing the Ministry of Food's 'Food Facts' articles which were published in newspapers. He remembers being given information on bread rationing and being told to design it in the 'Food Facts' format, but was warned that it was highly secret and he must work on it at home instead of in the office. Whether the Ministry feared an outcry at such a measure or whether it was merely to stop panic-buying of bread Eric cannot say. When rationing started on 21 July 1946, people had 'bread units' which they tore off when buying a loaf. It was a very unpopular measure and ended on 24 July 1948.

OATMEAL

The Government subsidized oatmeal so that everyone could afford to buy it. It was made from oat grain, kiln-dried and ground into meal (rolled out flat, the grain became rolled oats). Oatmeal's virtues were that it was home-produced, so it saved on shipping space, and it was nutritious. Housewives were encouraged to use it instead of flour for making scones, cakes and biscuits. The Ministry of Food also advised adding oatmeal to meat and vegetable dishes; using it for thickening stews, stuffing fish, meat and poultry and for coating fish cakes and rissoles. It had a slight drawback in that it did not keep for a long time, so everyone was told not to buy big quantities at a single purchase. If it did get musty, the remedy was to toast it in the oven.

Scotland was the main oat-growing area and the secretary of state for Scotland, the National Farmers' Union and Scottish Millers' Associations promoted it enthusiastically. Part of their campaign was to get Scots schoolgirls used to cooking with it, and to that end they initiated a competition for dishes made from oatmeal, with a section of the competition devoted to the other national product, potatoes. Girls from schools all over Scotland entered and the prize-giving ceremony took place at Edinburgh College of Domestic Science on 29 July 1943. The king and queen attended and the queen presented the prizes. Winning recipes and the queen's message of encouragement to prize winners are recorded in the 1944 publication, *Dainty Dishes for the Queen*. In her message the queen makes special mention of porridge: 'I can imagine now the many Scotsmen fighting so gallantly abroad who are thinking longingly of the familiar breakfast at home with a good bowl of porridge.'

Ruth, working for the Red Cross at Frilsham House, made porridge for the breakfast of convalescent servicemen, no doubt Scotsmen among them. She recalls:

> We used to get this allocation of oatmeal and we made porridge in a big steamer container with a bucket thing on top. We used to put it on at night to cook slowly all night. Well, I don't know what happened, but I don't think we ever really got it right. I don't know if anyone did afterwards, but one night you could stand on top of it and do a clog dance, and the next night you'd think, 'Well, we won't put as much oatmeal in,' and then you could fall to the bottom of it immediately! You couldn't seem to get a balance between the two. But I'm not an oatmeal porridge maker; I'm better with Quaker Oats or something like that.

OATMEAL GINGERBREAD

This recipe, submitted to an oatmeal cookery competition by Janet B. Henry of Mearns Public School, made her School and County Champion of the County of Renfrew and was published in *Dainty Dishes for the Queen*

2 oz flour
2 oz wheaten flour
2 oz oatmeal
1½ oz margarine
1 oz brown sugar
pinch of salt
¾ teaspoon ground cinnamon
¾ teaspoon baking soda
½ teaspoon ground ginger
¾ tablespoon syrup
¾ tablespoon treacle
boiling water to mix

Mix the flours and oatmeal, rub in the fat, add all the other dry ingredients and mix well. Add the heated syrup and treacle, stir into the mixture and add enough boiling water to make a soft consistency. Bake in a moderate oven for about 30 minutes till well risen and firm. Cool and store in an air-tight tin for a few days before cutting.

SWISS BREAKFAST DISH

8 level tablespoons rolled oats
3–4 tablespoons evaporated or top milk
2 level tablespoons sugar
4 apples, grated, or 4 tablespoons dried fruit or 4 tablespoons grated raw carrot + lemon substitute or 4 tablespoons fresh fruit

Mix the rolled oats with barely enough water to cover and leave overnight. Just before serving add the milk, sugar and fruit and mix well.

CHAPTER FIVE

WARTIME GARDENERS

PROFESSIONALS

In the autumn of 1939, when Harry was obliged to give up his job as garden journeyman at Ashburnham House and go to Chichester barracks to join up, young gardeners all over the country were having similar experiences. Only gardeners aged twenty-five years or over were exempt from call-up; from that age they were classed as 'reserved'. In September 1939 this reserved category applied to such horticultural workers as foreman gardeners, general hands, jobbing gardeners, fruit farm workers, nurserymen and bulb growers. By June 1940 the importance of food production had brought the reserved age down to twenty-one years, but certain jobs, including that of gardener and bulb grower, had their reservation status partly or wholly withdrawn.

If a man was called up but held a key post in a garden or nursery, his employers could apply to the local War Agricultural Executive Committee for six months' postponement. This allowed the employer time to find a replacement. A retired gardener, looking back recalls that he was lucky: after six months' postponement his case was reviewed and he was allowed to stay at his job; this happened every six months. He puts it down to the fact that he was working for some 'rather prominent people' who knew people on the War Ag. Committee. Others were not so lucky. Part of the late Ron Sidwell's job as Ministry inspector in the Vale of Evesham was to report on horticultural workers liable for military service. He remembered that with *bona fide* commercial growers he often agreed to one or two sons being put on the reserve list. However, sometimes a man would bring his family from Birmingham, buy a plot of land and then claim that the son should not be sent to join the forces. Ron had to assess the situation and generally the boy would be refused exemption.

These were topsy-turvy days for the headgardeners in large private gardens. Not only were they losing the core of their workforce but the remaining undergardeners were starting to earn as much as themselves. This came about because most garden hands were on agricultural rates and the Government, anxious to keep up food production, increased farm workers' wages substantially. By 1945 the agricultural wage had risen by over 90 per cent since the outbreak of war, which meant that whereas in 1939 an undergardener earned £1 14s 0d (£1.70) a week, by September 1945 his minimum wage was £3 10s 0d (£3.50). Headgardeners were not always treated so well and many employers, instead of raising their wages,

Facing page: Anya gathers broad beans at Chilton.

told them that they could have commission on sales of garden produce. To add insult to injury the Government expected headgardeners to spend any spare time they had training allotment holders.

In fact novices were a sore point to many headgardeners, for they found that they were having to contend with them within their working hours. An irate headgardener wrote the following to the *Gardeners' Chronicle* in October 1941:

> Many gardeners with life experience have now to train young lady gardeners sent out from horticultural schools, women's farm and garden associations, etc. to fill up the places of men called up. Some of these girls are very good, but others have had little or no training. A gardener is expected to give practical experience acquired by him during twenty or thirty years to these girls. The gardener is expected to do all this for the ordinary gardener's small wage! Yet men who train girls at the machine or bench are paid an instructor's wage of £7 or £8 per week. Is this fair?

If this was the general feeling, it is no wonder some young women got a mixed reception. Bridget Andrew of Newport in Shropshire went from being a student at Swanley Horticultural College, Kent, to work in the gardens of a big house near Wheatley, Oxfordshire. She recalls how at college all the girl students had been told that they should work under a good headgardener, but when this actually happened to her she found the headgardener a taciturn man. However, she says charitably, 'He probably didn't find the situation easy and it would I expect have been different if I'd been the normal garden boy.' Dorothy Pembridge of Malvern, Worcestershire, was a member of the Women's Land Army and during the war years worked in the gardens of Madresfield Court near Malvern. She remembers that the headgardener there saw a woman driving the bread van and said he 'didn't want any damn women around'. Dorothy goes on, 'But soon there were five of us, as the men were called up. After five years I heard the boss shouting at a deaf farmer: "What you want, Bill, is a couple of good land girls!"'

WOMEN GARDENERS

Women gardeners fell roughly into three categories: those who had studied horticulture in colleges such as Swanley in Kent or Studley in Warwickshire; those who had got their job through an agency known as the Women's Farm and Garden Association; and those who were members of the Women's Land Army.

COLLEGE STUDENTS

Owing to their horticultural training, female college students were often given glasshouse work, particularly at Kew Gardens which had been formerly a strictly male preserve (although a few women had been temporarily employed during the First World War). The students' other

WOMEN!

Farmers can't grow all your vegetables

BROCCOLI
POTATOES
CABBAGE
WHEAT
ONIONS
FODDER FOR DAIRY COWS
BRUSSELS SPROUTS
BARLEY for BREAD

YOU MUST GROW YOUR OWN

Farmers are growing more of the other essential crops — potatoes, corn for your bread and food for the cows. It's up to *you* to provide the vegetables that are vital to your children's health —especially in winter. Grow all you can. If you don't, they may go short. Turn your garden over to vegetables. Get the older children to help you. If you haven't a garden ask your local council for an allotment. DO IT NOW.

DIG
for Victory

ISSUED BY THE MINISTRY OF AGRICULTURE

advantages are recalled by Miss J. E. H. Dunn of Dorking, Surrey: 'Women gardeners were very much wanted – they did less damage than men and they were educated and could live with the family.'

This social asset is something that Anne Kenrick of Birmingham recalls. An ex-Swanley girl, she worked for two and a half years as headgardener at a public school, Winchester College, where she lived 'below stairs during working hours and upstairs after hours'. Anne had to do twenty-two hours of food production a week. This qualified her as 'reserved' and she did not get called up. Her job involved supplying the headmaster's cook with fruit and vegetables, producing flowers for the chapel and mowing lawns. The latter job she hated, particularly when it was in the courtyard in full view of everyone. She had an uneasy relationship with the cook, to whom lady headgardeners must have been a new phenomenon. Susan Cokayne of Wells, Somerset, worked in similar circumstances to Anne and agrees on a cook's power. In her experience the cook 'shredded the gardener; you were lower than the low. When you were given your coffee in the morning it was often banged down and your boots were looked on with disfavour.'

Ex-Swanley student Netta Shallcross examining rubber plants for bugs in a glasshouse at Kew Gardens. Her colleague Myrtle Speake syringes any finds.

Apart from their disfavoured boots, Swanley students wore breeches laced at the knee with long stockings, an Airtex shirt, a tie and a thick green pullover. Their tailored coats had leather patches. The breeches, Bridget Andrew recalls, were uncomfortable behind the knee when you were gardening. In summer the uniform was brown dungarees. Studley's outfit was similar: khaki breeches, also laced at the knee, and a khaki overall with a leather belt. Ex-Studley student Marion Hall of Dymock, Gloucestershire, describes her summer overall as being of a horrible sacking material, but eventually this was changed to dungarees. She also recalls that the uniform included a rather nice green coat.

Wages for professional women gardeners were not high and the work was hard. However, it appears that the students had a grounding in hard work. Swanley students of 1942–3 had to double-dig the college's tennis courts for vegetable growing. The ground was clay and they were given mattocks to help with the bottom layer. Even flower gardening seems to have been unduly laborious: when their rock garden full of couch and bindweed was dug, all the soil had to be sieved. Despite being used to hard work, once out at their various posts they occasionally found life depressing. Anne Kenrick says, 'When I was at Winchester I sowed some lettuce in a tray and when I was at my most gloomy went in to look at it. I thanked God, for among all the wartime dismalness the seeds had germinated. If they hadn't, I would have felt that all my knowledge had come to nothing.'

College-trained young women also found jobs as technical assistants, mainly working in plant protection. Joy Le Mare of Cumbria recalls that she was the first-ever female technical assistant at Hawthorndale Laboratories (ICI), Bracknell, Berkshire. She worked at laboratory, greenhouse and field experiments connected with the development of BHC (gammexane) as an insecticide on food crops.

When the war ended many of these professional women had proved their worth and career-wise had opened up doors for other women.

WOMEN'S FARM AND GARDEN ASSOCIATION MEMBERS

Members of the Women's Farm and Garden Association generally worked under college-trained women. They were often very young and had chosen the Association as their route to gardening because they were not old enough to join the Women's Land Army. The Association ran an apprenticeship scheme which gave six months' grounding under a headgardener in a private garden or on an estate. Once an apprentice was trained, the Association found her a place as an undergardener. In June 1941 there were forty apprentices and over sixty gardens on the Association's lists. Training costs at that time were borne by the president of the Association, Lady Lucas.

The Women's Farm and Garden Association, which is still in existence today, was founded in 1899. One of its main objects when starting was to unite all professional women interested in farming, gardening, poultry keeping and dairying. During the war years its head-quarters were in London (where members got the benefit of cheap accommodation in the Association's hostel when visiting the capital), but regional and local organizers arranged meetings for members in their area and occasional residential weekend conferences. In 1943 one conference at St Albans offered lectures which ranged from 'Market Gardening' to 'Advances in Farming Methods'. However, Viola Williams remembers that the WF&GA's role was not so much educational as placing women in jobs: 'It wasn't easy for women to get jobs, even during the war, if there was the option of a man or woman.' Viola, who later became a regional organizer, got her first two jobs through the Association.

WOMEN'S LAND ARMY MEMBERS

The Women's Land Army was first formed in 1917, and for the Second World War a similar workforce was recruited from May 1939. Its members came from all walks of life: some already had knowledge of land work, but many had spent their previous working days in towns and cities. At full strength during the Second World War, the Women's Land Army had approximately 90,000 members. Each member was allowed one week's holiday with pay per year and a wage (if aged over eighteen) of roughly £3 a week out of which had to come payment for digs.

Farmers had first call on employing Land Army members but they were also employed in large private gardens if their work involved so many hours a week on food production.

Before going to a garden a young woman had a month's training at a farm institute or college. Sybil Van Praet of Llanelli went for her month to Rodbaston Agricultural College in Staffordshire, then joined the garden staff at Broughton Hall, a big house on the Staffordshire/Shropshire border. The house held a boys' prep. school evacuated from Eastbourne; the garden staff had to grow produce to supply pupils and teachers. Sybil remembers that the staff consisted of 'headgardener Mr Lowe; one elderly gardener, Mr Sawyer; and me – a very "green" land girl.'

A cartoon from *The Land Girl* magazine.

Dorothy Pembridge spent her Land Girl days in the gardens of Madresfield Court near Malvern. Her mother had been nurse to the Beauchamp family, owners of the Madresfield estate. During the war years the garden grew a certain amount of produce for outside sale. Dorothy recalls that in May 1941, when all the young male gardeners had been called up, an ex-Studley girl and four Land Army girls (including herself) moved into the garden bothy, the house where the men had lived. They inherited the men's cat, Tiger.

Muriel Bushby (*née* Merritt) of Sidlesham, West Sussex, was working in a solicitor's office when she volunteered. She admits to having been puny and told the Land Army recruiting office that she did not want to go on to a farm and do milking but would like to work in gardens. She was sent to Warnham Lodge, a big house near Horsham in West Sussex. In fact there were two houses, for the owners had built a new one at the

Must you do homework every evening, dear?

back of the old. The old house and its outbuildings had been taken over by the Ministry of Food and used as a cheese store – 'very high at times', Muriel remembers. She found that she had replaced a gardener called Henry Burridge who had been called up into the army. She lodged with his wife in a house opposite the gardens.

Other land girls were sent to commercial nurseries and market gardens. One of these was Lillian Harbard (*née* Butcher) of Bow in London. Her father worked at Bryant and May, the match makers, and the family had a house in the works. Lillian also worked for the firm in their accounts department. She was living in Bow during the blitz and recalls, 'Meal times were interrupted by air-raid warnings and I rarely slept because I was a first aid/fire warden.' The cellars beneath the factory provided a shelter for the thousands of people who lived around Bow. Lillian can remember often being in the cellars when the top of the building was alight, calmly thinking, 'Well, this is it, this is the end.' For as long as she could remember she had wanted to work in the countryside, and despite protests from Bryant and May went to the Women's Land Army recruitment centre. The recruiting officers tried to persuade her not to join because she looked so frail. Lillian says they obviously thought that, like a lot of girls, she would leave after only six weeks, but she refused to be dissuaded and joined. Her friends thought she was mad, going to maroon herself out in the country miles from anywhere. When they heard that she had a posting just down the road to Slough, to work at the trial grounds of Sutton's Seeds, they roared with laughter.

A photograph from the album of Beryl Roke (née Jarvis) who worked as a land girl at a large market garden in Surrey.

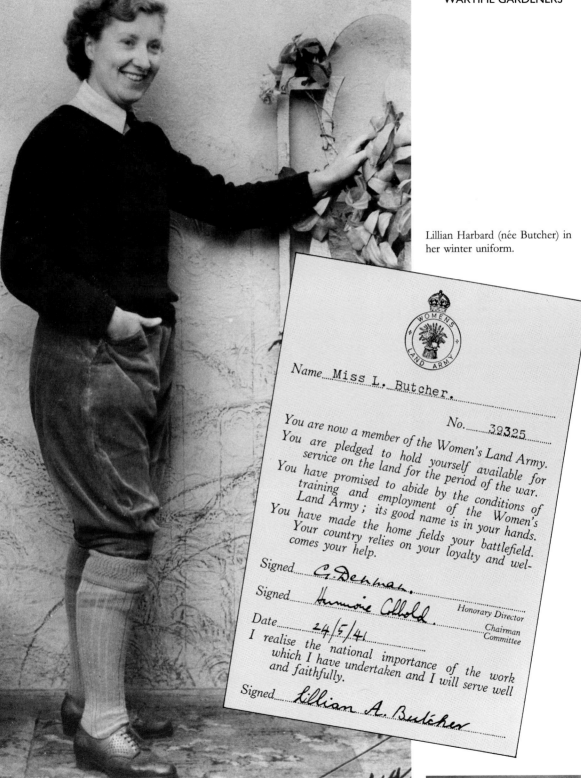

Lillian Harbard (née Butcher) in her winter uniform.

Name Miss L. Butcher.

No. 39325

You are now a member of the Women's Land Army. You are pledged to hold yourself available for service on the land for the period of the war. You have promised to abide by the conditions of training and employment of the Women's Land Army; its good name is in your hands. You have made the home fields your battlefield. Your country relies on your loyalty and welcomes your help.

Signed *C. Denman*.

Signed *Hermione Colhold*.

Honorary Director

Chairman Committee

Date 24/5/41

I realise the national importance of the work which I have undertaken and I will serve well and faithfully.

Signed *Lillian A. Butcher*

Tips from the Land Girl, the
Women's Land Army magazine

Make and Mend: Socks
Instead of darning wool collect
the soft cotton thread chain-
stitched across artificial manure
sacks and use instead; it wears
well and costs nothing. . . The
cotton thread will also do to
darn WLA shirts, being just the
right colour.

Elaine R. Bullard, WLA 28860,
Hampshire. February 1942.

Thermos Flasks
If your Thermos flask breaks and
you cannot replace it for a time,
here is a substitute. Take a pair
of really worn-out Land Army
stockings, cut off the feet, place
one leg inside the other and
seam up the bottoms from
inside. Measure a lemonade
bottle and cut cardboard or
corrugated paper the same
length. Roll into a tube and slip
between the two stocking legs,
forming a container with wool
inside and out. Put the hot drink
in the lemonade bottle, slip into
the stockings, pin over the top
and it will keep hot for several
hours.

B. Puzey, WLA 1453, Dorset.
January 1943.

For a healthy, happy job

Join the
WOMEN'S
LAND
ARMY

Above right: A recruiting poster
for the Women's Land Army.
Facing page: Anya gets used to
her *bona fide* land army dungarees
supplied by the BBC Costume
Department.

Lillian recalls that her first outing wearing her new uniform was to
Paddington Station. She had on breeches which were laced at the knee
and a pair of long socks which came up to meet them. Her chief worry
throughout the journey was trying to stop her socks from parting company
with the breeches! Later she solved this problem by making herself a pair
of garters.

Once a girl had resolved the garter problem, the Land Army uniform
was quite fetching. This was confirmed by a quote in a *Land Girl* magazine
of 1942. During that year there was a Warships Week, a week of events
to raise funds for building warships. The week usually started with a
procession and according to the *Land Girl* an onlooker at one particular
procession remarked, 'There is no doubt that the Land Army has the most

En route to a harvest festival service at Chichester Cathedral. From Muriel Bushby's album.

Old Oilskins

Cut off the arms below the armpits, make a hem at the top and thread elastic (or a bit of elastic eked out with string!) through the hem. They are very useful for picking sprouts or similar arm-wetting jobs.

E.M. Barraud, WLA 9600, Cambridgeshire. January 1944.

From Land Girl, *the Women's Land Army magazine.*

attractive uniform of all the women's services.' The winter uniform consisted of brown corduroy breeches; biscuit-coloured blouse; green tie; green pullover; shortish khaki overcoat; hat; mackintosh; little black leather boots with puttee-like gaiters and brown walking shoes with canvas leggings. Different-coloured arm bands with stars on denoted how many years a girl had been in the service. The summer uniform consisted of fawn bib-and-brace dungarees and the winter blouse which was in fact Airtex and short-sleeved. Muriel Bushby remembers that these dungarees were not so good for gardening because constant bending down caused the top buttons to fly off the bib. An extra item of uniform was rubber boots, but because rubber was scarce these were generally allocated only to girls who were on milking.

Replacing bits of uniform, particularly when the number of Land Army members was rising, was not always easy. Muriel further recalls, 'It came in dribs and drabs; everything was in short supply. I remember longing for some more stockings because we were forever darning.' Lillian Harbard remembers that breeches varied: she started off with corduroy but later had some twill ones like officer's trousers. Muriel Wildash, who worked at a market garden in Cornwall, has particular cause to remember breeches. When land girls left, those remaining had the option to buy items of their uniform – you gave your size and what you wanted and it was sent to you. Muriel asked for a pair of breeches but, despite giving her size, received an enormous pair: 'Why on earth they thought I wanted a pair of breeches that size, I can't imagine. I sent them back with a little note saying they were surely meant for "Freda Dean" and not me to wear.'

Another unsatisfactory garment was the oilskin first issued – it leaked. However, by 1943 new heavy kinds were being supplied. Rainy weather was the only time Muriel Bushby wore her hat: the usual headwear at work was a headscarf, tied turban-wise or under the chin. In summer some girls wore straw hats and on hot days rolled up the legs of their dungarees. Muriel went one better: when their dungarees wore through at the knees she and her colleagues simply cut off the legs above the knee. 'We originated hot pants,' she says with a twinkle.

Life was not all straw hats and cut-down dungarees. Many land girls had a hard initiation into the rigours of working outdoors in winter. Monica Haire of Yorkshire was in the ATS in London but on winter days, as she marched to her office, she used to think of her sister-in-law Hilda Haire and friend Annie Butler (in the Land Army together), knowing that 'these two girls were pulling frozen sprouts with no gloves – fields of them'. Gloves were useless because they got wet through and froze. Monica continues, 'Hilda, who died aged eighty-four, suffered terrible arthritis, as does Annie, now in her seventies.'

Muriel Wildash remembers,

We picked Brussels in the biting cold: we used to have to kick the snow off them. They were loaded on to lorries to be sent off to Covent Garden and we did the same with cauliflowers . . . When it rained the food still had to go up, so we still had to do it. The foreman used to say, 'You're not wet till the rain's running out of the arse of your trousers.' I lived in digs on a farm. We had a marvellous Scots landlady – we used to go in there so cold we couldn't undo our buttons and we'd stand in front of her and she'd stand there arguing (but really she'd got a heart of gold) and undo all the buttons.

Lillian Harbard also remembers almost crying with the cold when she started work at Sutton's in March 1942. The men told her and the other land girl, Elsie, who started on the same day, to run round the field to warm themselves up. She and Elsie used to take a flask, but because they were not allowed to stop, had to hide the fact they were drinking from it. This no-break regime was something that had always been in force and no one had ever challenged it, but eventually Lillian did and got everyone an official small break. She remembers too that she also asked for, and got, time to clean up before meals.

However, Lillian will probably be more remembered by her ex-Sutton's colleagues for her other exploits at this time. As Elsie came from Harrow and she came from Bow, the other workers called them 'Bow and 'Arrow'. 'Bow and 'Arrow's' inexperience at horticulture showed up painfully at first. For example, when pricking out seedlings, 'if you made a hole, popped a seedling in, then decided it wasn't the right place and moved it, that seedling always gave you away by looking the worse for wear beside its companions'. Then there was carrot hoeing. When the young women were first put on that, Lillian thought it was a lovely job, very different from the figures she had struggled with at Bryant and May. In the course of the afternoon both girls occasionally sliced the top off a carrot, but carefully placed it back on. Eventually the foreman said to them, 'If you cut the tops off, it would be better if you left them off.' They wondered how he had discovered what they had done, until they looked back down the rows and saw the collapsed foliage on top of every carefully reinstated carrot top!

With hoeing it was not inexperience which worried Muriel Wildash but the sheer boredom of the task. She and her companions used to sing all day to brighten themselves up: 'We would sing all the words to all the songs that were going.' Staying in London one weekend, Muriel and a fellow land girl learnt the words of a song that had just come out: 'Mairzy Doats and Dozy Doats'. When on their return they sang this to the rest of the girls, the reaction was: 'Rubbish, you've made it up!' However, it went on to become very popular. Muriel's dislike of using a long-handled hoe has endured. In her own garden today she would rather get down on her hands and knees with a small hoe.

You might be forgiven for thinking that the cloistered world of estate walled gardens was, if not boring, certainly evenly predictable. Such was not the case – at least, not on occasions at Madresfield Court. To begin with the building was earmarked as one of three possible country houses

War-time Adaptability
I have not used face cream for well over a year now but have instead a little bottle of glycerine and rose-water which is lasting indefinitely, for a tiny touch of it spreads all over the face and holds powder marvellously. I only use powder on Saturdays and Sundays – if I go out. Lipstick I must have all the week. If one is used to lipstick one must always wear it for the sake of morale! It is still quite easy to obtain – of a sort and at a price!

Hair curling is a problem. I have made a few curlers with a piece of copper wire cut into short lengths to replace ones that have broken. I roll my hair upwards round a ribbon and if I help this to stay up with pins on damp days it goes two or three days without curling. I have two shorter, flat curls on the side of my head and these I keep so firmly, though invisibly, pinned down that even the rain cannot harm them. I keep an old Land Army hat for really wet days.

D. Hudson, WLA 33083, Essex. April 1943.

From Land Girl, *the Women's Land Army Magazine.*

Mairzy Doats and Dozy Doats

Mairzy doats and dozy
    doats and
liddle lamzy divey.
A kiddley divey too,
    wouldn't you?

If the words sound queer,
and funny to your ear,
a little bit jumbled
    and jivey,
Sing 'Mares eat oats
    and does eat oats
and little lambs eat ivy.'

Oh! Mairzy doats and
    dozy doats
and liddle lamzy divey.
A kiddley divey too,
    wouldn't you?
A kiddley divey too,
    wouldn't you?

Written by Milton Drake, Al Hoffman and Jerry Livingston.

Above: Dorothy Pembridge with Cynthia and Pixie.
Facing page: A Land Girl in Kent preparing a meal for her mobile squad.

to which the royal family could escape if London became too dangerous. The plan was that, once at Madresfield, they would go from a secret passage below the chapel into the moat garden, cross the park, travel to Bristol and from there fly to the USA. One of Dorothy Pembridge's garden duties was to keep the boat moored on the moat baled out in readiness. In the meantime she used it for the more mundane task of transporting rubbish from weeding. Then there was the day when one of the land girls was working on the terrace by the house and a plane landed. The pilot walked up through the park and asked if the place was Madresfield. The young woman refused to answer, knowing that careless talk cost lives, but she was not able to stop the man, who wandered off towards the house. It is believed that he was a friend of the family.

Dorothy's employer, a charming countess of Danish birth, who partly through politeness and partly through her foreign upbringing referred to land girls as 'land ladies', was also wont suddenly to spring a surprise. Dorothy recalls the day when the countess went out to buy a hat and came back with a jersey – in fact two Jersey cows. She gave Dorothy a smock with red Scottie dogs on it and took her to the estate farm for a milking lesson. The cows, named Cynthia and Pixie, became part of her work routine. Their milking place was in the stables, which were reached through a kissing-gate that had to be lifted off its hinges. Cynthia, the larger of the two cows, nearly always squashed Pixie in her haste to get through. Combining gardening with dairying had its occasional mishaps. Dorothy sprained her wrist while clipping the garden's lime arbour and found it difficult to milk with a hand encased in plaster.

For all the rigours of their various jobs these ex-land girls remember the plus side of their life at that time. Lillian says she put on 3 stone in weight, eventually reaching 10 stone, and grew suntanned and healthy-looking. Muriel Wildash recalls enjoying evenings out: 'We used to pay in for a kitty and if it was anybody's birthday we used to walk down to the George in Newlyn and have a party that consisted of beetroot sandwiches. That was the only thing they could produce that we could eat!' Muriel Bushby remembers the bolt-hole she used to share in the evenings with other land girls. It was a shed loaned by a local farmer and converted by the girls into a comfortable place where they could sit and read, chat or play gramophone records. Dorothy Pembridge recalls the day the headgardener advised the girls to make cider out of fallen cider apples. He produced a tank which had previously held weedkiller, so they asked him for something to clean it with and he gave them the brush used to groom the garden pony! She set the event to poetry and can quote bits to this day:

The littlest land girl, she felt a bit sick,
Said boss, 'Don't be fussy. Come on now, be quick,'
For what did it matter how she felt inside her?
She'd soon like the smell when she tasted the cider!

Lady Denman poses with members of her army.

There is one sour note to the story of the Women's Land Army. In March 1945 Lady Denman, the Land Army's honorary director (and driving force), resigned. She did so to draw attention to the fact that, whereas all the other forces, including the Civil Defence, were to be given post-war privileges and rewards, members of the Women's Land Army were not. This treatment gave rise to its nickname, the 'Cinderella Service'. Lillian Harbard says, 'The Land Army girls had to fight for everything they had and none of them came out with a penny.' In fact, she recalls that a man bet her £5 she *would* get something when she left and she did not even get that £5!

PRISONERS OF WAR

Harry cannot remember working with land girls in gardens for, of course, they were replacing the likes of himself. Nor can he recall sharing his chores with conscientious objectors, who also did garden work. However, he does remember working with prisoners of war, both Italian and German. His first experience of this was in 1945 and 1946 when he was second in charge at the gardens of Lord Harcourt, Nuneham Park in Oxfordshire. The walled gardens there were given over to food production and every day six or seven prisoners of war would turn up for work.

Each group seemed to have a natural leader and if Harry explained what was required to him, he conveyed it to the others. At the end of the day, if the headgardener was unavailable, Harry signed a book to say that they had done their hours and their work had been satisfactory.

'I had no feeling against them,' Harry says. 'Two or three of them had worked in botanic gardens and parks in Germany in pre-war days and one of them especially was very interesting to talk to. He used to tell me the name of a plant in German and I'd tell him what it was in English.' However, one day things were not so happy. 'We had a lad in the bothy, an undergardener, who'd had a very rough time indeed at the hands of the Germans – he'd been a prisoner of war. One morning I suppose the poor chap flipped at seeing these Germans working in the same area as him. He came up through the frame yard in a terrible rage, swinging a rope round with a noose on the end – and if he could get hold of one of them he was going to string him up. The headgardener's wife came running out to me and said, "Harry, for goodness' sake stop him!" We managed to calm him down and got him in the bothy. A mess room had been set aside for the Germans and they scarpered into it and shut the door.'

Some British prisoners of war, of course, worked in German gardens. Retired gardener John Borthwick of Sussex remembers being in a prison camp in rural Saxony. On the other side of the village there was a paper factory owned by a German aristocrat. Most of the PoWs worked at the factory, but John, because of his knowledge of gardening, worked in the aristocrat's mansion gardens. The family was, he says, Christian and cultured and the daughter had been educated at Cheltenham Ladies' College. It was a wonderful garden alongside a river. He was happy there and learned a lot, for the garden was well equipped and the gardeners were doing many things he had not been able to do in England. He remembers that every evening overhead irrigators were turned on and water was sprayed all over the garden, with the exception of inside the kitchen garden glasshouses. 'In the morning when you came, the whole place was fresh and lovely.' He learned to look after bees too – the garden had cedar-built summer houses containing twenty-five to thirty hives in a block. He was also allowed to borrow good books. 'It was an oasis really,' he says.

In the spring the headgardener, knowing that John was not allowed out of camp at weekends, asked him if he would like to come to the gardens on the pretext of watering at weekends. Permission was granted and the headgardener used to collect him. John recalls, 'He had two little children, Heinz and Hilda. I used to adore them – they were really lovely kids – and when I was crossing the road one day I had one on my back and the other by the hand and along came this Czech commandant from the camp. Of course, he spotted that I was in British uniform and there was all hell let loose. He didn't say a word then; he went back to the camp. But an hour afterwards I was brought in and they were chastised at the house – what had I been doing there? It was a terrible situation. This chap stuck to his guns, but I couldn't go again after that.'

Not long after this John and his fellow prisoners of war left the camp, the demarcation lines were altered and the garden came within East Germany. The Russians used the glasshouses for the communal raising of plants for surrounding villages. John believes that those connected with the garden suffered terribly. One day he would like to go back.

For some time after the war Harry kept up a sort of oblique connection with prisoners of war and gardens. He was asked by William Rootes, the owner of Stype in Berkshire, to judge all the gardens on the estate once a year and award each marks out of a hundred. Harry used to go round with the headgardener of the estate and found it an embarrassing task, especially when he came to the stockmen's gardens. They, it seems, used to spend their spare time not in their gardens but at livestock shows! If a garden was found wanting, Mr Rootes used personally to contact the owner. However, never found wanting was the cottage garden tended by two Italian ex-prisoners of war. These men had stayed on after the war and, in fact, worked on the estate for many years. Their garden, Harry remembers, was always resplendent, especially with salad crops and garlic!

An Italian PoW's Tale

Emilio Ponti, an ex-prisoner of war living in Ledbury, Herefordshire, can fill in the interesting details of how some Italian PoWs came to Britain and how their work here was organized. As an eighteen-year-old NCO in the Italian army, he had been captured at Tobruk in Libya on 21 January 1941 and became one of 30,000 prisoners. Lack of shipping meant some forty days' wait at Tobruk in near-famine conditions before he was taken to a camp beside the Suez Canal.

One day the men in his camp were asked if they wanted to go to England to join working parties. The alternative was to go to India, South Africa, America or Australia. Emilio chose England because he feared ill treatment in some of the other countries and also because it was the nearest to Italy. The other incentive was that he and his colleagues were told that in Britain they would never be short of food because there were plenty of rabbits! He recalls helping to select men who had experience of working on the land, and then the wait until an empty ship coming from Australia or Alexandria could take them to England.

At his camp in Ledbury there were about 1,000 men and it was Emilio's job to liaise with the local representative of the War Agricultural Executive Committee, Stanley Smith. The system was that employers wanting prisoner-of-war workers went to Mr Smith and he in turn asked Emilio to select men for the job. The men went out to all sorts of agricultural and horticultural work. Their employers paid the War Ag. The men themselves received £1 a week pocket money, and for overtime they were paid in specially printed prisoner-of-war money which they spent in shops in the camps' canteens.

Left: Emilio Ponti (far right, front row) with two English officers and fellow prisoners-of-war at Ledbury Camp.
Facing page: Part of Emilio's repatriation papers.

AMATEURS

Wartime amateur gardeners included men and women whose age or occupation excluded them from call-up; service people in home bases; housewives; evacuees and schoolchildren, including scouts and guides – in fact the Government encouraged *everyone* to 'Dig for Victory'. The reason was the need for vegetables. Supplies from the continent had been cut and British farmers had switched from vegetables to growing corn for bread, and producing potatoes and other crops for animal feed. It was up to amateur gardeners to grow their own, and on 3 August 1940 the Government launched an award for home vegetable production. The award was a certificate of merit signed by the minister of agriculture. To win it gardeners had to prove they were using their land to produce food in winter as well as summer. Their gardens were inspected twice during the summer and the awards made at the end of the season.

A further (if unintentional) Government incentive to amateur gardeners was its announcement in November 1940 that British summertime would continue right through the winter months. This meant an extra hour in the garden or allotment on Saturday and Sunday afternoons. Another bonus, 'double summertime', started in May 1941: this was to operate during the summer months of the next few years. It was rather a mixed blessing. For amateurs it meant longer daylight hours in their gardens, but for professionals, particularly those employed in market gardens, it posed the problem that by the time conditions were suitable to do some jobs, it was time to go home! Even with extra daylight hours some amateurs, such as factory workers, found their working day so long that they had to rely on their families to cope with their gardens.

Right: A housewife thinks ahead and pots up parsley for winter. Facing page: A mother and her two children proudly show off their 'Dig for Victory' efforts.

Double summertime had some irksome effects. Rosemary Chip of Evesham, a 1943 Studley College student, remembers finding her best friend, who was on the College's poultry course, sitting on the stairs weeping bitterly because the hens would not go to bed!

In fact, in January 1942 the minister of agriculture, Robert Spear Hudson, launched that year's 'Dig for Victory' campaign with a particular appeal to women and older children to relieve their menfolk by working in allotments and gardens. They did. Fred Daw, wartime parks superintendent and food production officer for Oldbury, Worcestershire, remembers, 'There were a tremendous lot of women gardeners; 50 per cent of allotment holders were women.'

This certainly appears to have been the case further north. The amateur gardening magazine *Garden Work* told readers of its 20 June 1942 edition about the Preston Women Allotment Holders' and Gardeners' Association, 'the first of its kind to be formed in the country'. The Association included fifty women renting allotments in their own name and others cultivating plots for their absent husbands. Women's gardening achievements were also highlighted by the *Gardeners' Chronicle*. Its edition of 16 October 1943 carried a glowing account of the Nottingham Business and Professional Women's Club, whose members included policewomen, doctors and teachers. Not only had forty of them supplied themselves with fruit and vegetables from their own gardens and allotments but they had also shared their produce with friends and neighbours, contributed to works canteens and organized their own produce shows, netting £400 for charity!

Another enthusiastic woman gardener of the time, who cannot claim such spectacular results, nevertheless felt that her 'locum' work was an achievement, even if not quite in the style of her husband's. She recalls, 'I coped with quite a large garden for six years while my husband was in the forces, and by the time he returned the potatoes were full of calendulas – I couldn't pull up flowers. He wasn't pleased!'

CHAPTER SIX
WARTIME GARDENS

NO GARDEN

No plot was so small that it could not be turned into a 'Victory' garden. Indeed, with ingenuity you could even grow vegetables without a garden. The following story appeared in the *Gardeners' Chronicle* of 8 July 1944:

> A London flat dweller with no garden decided to grow a few Tomato plants on his balcony. First he got some plants from his father's garden in Wiltshire; then he found he needed boxes, so he begged or borrowed some from his greengrocer; next he found he needed soil, so he brought the boxes in a taxi to a demonstration allotment and begged a few shovelfuls; then he planted the Tomatoes.

The book *Cookery Under Rations* by H. T. E. Pearson (1941) suggested that people without gardens grow mustard and cress in seedboxes and tomatoes in flowerpots on sunny windowsills. For further advice on how to utilize windowsills, those without gardens could consult a Ministry 'Dig for Victory' leaflet called 'Roof and Window-box Gardening'. This lists suitable crops for windowboxes – for example, lettuce, radishes, tomatoes and dwarf beans – and suggests varieties of compact growth such as 'Tom Thumb' lettuce and 'Osborn's Forcing' beans.

For those branching out into roof-top gardening the leaflet advises soil containers made from boards or simply wooden boxes. Tomatoes, marrows and climbing beans could fare well in an old metal bucket with a drainage hole punched into the base. With space restrictions in mind, roof-top gardeners are advised to choose root vegetables usually grown in garden frames and to opt for bush rather than trailing marrows. A suggestion for those with plenty of roof space is to have an ordinary Dutch light (a type of garden frame). However, the leaflet warns that care should be taken to fasten the top securely lest it be carried off by the wind. Wind also has to be considered when plants begin to grow, tomatoes need strong stakes and climbing beans secure sticks or string fastened to wire.

SMALL GARDENS

Perhaps the toughest decision for 'Victory Diggers' with small conventional gardens was whether or not to dig up the lawn and turn it into a vegetable patch. Gardening experts of the day offered comforting words

Facing page: Harry's garden at Chilton laid over with rows of vegetables as it was during the war years.

that when the war was over the lawn could be re-instated and would be all the better for having been dug and re-seeded. People were advised that the best first crop for ground that had been grassed was potatoes or perhaps well-grown cabbage plants, but first the lawn had to be double-dug and its turf dropped face downwards into the bottom of each excavated trench.

In October 1940 it was Mr Hudson the minister of agriculture's express desire that every householder convert a portion of his or her flowerbeds to vegetable growing. Stephen Chevely, in a book about his garden called *A Garden Goes to War*, worked out a way to do this fairly painlessly:

> Our general plan will be to discard a large number of perennials and have fewer annuals. This will free the front half of each border for vegetables. The remaining perennials will be transferred to the back of the borders, so that one can imagine, next summer, dwarf vegetable crops against a background of flowering plants.

Mr Chevely also suggests that gardeners can save excavated flower bulbs by dropping them into trenches.

For those who still wanted the beauty afforded by flowers but who had turned their garden over to vegetables, all was not lost. There was the option of having attractive herbs instead, or of choosing some vegetables with ornamental features. A correspondent to the *Gardeners' Chronicle* had suggestions for the latter: borecole or kale because it was 'crisped and incised like a giant fern'; beetroot for its purple leaves; scarlet runner beans for their flowers; and carrots for their feathery foliage.

As war clouds gathered, the Government began distribution of Anderson shelters. This photograph was taken in a street in Islington, London, on 25 February 1939.

Practically every small house without a basement, and which was in an area vulnerable to air raids, had an Anderson shelter in the garden. These shelters, made out of corrugated steel plating, were sunk into the ground, and the earth dug out to make the hole was thrown over the top and sides and patted down. The earth was added protection and it served to make the shelter less noticeable. On that score *Garden Work* (10 August 1940) considered that even the disturbed soil might draw machine-gun fire and applauded the camouflage efforts of two of its readers, Mrs Prendergast of Clapham and Mr Lamb of Forest Gate, both in London. Mrs Prendergast was growing lettuce, beetroot and marrows on her shelter and Mr Lamb had sown grass on the sides of his and planted the top with flowers. The following year the same magazine berated those garden owners who had simply left their Anderson shelters with their covering of soil so that 'something closely resembling an Eskimo's igloo is left standing nakedly in full view of the houses'. It suggested that they turn their shelters into rockeries, taking care to use plants suitable for both the sunny and shady side, and gave the name of a nursery which advised on shelter rockeries.

Flowers aside, most gardeners grew marrows on their shelters. If there were sage and thyme nearby, the three could be combined in the kitchen to make 'mock goose' (stuffed marrow). However, shelter horticulture was not always successful, for when the shelter was built invariably a fair amount of sub-soil became mixed with the soil patted over it. Rachel Thorpe recalls that this happened to the shelters at Wigston Girls' Grammar in Leicester, where from 1941 to 1943 she looked after the grounds and taught gardening to the pupils. Complying with the headmistress's request, she planted vegetables on the shelters, but disappointingly the cabbages grew only to the size of Brussels sprouts.

Mike Benson, who was brought up in Liverpool, recalls that his father's rhubarb was unsuccessful for the same reason. Mike would be despatched on his bicycle, with a couple of canvas bags on the handlebars, to a pub called the Horse and Jockey. When the big brewers' dray horses arrived on their delivery round, they used obligingly to relieve themselves and Mike had to scoop up the proceeds and bring it back in the bags. Their contents would then be used to enrich the soil on the shelter. Mike's mother also played her part by keeping an apple and a bucket and spade ready for the milk delivery horse.

Some people actually grew their rhubarb *inside* the shelter. A crown in a well-manured bucket yielded tender shoots in the darkness. Another bucket or box crop which responded well to shelter gloom was mushrooms: eggs being scarce, these were valued for frying with the modest bacon ration.

STUFFED VEGETABLE MARROW

1 onion
3 tablespoons brown breadcrumbs
1 tablespoon Soyolk (trade name for prepared soya flour)
4 oz nuts, chopped (or 4 oz grated cheese or cooked lentils)
2 tablespoons minced parsley or mixed herbs
a little stock or 1 made-up egg (if available)
1 medium-sized marrow
2 oz cooking fat

Chop the onion and mix with the breadcrumbs, Soyolk, nuts (or cheese or lentils), herbs and stock (or egg). Wipe the marrow, but do not peel, and scoop out the pith and pips. (Cut it in half to do this, or, better still, if possible, cut off one end and scoop out the inside with a long knife.) Stuff the marrow with the mixture, then tie the two halves together with clean string. Bake at 350°F or gas mark 4 for 40 minutes in a well-greased tin: lay some of the cooking fat on top, scoring lightly with a knife, and baste frequently until done. It should brown well.

From Health for All Wartime Recipe Book by Margaret Y. Brady (1945 edition).

Overleaf: Anya cuts a marrow grown on the Anderson shelter built for the television series.

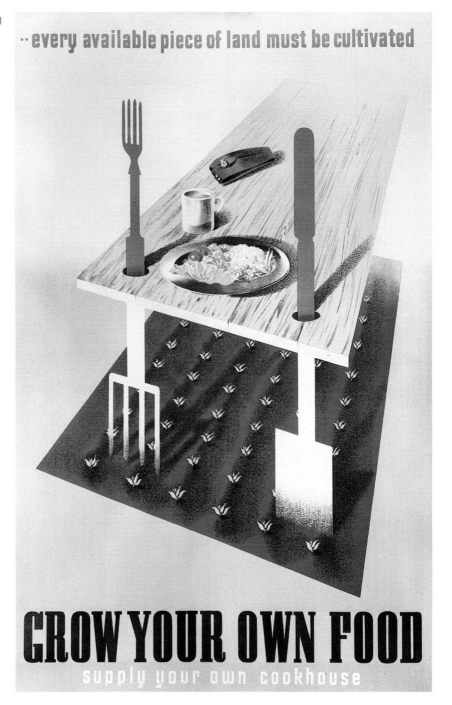

A poster with an inventive link between garden and dinner table.

Many household gardeners took the propaganda phrase 'Grow Your Own' very much to heart, and when in April 1942 a 'Sacrifices for Victory' budget sent the price of a packet of twenty cigarettes up from 1s 6d (7½p) to 2s (10p) they did indeed resort to growing their own. A 6d (2½p) booklet sold by W. H. Smith encouraged them. It was called 'How to Grow and Cure your own Tobacco at 2d a lb', and if you bought the book you got a free packet of seeds.

By all accounts cultivation of tobacco was relatively simple. The seeds had to be sown under cover in April and potted off as soon as they were big enough to handle. Planting out into the garden could take place at the beginning of June – any earlier and a frost might stunt their growth. The plants needed to be 2 feet apart in rows 3 feet apart and appreciated plenty of water and liquid manure. Newspaper gardening columns advised breaking the flower head and suckers off and not letting a plant have more than ten leaves. Given good weather, the leaves could be harvested in mid-September when they were beginning to turn yellow. Curing was a bit of a problem and had to be done carefully: the ideal conditions were dry but not too hot as the leaves needed to dry slowly. The usual answer was to peg them on to a piece of string strung across the inside of a shed. When the tips of two leaves stuck if pressed together but separated at a slight shake, it was time to cut out the central rib and tie the leaves into bunches. These had to be hung up for two weeks in the sunniest possible position. The penultimate stage was to hang them in a cool, dark place to mature, which took a minimum of three months. Any time from then onwards you could take the leaves to a local tobacconist and have them cut for pipe or cigarette.

Harry planting out tobacco in garden frames.

A member of Winford Amateur Gardening Society, near Bristol, recalls curing his own tobacco leaves with molasses. However, this method had a drawback. He had to have two pipes because after one smoke a pipe got clogged up.

Facing page: The tobacco plants making good growth.
Left: Leaves being picked.
Above: Harry hangs the leaves up to dry.

At first gardeners had to obtain a licence to make their own tobacco. Those without were prosecuted. In February 1941 Airdrie sheriff court imposed a fine of £2 each on defaulters. In the later years of the war the need for a licence was dropped if you were growing just for your own consumption but you had to be sure to tell the local excise officer what you were doing.

ALLOTMENTS

The custom of tenanting and cultivating a piece of land less than 2 acres in extent started in rural parishes at the beginning of the nineteenth century. Urban allotments became prevalent after the 1887 Allotments Act empowered local authorities to provide them. The First World War gave a huge boost to the allotment movement. Numbers declined after the war, but local authorities made headway in creating better tenancy conditions and more permanent allotment sites.

In September 1939 the minister of agriculture, aware of the food production achieved by allotment holders during the First World War, started a campaign to increase the number of allotment holders by 500,000. An order was made granting urban authorities wide powers to take possession of land which they could either cultivate themselves or let out to individuals, generally one tenant to a 10 square rod (90 × 30 ft) plot. By January 1940, however, it was evident that the campaign had not succeeded in stimulating enough industrial workers to take allotments and propaganda was stepped up.

In September 1940 the minister of agriculture asked for *another* 500,000 allotments to be under cultivation by the following spring, stating that this would go some way to making up for the vegetables normally purchased from the continent. He estimated that these extra allotments would provide six to seven million adults and nine to ten million children with vegetables for the greater part of the year. On 6 October a special allotment service held at St Martin-in-the-Fields church in London was broadcast on the wireless. It included blessings to increase production and Mr Middleton, the well-known gardening adviser, read the lesson.

The numbers of allotments began to rise. For example, at the end of May 1941 Bristol had more than 15,000; Nottingham had 6,500 occupying 570 acres; Swansea had doubled its total since war began; Norwich had 4,000 on 40 acres and in Enfield, Middlesex, it was reported that one householder in every six was working an allotment. Perhaps the biggest strides were made in Tottenham, London, where by January 1942 there were almost 3,000 allotments covering an area of 150 acres.

Most allotment societies bought supplies of seeds, fertilizers and tools in bulk and sold them to members at cost price. Allotment holders who could not avail themselves of this facility could usually get their supplies from the local council and also buy seedlings and plants raised in corporation glasshouses. Section 21 of the Land Settlement (Facilities) Act 1919 had given councils the power to sell to the public in this way and during the war years the Government encouraged them to adopt the practice.

Wartime allotments were not confined to specially provided council sites; they appeared all over the place. Schoolchildren tended allotments made from school playing fields; members of the fire service tilled land attached to their stations; individuals rented plots from farmers or dug up

My Uncle Jack's allotment was a magical place. I can still see the neat rows of cabbages, beetroots, lettuce, spring onions, etc. I remember how thrilled we were to pick strawberries and tomatoes. Often after school my brothers and I would take along a 'gang' and Uncle Jack would provide us with a stick of rhubarb and some sugar in a screw of paper. What a place to be, though, on a summer's day, just to lie there and listen to the buzz of bees and watch butterflies and ladybirds!

My uncle gave me a great love of gardens and all things that grow.

Sheila Henry, Bury, Lancashire.

bits of village green; on-duty ARP wardens 'Dug for Victory' on land around their posts (Post B.20A. in Bournemouth had its own specialists in onions and radishes); and there were even allotments laid out on royal premises. The latter came about when the king allowed keepers on Windsor Castle estate to have plots in the gardens there, so that they could feed their families the year through.

Firms also allowed employees to make allotments on their premises. For example, workers at Wolseley Motors reclaimed the factory's scrap heaps and even made marrow and cucumber frames from the windscreens of old cars (a sensible move in wartime, given the glass's non-splinterable quality). Pilkington's glassworks at St Helens in Lancashire made their greenhouses in their factory, using them to grow tomatoes and cucumbers, and had fourteen allotment sites on the works' playing fields.

Perhaps the largest number of allotments owned by commercial enterprises belonged to railway companies. In 1943 LMS Railway had

Working an allotment on Hampstead Heath, London.

ON THE ALLOTMENT

From being a pleasant, healthful hobby, allotments have now become a national necessity. C. H. Middleton will bring the Secretary of the National Allotments Society, G. W. Giles, to the microphone with him in his gardening talk on Sunday, December 17.

Above: The radio gardener Mr Middleton encouraged listeners to take on an allotment.
Above right: Part of a display staged on 14 February 1941 by the Parks Department of Cheltenham Corporation. It showed how carrots and potatoes could be stored in clamps and kept over winter.
Facing page: An ingenious way of encouraging gardeners to grow winter vegetables.

22,000. A quirky-minded statistician estimated that, placed end to end along the line, they would stretch from London to beyond Dumfries!

In a perverse way even Hitler helped the spread of allotments. Manchester Corporation turned the gardens of bombed houses into allotments, and in Bethnal Green, East London, locals formed a Bombed Site Producers' Association. In August 1942 the Association had 300 adults working thirty sites. Air-raid wardens had done initial work to clear the ground; and, to stop any precious soil being carted away, punched holes into dustbin lids and used them to sieve the rubble. Bombsite rubbish itself was put to good use in some places. In Romford, Essex, allotment holders broke up and sieved ceiling fragments as a substitute for lime and in the Middlesex districts of Hayes and Harlington they made their huts out of material salvaged from bombed buildings.

In the summer of 1942 the Ministry of Agriculture expressed concern that average production from both small gardens and allotments was only half what it should be. One of the major problems was that cultivators, through inexperience, were getting a glut in summer but had nothing on their land in winter. Amateurs were urged to obtain a copy of the Ministry's cropping plan, which outlined crops and cultivation methods for a plot of approximately 10 square rods (90 × 30 ft). They were also advised to visit demonstration plots laid out in local parks and to seek advice from allotment societies.

Inexperience was not the only impediment to maximum production; even old hands had their difficulties. Home Guard, firewatching and other voluntary work took them away from their plots. Then there were allotment problems such as soil infertility. A soil sample taken in 1941 from allotments in St Georges, Bristol, was analysed and found to contain ash and abnormally high amounts of zinc, copper and nickel; the latter three were having toxic effects on plant growth. In Yiewsley, Middlesex,

6 STARS FROM the WINTER GARDEN

SAVOY THE BIG-HEARTED TENOR ★

KALE
THE EVER GREEN

SPINACH
THE STRONGEST MAN IN THE WORLD

THE LEEKS

THEY KNOW THEIR ONIONS

THE SPROUT SISTERS
Very tasty – very sweet

IF ITS HEALTH YOU'RE AFTER
CABBAGE
YOU LUCKY PEOPLE

GROW THEM IN *your* WINTER GARDEN

ALLOTMENT SOUP

3 carrots
3 turnips
3 onions
3 leeks
5 potatoes
2 oz Stork margarine
2 quarts water
salt and pepper

Scrub the vegetables; peel the turnips, potatoes and onions; scrape the carrots; wash the leeks. Cut the leeks and onions into fine rings and the turnips, carrots and potatoes into dice. Melt the Stork margarine in a large saucepan, add the vegetables, put on the lid and leave them to sweat in the hot Stork for 15 minutes, shaking the pan from time to time. Then add 2 quarts of boiling water and a little salt and leave the soup to simmer gently until the carrots are tender. If the vegetables are old, or dry, the cooking may take 1–1½ hours. Season with salt and pepper and serve hot. Other vegetables from the allotment may be added to this soup, such as cabbage, green beans, celery, etc., but they should all be cut in small pieces or shreds before cooking.

From Cooking in War-time *(1940) by Elizabeth Craig.*

the soil was so poor that the council was forced to give allotment holders a free bag of fertilizer to encourage them to carry on. Lack of humus in soil was another problem: the answer was to dig in farmyard manure, but that was expensive and scarce. The Ministry advocated making compost as a substitute, but an inspector visiting some allotments in one of the home counties in September 1944 reported back that 'a good compost heap is almost as rare as snow in summer!' Potash was also in short supply as unfortunately most of the main deposits of natural potash were in Germany. On some sites eelworm ravaged crops and at others, which had no water supply, drought at planting-out time spelt disaster to young plants.

Two other major problems beset allotment holders: damage by trespass and pilfering. The former prompted a parliamentary debate at which the minister of agriculture remarked, 'Everyone must know and recognize when a piece of ground is being cultivated. It may not be easy to define what an allotment is, but it is like an elephant – you recognize it when you see it.' This may have been true for humans, but animals were also trespassers. Dog owners were fined £5 if their animals strayed on to allotments, and in June 1943 a Caernarvonshire farmer was fined £20 plus costs for letting his sheep eat a crop of winter vegetables. Elizabeth Hess recalls that when her advisory work for the Ministry of Agriculture took her to Wales, she was always asked if she could get the Ministry to send down wire netting so that it could be put up to keep out sheep. 'I had to say I didn't really think I could, but that I would mention it – they were rabid, these allotment holders, sitting around glaring at me. But of course there was no wire netting available. I did have every sympathy with them and did send notes to the Ministry of Agriculture. I don't know if it did any good; I only hope it did.'

Obviously not a lot of wire reached the Monmouth area, for in June 1945 the council there decided to employ a shepherd and his dog to keep sheep from allotments and gardens.

Cats, rats, mice and rabbits were other unwelcome allotment visitors. Ken Allen of Teignmouth in Devon was a boy in 1940 but remembers how his family kept rabbits off their allotment. As 1-in. mesh wire netting was obtainable only if you had an agricultural permit, they used instead the mesh wire frames which were supplied to householders for the sides of their Morrison table shelters! The shelters, named after the minister of home security, Herbert Morrison, were designed for indoors and people had one either in a spare room or in the living room. The top part was a flat piece of steel plate and wire mesh was fitted to the sides to stop rubble getting in.

To deal with theft many allotment holders arranged 'plot watchers', both paid and voluntary. Courts imposed harsh penalties on offenders. For example, in September 1941 a Penryn man was sentenced to two months' hard labour for stealing potatoes and onions from a railway embankment plot, and in October 1942 Ipswich magistrates sent a man to prison for a month for stealing growing vegetables worth 1s 6d (7½p).

Vegetable theft was taken so seriously that when Fred Daw found gaps in the rows of carrots in his demonstration plots at Barnford Park, Oldbury, in Worcestershire, the following took place:

1 A detective constable took plaster casts of large footprints on the plots.
2 A police constable obtained the names of nineteen Home Guards on duty at a post where two carrot tops were found.
3 The boots of each man were compared in turn with the casts until a pair was found to correspond.
4 A police constable made a number of enquiries and took down several statements.

The upshot was that three men appeared at Oldbury magistrates' court charged with stealing three pods of peas and three carrots. It was not evident that the pea pods had been taken, but the value of the carrots was put at 4d (just over 1½p) apiece, making a total of 1s (5p). The case was dismissed under the Probation of Offenders Act, but the Home Guards concerned had to pay 4s (20p) each.

In spite of all their difficulties, allotment holders did contribute greatly to the amount of vegetables consumed during the war years. Their peak year was 1942–3, when they grew nearly 1,000,000 tons. After the war, allotment ownership declined, largely because much land went back to its original use or was bought for building.

MANSION GARDENS

The cultivation of mansion gardens during the war years did not conform to a pattern. In general it seems that the owners were not formally compelled to turn them over to the 'Dig for Victory' effort and, indeed, despite restrictions on fuel and manpower, some carried on very much as in pre-war years. As an illustration of this, Viola Williams remembers leaving her job in a mansion garden near Witney in Oxfordshire because, she says, 'we were growing arum lilies when we *should* have been growing tomatoes'. On the other hand some mansion gardens changed their regime completely as they found themselves having to service a household of evacuees. Then there were gardens which fell between the above two extremes. These put up a credible 'Dig for Victory' effort either by selling off surplus produce or by growing crops specially for sale.

In retrospect it is not surprising that some large private gardens were reluctant to go wholeheartedly into producing for outside sale, for the problems involved in doing this seem to have been many. First there had to be a change of crops. Sturdy commonplace kinds had to replace the delicate sorts gardeners had been used to carrying carefully to the cook in the mansion. Also quality had to give way to quantity because traders were only interested in large quantities, and to produce them sizeable clear growing areas were needed. Mansion gardens, however, built for beauty and convenience, did not have these: their plots were intersected by pathways. To overcome the problem some owners allowed their tennis courts and bowling greens to be dug up, although even this, in some cases,

Master Gerald Baldwin of Corie Road, Norwich, is probably the youngest allotment holder, for he is only ten years old. He is actively cultivating a 5-rod plot, which had not been dug over for several seasons when he took it in hand. Master Gerald has already sown seeds of Carrots, Peas, Turnips and Cabbages.

From Garden Work, 5 April 1941.

Mr Edward Mills of Northfleet, Kent, is probably Britain's oldest allotment holder. Ever since he retired from his work as a Trinity House pilot twenty-one years ago, most of his time has been spent on his allotment.

From the Gardeners' Chronicle, 24 March 1945.

was not entirely the answer. For example, when the bowling green at Levens Hall, near Kendal, Cumbria, was ploughed, so much clinker was thrown up that only a poor crop of vegetables could be produced.

Gardeners in private mansions were also faced with the obstacle of having to combine their efforts at commercial enterprise with continuing to provide their employers with choice produce. The difficulties this entailed used to be evident on certain days at Madresfield Court gardens. Dorothy Pembridge recalls that produce would be all weighed and packed ready for market when word would suddenly come down from the house that Countess Beauchamp was going to have a dinner party and wanted, say, a certain quantity of fruit.

Perhaps the final and biggest problem which faced private gardens doing their bit for victory was actual disposal of produce. For some houses in remote areas transport costs cancelled out any profit and it was no use selling or even giving the produce away locally for practically all country cottages had their own good vegetable gardens. This 'disposal' problem was the source of much frustration to gardeners and many columns of print were devoted to it in gardening periodicals, the general tenor of them being that the Government should organize some scheme to help gardeners, particularly over 'specialized' crops like onions, carrots, beets, leeks and salads, which private gardens produced in far better quality than farms. The way gardeners did manage to dispose of crops depended on quantity. Small amounts could either be sold through village produce associations (an association member collecting and delivering to a nearby town), taken to a Women's Institute stall or sold to local shops. Individuals also came to purchase direct from gardens. Muriel Bushby remembers a queue of people waiting as she dug new potatoes at Warnham. When she moved to work in gardens belonging to Plant Protection Research Station, Fernhurst, Surrey, Muriel recalls that produce from there went off on a lorry. This happened at most gardens which had seriously turned over to food production and were operating like a market garden. Usually the lorry was arranged through a co-operative scheme and would call several times a week.

Harry recalls that the lorry system was in operation at Chilton when he became headgardener there in October 1947. Chilton's produce went via the lorry to 'the pool' in Newbury which was fed by a number of gardeners, all of whom had registered with the same wholesale dealer. The dealer himself was registered with the Ministry and he distributed all the pooled produce to shops at controlled prices.

Harry recalls that as Chilton was officially registered as being on food production, he had to fill in quarterly returns detailing what the garden was producing and what amounts were being sent to the pool, and this was checked from time to time by the Ministry. He explains that if a garden elected to go on to food production it meant that practically all the garden land and glasshouses had to be growing eatable crops. To assist, the Ministry granted him a certain amount of fuel, mainly to help with tomato crops. There was no fuel allowed for the garden's vineries and peach

Facing page: The ornamental Rose House at Chilton was stripped of most of its roses in the war years and cauliflowers were grown in their place. Harry shows that the old house can still raise a good crop of caulis.

A lorry being loaded with produce from the garden at the Plant Protection Research Station, Fernhurst.

houses, and Harry says that in some gardens vines and peach trees were pulled up altogether. However, the ones at Chilton were spared because the heating pipework was such in their houses that even if the fruit had been pulled up there would not have been sufficient room to grow many tomatoes. Even so, and despite lack of heating, Harry raised lettuce, cabbages and dwarf French beans in these houses and also had some tomatoes growing up the back wall of the vinery.

Harry remembers with admiration the way in which the peach houses at Nuneham Park were used when he was there in 1945 and 1946. Nuneham had also been registered for food production. He explains,

> There was a very long peach house and the trees were planted *across* the house instead of in borders up the sides. This meant that the peach trees were smaller than conventionally planted ones would have been, but you did get a space of about 9 ft between each tree and those spaces took first a crop of radishes, lettuce and carrots and, when these were cleared, tomatoes. You could get three rows of tomatoes, five plants to a row. They were treated as a coldhouse crop and came into bear in late July with a full crop during August and early September. The peaches were left there undisturbed and there was a ready market for both peaches and tomatoes in Oxford.

Harry believes that using the house in the above way and getting the early salading made a worthwhile contribution to war crops.

Nuneham's main war crop was tomatoes. Unlike Chilton's the vines there had not been spared and their four large houses, each with an 18-ft bed running its length, were turned over to tomato crops. Harry remembers that another wartime conversion at Nuneham was a big, old, gable-ended glasshouse. It had formerly been filled with displays of potted ornamental plants but, with the coming of war, the staging had been taken out and the whole floor space given over to lettuce, early carrots and radish; then, like the vineries, it was filled with tomato plants.

Elbowing out flowers for vegetables was a sad fact of war production, and when Harry left Nuneham and came to Chilton he found that the rose house there had been denuded of all its roses but those which scrambled over the back wall. The main body of the house was given over to early cauliflowers. These were cleared out by the end of May and followed by tomatoes. After Harry had been at Chilton a couple of years he also managed to get a 'catch' crop of chrysanthemums after the tomatoes had been cleared. These flowers had been grown outside but, when lifted and brought into the house, bloomed during November and December.

Harry recalls that when he first went to Chilton he had a visit from a ministry inspector, but it was amicable. Dorothy Hinchcliffe, who was a ministry inspector during the war years in Cheshire and Lancashire, concurs that in fact there was little friction between inspectors and headgardeners. 'People knew the urgency and really did things of their own accord,' she says. 'I didn't go round saying, "You must do this and the other;" I'd go round saying, "Are you doing so and so?" and I'd generally find they were well ahead of me.' However, there is always an exception to prove the rule. Gardener Harry Fox, who started work in the gardens of Lulworth Castle, Dorset, in 1941, aged fourteen, remembers the day when a young woman inspector from Dorchester made an unannounced visit. The garden had a large span-roof vinery which had vine rods on each side with their tips meeting at the roof apex. In summer, when the leaves were on the vines, the interior was pretty gloomy. The lady looked into the vinery and, says Harry, was shocked and cross that the large borders beneath the vines were empty. The headgardener protested that nothing would grow in them because of the gloom but the lady insisted that tomatoes be planted. With grumblings the gardener planted eighty tomato plants. Harry takes up the tale:

> Some time much later the 'adviser' asked what kind of crop the tomatoes yielded. 'Oh! I'm glad you asked,' said the gardener. 'You must see them.' He opened the vinery door and pointed to the rows of tomatoes, all very pale green, stems as thin as pencils and nearly 8 feet tall with fruit very green and the size of gooseberries. To the old chap's dismay she calmly said, 'You obviously haven't fed them'!

It would be an injustice not to mention the achievements of gardeners in mansions which were taken over by evacuees. The evacuees came in many forms: they could be the staff and patients of a hospital, a convalescent home, the employees of a city firm, a factory, military authorities or a college or school. In some cases where the house had been rarely used by its owners and only a skeleton staff kept, it must have been a shock for the gardeners suddenly to have to feed a mansionful.

Even when a house had been in regular use, catering for an establishment like a hospital or school was rather different from supplying produce for the owners and their guests. Gardeners had to turn their hand to providing in bulk the year through and also had to be able to gauge how much so many adults or small children would eat. Garden periodicals came to their rescue with snippets of advice: adults of education and refinement, for example, were said to eat plenty of salading crops, sprouts, peas, French beans and good-quality potatoes; children, on the other hand, needed all the common vegetables which could be prepared quickly plus, for soups and stews, turnips, carrots and onions, and, because of its laxative qualities, rhubarb. One periodical helpfully explained that children aged three to six years would not consume many vegetables and that six large cabbages or cauliflowers were sufficient to feed over sixty children for one day. Sybil Van Praet remembers that, at Broughton, four cabbages were sufficient 'greens' for the whole of the Eastbourne prep. school (staff and pupils, numbering approximately 120 people) evacuated into the mansion. She emphasizes, however, that these cabbages were extraordinarily large as a result of Mr Lowe the headgardener's policy of plenty of organic manure and hoeing!

Finally, to add to their troubles, some headgardeners catering for evacuated establishments found themselves at the whim of one or several of the following: medical officers, stewards, matrons, cooks, quartermasters, headmasters and canteen supervisors.

MARKET GARDENS

When war broke out, officers employed by their local War Agricultural Committee visited all market gardens. They recorded the acreage and crops and found out from the grower what future crops were planned. The information, which would help the Ministry of Agriculture assess the potential of a holding for producing food crops, was not always easy to obtain. Hubert Taylor of West Sussex was an agricultural advisory officer of the time and recalls that at a few holdings he was met by a gun. In these cases he returned with a War Ag. Committee member, who was usually another grower, and they managed to sort things out.

In order to maximize the production of vegetables the Ministry imposed cropping orders which stipulated which crops had to be grown and which not. The axe fell on 'luxury' crops. From 1940 no grower was allowed to use a glasshouse for raising strawberries – a particular blow to some south-coast growers, whose holdings were 100 per cent strawberries. Further orders were issued which prohibited the growing of cucumbers under glass (their nutritional value was not deemed to be worth the cost of the fuel needed to raise them), and in 1943 no grower, except with special permission, could produce asparagus, because land was short and this crop took three years to raise. In fact the ruling on asparagus was not a particular hardship, for growers were generally only too happy to concentrate on quicker-growing crops which paid better.

The cropping orders which caused most heartache and consternation were the ones relating to the commercial cultivation of flowers. From 1931 the British flower-growing industry had expanded considerably. A survey taken in the late 1930s put the area of outdoor flowers, including bulbs, at 12,340 acres and the acreage of indoor flowers at 12,497. Flowers, however, were not food and as the war progressed the Ministry issued cropping orders which cut their production. In 1942 it offered flower growers £20 for each acre put over to food production but in many cases this was small compensation for destroying a lifetime's work. Growers had to plough in fields of bulbs (some of the bulbs were steamed and fed to pigs) and grow instead wheat, potatoes, carrots or onions. Lincolnshire growers were particularly badly hit by this ruling, for the county had over 2,000 acres of daffodils. A diary entry for 1943 records: 'All around Spalding there are fields of young corn where daffodils used to be – and every here and there in the corn a daffodil!'

Around the country acres of roses and other shrubs had to be ripped up to make room for wheat and barley. Roses grown under glass were destroyed, a hardship to growers in Hertfordshire who had over 70 per cent of the country's total. The majority of lilies, orchids and other pot plants had to be taken out of glasshouses, although growers were allowed to keep rare collections. A certain amount of stock material was also allowed to be kept so that business could be built up again after the war. By January 1944 the official ruling on flowers under glass was that only 10 per cent of the area was to be allocated to permanent flower crops. Also at this time growers could sow and raise flowers on no more than a quarter of their open land. By the end of 1944 Government statistics recorded that hardy nursery stock had been cut by half its pre-war total and outdoor bulbs and outside flowers by three-quarters.

Yet in some nurseries appearances could be deceptive. Ron Sidwell remembered that during the war years flower growing was profitable and nurserymen could be wily. On his visits as a ministry inspector in the Evesham area he used to encounter a glorious mixture of boxes of cabbage plants and asters along greenhouse benches, so much so that it was difficult to assess whether the amount of flowers complied with the restriction on their number or not! He recalled, 'It was uneconomic in terms of officials' time to calculate the relative quantities of the two categories of plants, and game set and match went to the grower.' He also remembered a grower who was building up his stocks of gladioli for the cut-flower trade. In order to keep within the restricted acreage the grower put corms closer and closer together. When eventually the restrictions were lifted, his acreage of gladioli jumped fourfold.

When it came to producing food crops, some flower growers endured a restriction additional to those imposed by the Ministry: their glasshouses. George Brown, now living in West Sussex, worked at a nursery near Brighton which specialized in such pot plants as calceolaria and cineraria. He says that because their glasshouses were built for pot plants, they had to grow tomatoes and lettuce in pots. One year they had 100,000 pots of

K. Squirrel describes how cress is grown on the market garden where she works:

The houses are prepared for the cress by the men who work here. Each house is dug, and 3 or 4 in. of sifted soil is spread on the surface, which is levelled and made firm, and is then ready for the seed, which is soaked, scattered, then watered well and a wet sack laid on the top. The seed germinates in about five days, the sacks are removed on the sixth day and the cress is cut on the seventh. This goes on from November until March. I had been here about three weeks before I was shown how to cut. It was difficult at first, but after a few days one soon gets used to it.

From Land Girl, *September 1944.*

cabbage lettuce. Also in some houses side benches were dug up and mustard and cress sown. Outside they grew tomatoes and brassicas. Flowers (from the 10 per cent they were allowed to keep) and vegetables went to Brighton market twice a week.

Willie Barker despatched produce from his market garden at Walton-on-Thames every day. He was not affected by the flower-cropping orders because the 100 or so acres he cultivated had always been under vegetables. Picking began at five o'clock in the morning and his two lorries would leave for London's Covent Garden Market at 1.30 am. It was a journey of about 15 miles to Covent Garden and once there some of the produce was put on display, but selling was direct from the lorries with a desk set up on the cobbles. Willie says that during the blitz it would have been madness to make the journey to London at night, so his lorries went in the daytime instead and buyers also came to his yard at Walton. Even on days after the blitz his journeys were not without incident. The route took the lorries through Putney where there was a stone obelisk in the middle of the road and drivers were made aware of this obstacle by a circle of warning lights. One night a land mine went off, extinguishing these lights, and one of the lorries went smack into the obelisk. The front wheels were pushed back under the cab and the load had to stay where it was until he could send another lorry next day.

Willie Barker had 4,000 Dutch lights (a type of garden frame) producing early crops, like marrows and cauliflowers, and 3½ acres of his ground grew outdoor tomatoes. He remembers that one day he sent off 2,000 wooden boxes of produce (returnable boxes, as a deposit was paid on them), which he believes is something of a record for those times. When the war began he had horses, Welsh cobs, working in the fields and hauling in produce, but he replaced them with a Ferguson tractor. This machine, which had come over from America on Lend-Lease, had hydraulics, could do twice as much work as the horses and, unlike them, did not need looking after at weekends.

Willie's workforce included members of the Women's Land Army and the wives from a nearby Romany encampment who brought their prams and children with them when they came to work. (The Romanies used to spend part of their year in Bristol and part in Walton.) At one time twenty Welsh Guards, who had just returned from Calais and were recuperating at Sandown Park, turned out to pick his tomatoes. Members of the Surrey Land Club also helped out on a temporary basis. This club had been formed during the war and its members included a lot of women office workers. Willie says that, although their hearts were in the right place, the ladies were totally at a loss when it came to jobs like thinning out beetroot or telling the difference between a weed and a young carrot. At the time he was in the Home Guard but says that he had to get special permission to be excused from parades as he could not leave his willing but inexperienced weekend workforce!

During the war years market gardeners could apply to the Ministry of Works and Building for sufficient paint to keep their glasshouses in 'good order'. The owners of some, however, needed more than a coat of paint to do this – for example, Gordon Veitch and his partner who ran a market garden in Birmingham. Gordon recalls how, during the first winter of the war, forty bombs came down within 400 yards of their premises and the partners found themselves spending most of their day repairing glass. He remembers also bomb blasts knocking him off his feet when he came up from his nightly ritual of stoking the heating boiler. Stones, building materials and shrapnel used to rain down all around. The shrapnel came from our anti-aircraft guns and was hot, like a car exhaust, when it came down. On a day when a German bomber dropped his bomb near the Austin Motorworks, Gordon and his partner moved from the spot in the garden where they had been standing and as they moved a 1-ft piece of shrapnel hit the spot.

Inevitably during that winter splinters of glass used to get into the glasshouse crops. One Sunday Gordon's whole family spent the entire day taking pieces of glass out of chrysanthemums. After a time the gardens accumulated a heap of broken glass roughly 20 ft long and 3 ft high. Despite Gordon's attempts to get rid of it, no one wanted the glass and finally the council came and took it away.

Greenhouse damage was not confined to broken glass. One night a house literally fell apart when its two 100-ft-long sides were blasted off their support stanchions. Extraordinarily not a pane of glass was broken, and when it was jacked up and together again the only damage was one cracked pane!

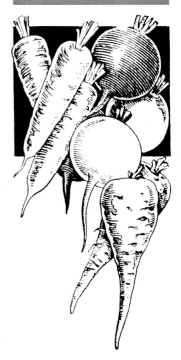

Land Army girls pricking out seedlings at a market garden.

Fruit picking and spinach thinning with babies in the background.

During the worst part of the blitz Gordon recalls that the pipeline which brought water from Wales into Birmingham was destroyed. There was no water in Birmingham for ten days: 'We had a well at the nursery and I spent all my time filling up bottles and buckets for queues of people.'

The nursery might have had water but it was low on another essential, fuel. In an attempt to keep the heating boiler running Gordon used to pick up coke which had fallen between railway lines.

Bedding plants had been part of their output, but after the imposition of flower-growing restrictions, it sold only salad and vegetables. Gordon remembers that they picked tomatoes on Friday nights – all they could lay their hands on – and weighed them into 1 lb bags. The next morning there would be a queue of people 200 yards long waiting to buy them!

PARKS

In addition to managing demonstration allotments and keeping their grounds in a semblance of order, park superintendents turned their nurseries into market gardens. Glasshouses normally used for raising young stock for flowerbeds were largely given over to tomatoes and cucumbers, and vegetables filled coldframes. Some park supervisors also found themselves responsible for ploughing up and cultivating golf courses, sports pitches and even bits of farmland.

Park staff sold young vegetable plants to gardeners and allotment holders, and produce like tomatoes and cucumbers was sold to the general public. Park produce also went to supply school kitchens, British restaurants (see p. 197), local hospitals, ARP canteens, and shops. Ada Hutchinson of West Sussex was one of the many women taken on as park gardeners during the war years. She worked in the parks around Ilkley in Yorkshire and remembers taking produce from the parks' nurseries to local shops. The shops were a mile or so away and, because petrol was rationed, she had to push the produce along on a trolley!

In many parks ornamental gardens were closed off to the public and gardeners did just sufficient to stop them running wild. In some cases trees and shrubs had to be cut down to make room for anti-aircraft and barrage-balloon units. More damage was caused by heavy lorries cutting into the turf and by night-time trespassers. The latter gained easy access, for parks had had their railings removed by the Ministry of Supply. It was said that the railings were to be melted down and the metal used for munitions.

Park beds also suffered when air-raid warnings sounded, for understandably people took the nearest direct route to a park's public shelter. Schoolchildren who had not been evacuated found these shelters a wonderful playground much to the irritation of park staff. However, parks' people did have a soft spot for youngsters, for when Portsmouth schoolchildren collected bits of shrapnel in the park and sold the biggest for 2d (1p) apiece, the superintendent recorded, tongue in cheek, 'On these occasions the by-law prohibiting the selling by unauthorized persons in the parks is left in abeyance.'

Railings being removed from Battersea Park, London in May 1940.

CHAPTER SEVEN
WARTIME GARDENING

WAR ON PESTS

'Pests didn't know there was a war on,' a gardener of that time remarked recently. To stop them ravaging 'Victory' crops, they had to be sprayed, dusted, steamed or physically removed.

The battery against invading fungi and insects involved some poisonous remedies. Arthur Hooper, who gardened to feed a psychiatric hospital and also produced flowers for locked wards, remembers using a mixture of cyanide and sulphuric acid against scale insect (a small sucking insect) on indoor flower crops. He would put the acid into a metal container, add enough water to make it boil and then drop in the cyanide. He used cyanide to keep whitefly at bay too: the method was to sprinkle it on a wet floor and 'get out quickly before you had a smell or sniff of it!'

Harry also used to employ a particularly potent remedy for killing whitefly, called 'Cory's White Fly Fume'. On one of the filming days for the television series he routed through his office cupboard and found a bottle of it. The stopper had not been removed for some thirty years, but the strength of the liquid inside was still such that no one could stay anywhere near it without extreme discomfort. Harry demonstrated how the 'Fume' was put to work. He got several sticks and fixed a piece of linen (although he said flannelette was best) on to each one, rather like a flag. Then he dipped the material into a bucket of water, wrung it out so that it was damp and tipped some 'Fume' on to it. Half a dozen of these lethal flags stuck into the bedding in various places around the tomato house, plus perhaps a little 'Fume' on a damp floor, worked wonderfully well. By the next morning the floor would be, as Harry put it, 'pretty well carpeted with whitefly'. However, because the fumes did not kill the pest in its unhatched state, he remembers having to follow the treatment up every three or four days.

Interestingly the modern whitefly treatment of putting the parasite *Encarsia formosa* into tomato houses was being researched during the war years. The parasite does its job of control by laying its eggs in the eggs of whitefly and thus destroying them. During the 1940s tomato plants were being specially grown as hosts for *Encarsia formosa* at an experimental and research station in Cheshunt, Hertfordshire.

Nicotine was another lethal substance well used as a pest control during the war years. It killed most insects but was used particularly against

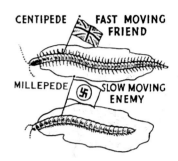

One wartime way of reminding gardeners that centipedes prey on soil pests but millepedes eat vegetables.

Facing page: Harry filling a syringe in order to spray blackfly on broadbeans.

123

Facing page: Making up
Burgundy Mixture (see page 129).
Left: Spraying the mixture on to
potato foliage.
Above, top: Harry with bottle of
White Fly Fume and home-made
'fumigator flags'.
Above: The soil sterilizer gets up
steam.

greenfly. It could be bought in powder form or as a proprietary preparation, but an alternative was simply to collect cigarette ends and soak them in a bucket of water with a bit of soft soap. Anne Kenrick remembers doing this and using a stirrup pump, supplied to put out incendiary bombs, to spray the resultant liquid on to plants. Of the pump she says, 'I've never had a better, more trouble-free tool for spraying' – sentiments echoed by numerous wartime gardeners!

Nicotine in another form actually did more harm to plants than good. This was when it was being consumed by a gardener either as a cigarette or chewed in the mouth. Research in 1940 showed that in either form it played host to the mosaic disease virus which affected tomato plants. The virus remained in tobacco even after it had been cured and a worker smoking while he or she worked with tomatoes could spread it from plant to plant.

A pest and fungi control method that was not exactly lethal, but certainly dangerous if done without care, was soil sterilization. This could be carried out with either chemicals or steam. Commercial growers preferring the latter method could ask their local War Ag. Executive Committee to send a man with a special steaming machine. If the grower supplied the fuel and water for the boiler, the operator would put a pipe underneath the soil, cover the soil with tarpaulin and then, by steam, heat the soil to 212°F. No bugs could withstand this high temperature and the soil could then be safely re-used for plants. The wartime price for steam sterilization was a hefty £240 an acre, but it needed to be done only every three years.

Private gardeners who needed less soil sterilized could carry out the operation themselves. Harry still has two wartime vintage sterilizers at his gardens. One is 'the Terrorizer' – its proper name is in fact 'Terra Force' but Harry's men re-named it because of its fearsome habit of throwing out a shower of sparks if not enough soil was fed into its drum. Harry says it had to be fed with a shovelful of soil every 5–10 seconds and required four pairs of hands to keep it fed at one end and cleared of sterilized soil at the other. Today the Terrorizer, perhaps fortunately, is rusted beyond resuscitation but Harry's other sterilizer is still usable with care. It takes the form of a galvanized oblong tank of which the bottom quarter is a sealed compartment for water. The tank rests on a firebox. Water is fed into the bottom compartment and the soil for sterilizing placed in the top part of the tank. Once a fire is stoked up beneath, the water boils and sends steam through a vent into the top chamber and through the soil. Smoke from the fire escapes through a flue in the back of the pot shed. Harry got the old sterilizer working well for the television cameras but warned Anya, his 'land girl' for the series: 'If it starts bubbling at the back, stand well clear because if there's a stoppage and the steam is unable to get through, the back will blow off and hot steam and water will rush out.' Fortunately this did not happen, and Harry said with pride (referring to the sterilizer), 'She's a good old lady who's done a lot of service and there's life in her yet!'

How to Keep Cats off Allotments and Gardens
Like rabbits, they have runs. If you look carefully round, you will find tracks in the places at which they enter. Sprinkle these thickly with garden pepper and here and there on the plot bury, all but the neck, a few medicine bottles, putting about three teaspoonfuls of ammonia in each. Cats are nothing if not inquisitive. Seeing the bottle necks, they will take a sniff at them, and will naturally receive rather a shock when they smell strong ammonia fumes. They won't come again for some time.

From The Smallholder and Home Gardening magazine, 29 March 1941.

The less dangerous side of wartime pest and disease control included lots of sulphur to combat mildew and Derris powder (from Derris root) for destroying caterpillars on cabbages or flea beetles on seedlings. Unfortunately Derris came principally from Malaya and the Japanese occupation of that country from the end of 1941 meant that the powder was in short supply. In fact, it was by trying to find a substitute that scientists perfected the insecticide HCL (hexachlorocyclohexane).

A simple wartime way of dealing with slugs was to paint the underside of an old plank of wood with syrup or bits out of the bottom of a jam pot, then turn the plank over twice a week and squash the slugs attached to it. Carrot fly could be kept away from its prey by stretching a creosoted line above the carrots. Put off by the smell of the line, the fly would bypass the crop.

Collecting pests was ecologically safe if unsavoury. Many an ex-land girl recalls with revulsion the writhing mass of caterpillars in her bucket after a few hours' solid hunting. Children were encouraged to collect cabbage white butterflies. A 1943 show schedule has a class for the 'largest number of White Butterflies to be taken to school', and Fred Daw remembers that children were paid 1d (½p) for every cabbage white they brought to the advice bureau set up in his park.

While his schoolmates tend their Victory gardens the boy, centre, nets butterflies.

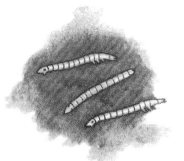

WIREWORMS

CUTWORMS

MILLEPEDES

LEATHER JACKETS

be destroyed. *'P.P.' Calomel Dust* (4%) is a very good control. This should be used in the seed beds and again after planting out from the end of April onwards. Give a matchbox full to each plant. Be sure to surround every plant, completely touching the stem all the way round, to prevent the egg-laying of the female. Always apply the Dust within four days of planting.

CABBAGE WHITE BUTTERFLIES

These pests are perhaps as well known to gardeners as the black fly of beans. It is, however, easier to control the caterpillars of the various Cabbage Butterflies and Cabbage Moth than is commonly supposed.

The Cabbage White Butterfly is familiar to everyone. It lays its eggs in spring and early summer. Stocks, nasturtiums and shepherd's purse, as well as cabbages, are host plants. The dull yellow eggs are quite conspicuous and can be destroyed by hand. If allowed to hatch, the young caterpillars feed together, grow rapidly and cause much damage. The pupæ or resting cases of the insects can be found hanging on fences, posts and walls in winter and early spring. They are about an inch long, of a silvery colour, shaped not

12

Children also played an invaluable part in collecting Colorado beetles. This may come as a surprise to those who believe that the pest, which could wipe out potato crops, was non-existent in this country or at least rare. In one respect they would be right, for anyone spotting or believing that they had seen a ½-in.-long yellowish beetle with black stripes on its back had to inform the Ministry of Agriculture directly. However, children *did* collect these insects on the Isle of Wight after German planes dropped boxes of them on to the Island's potato crops. Richard Ford, a wartime horticulturalist, remembers this happening. He recalls that farmers used to find the burst boxes and alert the police who contacted him. He then organized large numbers of schoolchildren to spread out across the field and walk up and down searching for the beetles. The Germans helped collection, for they always dropped boxes containing either fifty or a hundred beetles. If fifty-one beetles were found, Mr Ford knew that the children had to keep searching for the other forty-nine. Colorado beetles were also dropped in Kent. Whether these deliveries from the skies contributed to the outbreak of the pest in the late 1940s is not known, but their presence was then sufficient for the Ministry of Agriculture to equip special units across the country, which, rather like fire brigades, once alerted rushed off to spray.

Although saved from Colorado beetles, potatoes suffered other ills. The worst was wart disease which turned the tubers into a warty mass. This had become prevalent in the First World War when people exchanged potatoes and grew them too often on the same ground. The presence of the disease had to be reported to the Ministry. Eelworm was a pest which infected many wartime potato plots. The only remedy was to starve it by not growing potatoes: a difficult solution for some small plot holders, who simply added a lot of nitrogen, continued planting and hoped for the best.

Potato blight, which rotted foliage and tubers, could be treated by spraying with Bordeaux mixture (copper sulphate mixed with water and dissolved quicklime) or Burgundy mixture (copper sulphate mixed with dissolved washing soda). The strength of either could be tested with a pocket knife blade: if, when immersed and withdrawn, the blade darkened, the mixture needed more quicklime or soda solution. Application could be by stirrup pump or back-pack sprayer.

Coating onion seed in a mixture of starch paste and calomel, or dusting calomel along the rows, helped to deter onion fly, whose grubs burrowed into onions. Onion eelworm was more of a problem: the tiny worms caused the onion stem to thicken and rot. Because there was a shortage of overseas seed, a lot of English seed was grown. Unfortunately, the flower heads from which some of this seed was gathered had been infected and the seed carried the eelworm. The National Institute of Botany in Cambridge offered a service of fumigating onion seed with methyl bromide, but it was on a limited scale.

Where waste land or grass land had been newly brought under cultivation, the worst soil pests were wireworm and leatherjackets.

Facing page: Some of the most common soil pests which troubled wartime gardens.

Wireworm ate its way into potato tubers, tomato plants and carrots, and leatherjackets (the grubs of the daddy long legs or crane fly) damaged plant roots and ate into the underground stems of lettuce and spinach. One recommended method for destroying wireworm from the onset in newly dug grass land was to double-dig, then immediately to sow a crop of mustard. When 1 ft high the mustard was to be dug in. As well as acting as a green manure, it also apparently deterred wireworm. The more usual way of dealing with wireworm was to trap it in a potato or carrot which had been stuck on to a stick and then buried 4 in. deep with the stick protruding from the soil. Every three or four days the stick could be pulled up and wireworm inside the potato or carrot destroyed. Leatherjackets, once their presence was evident by a wilted plant, could be done to death by a knife point prodding into the soil in a circle around the plant.

A special effort against garden pests was made on 28 June 1941, designated National Spraying Day. No doubt garden syringes, ARP stirrup pumps and heavy metal back-pack sprayers did their bit. At the same time a high-pressure bug bomb developed for the Second World War was paving the way for less cumbersome spraying. Its principle was adapted for the first ever high-pressure aerosol insecticide marketed commercially in 1945.

FERTILIZERS

At the outbreak of war the Ministry of Supply set up Fertilizer Control to fix prices. With so much land in Britain under cultivation, the demand for fertilizers was high and meeting it was not easy. The fall in the availability of imported animal feeds reduced the amount of stock and made farmyard manure scarce and costly. Supplies of imported fertilizer were affected by shipping shortages and, in some cases, by their source being cut off.

Potash in particular was scarce. Almost all Britain's supplies had come from a belt of deposits running across France, Germany and Poland. When these sources were cut, limited amounts were brought from the Dead Sea, Spain and the USSR. In the summer of 1940 Britain's stock was half its peacetime level and the use of potassium fertilizers was carefully controlled. Professional growers could have supplies only for priority crops, with an amount stipulated for each crop, and holders of 10-rod allotments growing vegetables could have 3½ lb of muriate of potash. Small gardeners could still obtain supplies through horticultural merchants, but often purchase was dependent on the assurance that the potash would be used only for raising vegetables.

The Ministry of Agriculture encouraged gardeners to eke out their supplies by getting their potash from other sources. Wood ash was one: provided that it was not allowed to get wet, which would wash the potash out, a bushel of bonfire ash contained 4 or 5 lb of this nutrient. Harry remembers collecting up every bit of ash from open fires almost before it had time to cool. The ash was stored in a dry shed and used

Harry sprinkling wood ash around tomato plants.

liberally, especially on tomato crops. Ash from burnt, dry bracken was also a good source of potash and burnt ivy leaves yielded both potash and phosphates.

'Don't give Hitler the sack' was the message carried by advertisements in garden periodicals and followed with the instruction to open all jute and cotton sacks and bags carefully and return empties to your retailer. This was because war in the Far East had seriously affected supplies of sacks and bags.

'Bag' fertilizers at this time were either 'straights' (that is, containing one nutrient) or 'compounds' (containing several nutrients). The compounds came in a bewildering variety, for different merchants made up different mixes. However, in 1942, after being subjected to Fertilizer Control Committee field experiments, the first standard compound fertilizer was issued. Called National Growmore, it was made up specially to meet the needs of private gardeners and allotment holders who wanted a reliable fertilizer containing potash. National Growmore was 7 per cent nitrogen, 7 per cent potash and 7 per cent phosphates and, as Ron Sidwell remembered, 'did everything you wanted if the ground was in reasonably good heart'. It was also economically priced: in 1944 a 14 lb bag cost 4s 6d (22½p). Allotment holders were allowed 42 lb per year. The Ministry estimated that 30 lb of this was sufficient to dress a 10-rod allotment and the remaining 12 lb could be used as extra dressing for potatoes, winter green cabbage and spring cabbage. Interestingly, just after the war, scientists from Long Ashton Research Station in Bristol published a report which revealed that, from their own experiments carried out on allotments, this 42 lb allowance was barely enough to keep up crop production. They believed that the amount would have to be increased to maintain crop yields and soil fertility.

In June 1940 the Ministry stepped up its propaganda on compost heaps. Wireless announcements outlined the process of composting and gardeners were urged to read the new 'Dig for Victory' leaflet called 'Manure from Garden Rubbish'. The principles of composting – that is, putting vegetable and kitchen waste into a heap and inducing it to ferment and decompose into organic manure – might have been unfamiliar to some gardeners, but others were converts before the Ministry's prompting. Of this latter school was Sir Albert Howard, who had been director of the Institute of Plant Industry at Indore, India. When he returned to England he had great support, particularly in the county of Cheshire, for his theory that people's health depended on how soil was treated, and many followed his method of composting. This method was called the 'Indore Process', for it had been perfected there.

The Indore Process involved using not only garden rubbish but also, after they had been soaked in water, clothing, leather and sacking. Animal, bird and human dung was also a component part, plus earth and sufficient water to keep the heap at the consistency of a wet sponge. In October 1940 Sir Albert moved from Blackheath in London to a house at Milnthorpe near Kendal and became acquainted with F. C. King, the headgardener of nearby Levens Hall. Mr King read about the Indore Process in Sir Albert's book *An Agricultural Testament* (1940) and, according to Sir Albert's introduction to Mr King's own book, *Compost Gardener* (1943), 'not only adopted the Indore Process of composting but has incorporated the principles underlying the operations of Mother Earth in his outlook on gardening and life'. Dorothy Hinchcliffe actually remembers Mr King's composting. She says that everything he could find went into wooden bins. It was a rough sort of mixture containing garden waste, household waste, as much animal manure as possible and even tin cans to improve aeration.

With the fervour of the converted Mr King wrote of his composting to the *Gardeners' Chronicle* and received 'dusty' comments from other gardeners who doubted that inorganic matter such as cinders, ash or clinkers could be converted into 'humus as pure in its way as refined gold'. Harry recalls the columns of controversy over Mr King's methods, particularly his 'no digging strip'. This recommended sowing vegetables not into land which had been dug but on to soil on which 3 or 4 in. of well-prepared compost had merely been spread. Harry says that at the time, like a good many others, he was sceptical of this method, although he had never put it to the test as fortunately he had always had plenty of farmyard manure and had not had to rely on compost. However, having demonstrated for the television cameras how conventional compost heaps were made, he gamely volunteered to deplete one of his heaps by covering a strip of undug garden with about 4 in. of compost. Harry has now revised his ideas on Mr King, for the celeriac he planted in this mattress of compost became huge, and the New Zealand spinach and marrows 'went mad'. In fact, marrows planted in mid-April were ready for cutting before May was over.

The present owner of Levens Hall, Hal Bagot, is not so impressed with Mr King's devotion to compost gardening. Despite the gardens' immaculate appearance today, he says ruefully, 'The system quite clearly encouraged all kinds of noxious weeds, including bindweed, ground elder and creeping thistle. We've been struggling ever since to eradicate these.'

Wartime manures came in many guises. Ex-Swanley Horticultural College students recall working in the 1940s with 'London dung'. This, which arrived by lorry, was the sweepings of London streets. It was dark brown and had a peculiar pungent smell. The students had to single-dig it in. Among its plane leaves and rotted paper, the manure occasionally revealed old pieces of corset which had defied decomposition and the occasional coin.

Plymouth Corporation used to sell sewage at 1s 6d (7½p) a ton. It was also sold in other parts of the country, for Mary Caswell of Norfolk remembers that her father had sewage sludge delivered to his West London garden. It was a great success until the spring, when the whole garden was covered in tomato seedlings. The seeds from which these had sprung had passed unscathed through the human digestive system and survived treatment at the sewage works.

Below: 'Growmore', the first-ever standard compound fertilizer. Facing page: Onion seed, in wartime, as sought after as gold dust.

Gardeners were encouraged to ask the sweep if they could keep the sweepings from their chimney, for soot contained up to 4 per cent nitrogen and, mixed with wood ash, produced a well-balanced fertilizer.

Poultry, pig, goat and rabbit owners could gain manure from their livestock. This was not only in the form of droppings: feathers, if chopped and buried, provided humus and nitrogen, and rabbit waste and skins placed in a compost heap and covered with vegetable waste eventually yielded nitrogen and phosphates.

Muriel Smith of Cirencester recalls using a rather personal nitrogenous material:

> After school I was apprenticed to ladies' hairdressing . . . There was a patch of garden at the rear of the salon, and here we dug deep trenches lined with newspapers, plus thick layers of hair cuttings. We saturated this well, filled in with earth and planted runner beans. They did remarkably well . . . the yield kept us busy, slicing and salting down whenever there was a moment to spare between clients.

For the scientifically-minded, $15\frac{1}{2}$ lb of hair produces about $2\frac{1}{4}$ lb of nitrogen.

Perhaps one of the most enterprising conversions of waste into manure was that employed by Mary Smith's mother. Mrs Smith, who now lives in Louth, was in the Women's Land Army doing farm work during the war years. Her dungarees used to get stiff with pig swill and cow and pig manure, but her mother, instead of being annoyed when she sent them home for washing, was delighted, for she would soak them and then use the water on her tomatoes!

SEEDS

Compared to their peacetime editions, wartime seed catalogues were austere and thin. Illustrations were minimal and vegetable seeds, usually put at the back, were brought to the front and flowers relegated to their place.

In the early war years seed merchants had ample supplies in stock – in some cases too ample, and pleas were put out for people to order in case storage sheds suffered air-raid damage. However, in the summer of 1942 worries over shortages were being voiced by some leading members of the seed trade. The reason for this was that a large percentage of seed had formerly come from Holland, Italy and North Africa, areas where the climate could be guaranteed (in fact cauliflower seed could not be grown in Britain at all, for the winter killed the seedhead), but war had cut communication with many overseas sources.

British seed growers endeavoured to augment supplies by concentrating on vegetable instead of flower seed. Lillian Harbard, who worked at Sutton's in Slough, recalls cutting piles of beetroot and laying it out to dry, also brassica seedheads and beans and peas. She remembers that some

ONION, JAMES' KEEPING

Bees' Guaranteed Seeds

Tomatoes
It is better to save seed from a fruit containing 20 seeds than on containing 100. The plants from the former will give a far heavier yield. The best way to dry tomato seed is on a sheet of glass.

From The Smallholder and Home Gardening *magazine, 1942*

seedheads were dried over frames which looked like flag poles. Beetroot seed was threshed by machine in the field, while fine vegetable seed was hand-threshed with a flail in a barn.

British seed growers' output was stepped up to such a pitch that by November 1945 the Association of Pictorial Seed Packers estimated that sufficient vegetable seeds had been produced to fill 650,000,000 packets! Yet this colossal quantity was insufficient to supply all 'Victory Diggers', and the Ministry of Agriculture urged gardeners to save their own.

The safest seeds for amateurs to save were from vegetables that produced seed which came 'true' to type. The best results came from beans, peas, tomatoes, marrows, lettuce, onion and leeks. The shortage of onions in the 1940s (pre-war Britain had relied on overseas crops) made onion seed particularly valuable. But in the period before home-raised seed was ready, onion seed, particularly in large amounts, was difficult to find. Elizabeth Hess, who was responsible for organizing special seed packs for Women's Institute members, recalls the problem she had in getting onion seed. However, an unexpected solution presented itself. Her travels around the countryside took her one day to Ilkley in Yorkshire. Stopping for a cup of coffee, she noticed a small seed shop on the corner of a street. She decided to try her luck and, going in, asked for some onion seed. The shopkeeper enquired how much she wanted, to which she answered, 'Rather a lot. I want to supply all the Women's Institutes.' To her surprise the man replied, 'Oh yes, I might be able to do that.' He did, and WI members had onion seed when it was at its scarcest. In fact the tiny Ilkley shop supplied them the whole war through!

The WI was also lucky as far as other seeds were concerned. In April 1941 its headquarters received 40 tons of vegetable seeds as a gift from a New York association closely connected with Eleanor Roosevelt, the US president's wife.

In the ensuing war years American benefactors were to contribute seeds to many British gardeners. By January 1943 90 tons of American seeds were being distributed among members of the National Allotment Society. Their delivery was financed by the British War Relief Society of America. The seeds came in boxes which held seventeen or eighteen different varieties. Each box bore the name and address of the American donor and a lot of pen pals were made when British gardeners wrote their thanks. Gifts of seeds also came from Canada, Australia and New Zealand.

Occasionally certain varieties perplexed the British gardener. A number of gourds and squashes were unfamiliar, and maize, so easily grown by the donor, presented a problem in the British climate. Harry also recalls that some short-day and long-day lettuce varieties did not fare well in the daylight hours of Britain. Instead of making good hearts, they became blowzy.

Donations of seeds from particular organizations in Canada and South Africa went to the Royal Horticultural Society too. These, combined with gifts from professional British seed growers, were parcelled up by the Society and sent under Red Cross labels to prisoner-

WANTED FOR SEED DO NOT TOUCH

of-war camps in Germany and Italy. The parcels were addressed to camp leaders. A similar scheme had been carried out successfully during the First World War. All the common vegetable seeds except peas, beans and leeks were sent, though whether these three were excluded because of the 1940 Ministry ruling banning their export is not clear. Pumpkin seed was despatched particularly to camps containing South Africans. The flower seeds sent consisted of a good range of annuals and biennials.

The Society received back many letters of appreciation. This came from a prison in Stalag VIII-B: '. . . You ought to see the garden the lads have here, Cabbage, Peas, Beans, Tomatoes, Potatoes, plenty of everything . . . nice show of flowers, fifty Tomatoes on one plant, and more to come.'

Some prisoners of war did not confine their gardening to the purely practical. Helped by study material sent through the Red Cross Educational Books Section, they entered and passed Royal Horticultural Society exams!

Follow the Moon
In regard to the call for production of more home-grown food, I would recall the wise old country hint: 'Sow every form of seed by the moon.' The meaning is that seed sown during the days preceding the full moon germinates more readily and produces more prolific crops than seed sown during the waning moon. Those who smile unbelievingly might experiment; no harm can be done by doing so.

A letter from S. E. G. Ponder printed in Garden Work, 19 April 1941.

WEEDS

The month of August, once known by the old English name of *Weodmonath* because it was the time when many pernicious weeds seeded, prompted the Ministry writers of the *Allotment and Garden Guide* (August edition) to remind readers: 'Keep the hoe going. What feeds a weed will feed a cabbage to feed you.'

In a different, sterner bulletin the Ministry reminded householders that it was a matter of duty to keep down injurious weeds, especially those likely to spread seed to a neighbour's property. Not to do so would result in a fine. Even evacuated premises were not exempt. Fines *did* occur – for example, in the autumn of 1944 a North London man was made to pay 40s (£2) because he had failed to destroy thistles and docks growing in his garden.

As well as by hoeing, weeds could be discouraged by constant cutting; by hand-pulling and burning; and by suppressing with a smother crop like vetches. Horticultural chemical weedkillers were in their infancy, but in 1940 one which had been proved in agriculture – sulphuric acid – was used in gardens on onion and leek crops. It could be applied twice, once before the crop came through (weeds germinate more quickly than the crop) and again when the crop seedlings were above the ground. The seedlings were protected by their thin upright shape and waxy leaves which caused the sulphuric acid to run off and leave them unscathed.

Not quite so lucky were some land girls whose job it was to spray the acid. The young women, four of them, used a special barrow sprayer which had been developed at Long Ashton Research Station. This had a bitumen-lined tank, but the girls' own protection was not so well thought out. Ron Sidwell remembered that at first they just used to wear dungarees. They lodged in a hostel called Avonbank (now Pershore College of Horticulture) and after a day's spraying Ron would drive them home. On those return journeys he was treated to the sight of more wartime women's underwear than he had ever seen in shop displays!

Acid-proof clothing was eventually issued to sprayers.

PRACTISING ECONOMY

Large gardens faced with coke shortages had to close the valves on many of the hot water pipes usually fed by the garden's boiler. Glasshouses and frames were forced to remain cold and the heating pipes drained to avoid frost damage. Estates with ample supplies of timber could supplement their coke supply with logs, but even so it was wise economy to gather all exotic plants which needed heat into as small a space as could possibly be achieved without their coming to harm.

With supplies of fuel limited, maximum use had to be made of nature's heat. There were various ways of going about this. Crops grown within coldframes could be made to feel the benefit of winter sun long after it had gone in if the frames were closed and covered with a sack. A hot-bed of fermenting manure capped with fine soil would create sufficient heat within a frame to germinate sought-after early crops. Sales of cloches, which protected crops and trapped warmth, were high – not so much of the old-fashioned bell glass ones but of the newer types which were built up out of panes of glass and which could be joined to make a continuous shelter over a row. Harry's first experience of these panes-of-glass cloches was when he arrived at Chilton in 1947. The garden had a couple of hundred of them which were being used for war-effort crops, mostly early lettuce followed by dwarf French beans. After the French beans the cloches were used to germinate runner beans. Harry fell in love with using them and persuaded the garden owners to buy more. Placed in sunny south borders, the cloches soon paid for themselves.

For the television series Harry got Anya, his 'land girl', to go around the gardens and gather up every old cloche frame and pane of glass she could find. Cleaned and fitted together, these helped to swell the ranks of those already in line over his 'Victory' crops. Harry gave Anya the tip that a cloche placed on ground several weeks before sowing beneath it warmed up the soil and so helped germination. He remembers that another benefit of the cloches for a garden on wartime food production was that they enabled the production of three crops instead of two from a piece of land: the extra crop was an autumn one.

Besides cloches there were two other methods which gardeners could use to coax the maximum quantity of produce from their ground: catch-cropping and inter-cropping. Catch-cropping was growing a quick-maturing crop between main crops; inter-cropping involved cultivating two main crops together. Spinach, lettuce, early turnips, radishes, early carrots and globe beet could all be grown between rows of peas and broad beans. In an effort to use every yard of ground, vegetables were even inter-cropped between fruit trees. However, it must be said that inter-cropping was not liked by all gardeners. Some believed that it led to overcrowding and a reduction in yield of one or both crops.

A space-saving wartime ploy was to remove ornamental climbers from arches, fences and arbours and replace them with climbing beans, gourds, marrows and squashes. This had the benefit that it partially

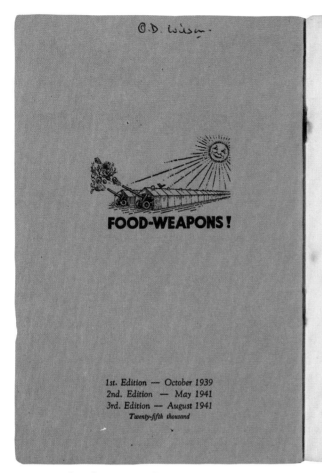

FOOD-WEAPONS!

1st. Edition — October 1939
2nd. Edition — May 1941
3rd. Edition — August 1941
Twenty-fifth thousand

CLOCHES versus HITLER
3rd EDITION

The first edition of this little book was published in October 1939, for it was realised even then that this was to be largely a food war. Now that more than eighteen months have passed, it is a commonplace that the battle of the Atlantic is being fought not only on the sea and in the air, but also on land in every garden and allotment in the country.

The ships, which formerly brought cargoes of fruit, meat, and other foodstuffs into this country, are now bringing us tanks, aeroplanes and shells from America. But it is quite possible to live on vegetables, and cloches can help you to crop a large variety in every month of the year. They can do more than this. They can help you to save two-thirds of your seed, for you must sow much more thinly under cloches, and almost every seed will germinate. They will save your seedlings from frost and excessive wet, the two greatest enemies of the English gardener. And lastly they will protect from wind and birds, and also from dogs and cats, which often do so much damage in the private garden.

Cloches are therefore true food weapons with which every gardener should arm himself. They are not luxuries, but rank with seeds, manures and. garden tools, as part of the equipment essential for successful all-the-year-round vegetable growing.

August, 1941.

converted a flower garden into a vegetable plot with the minimum of labour.

Economy on labour itself was a necessary wartime practice. In some mansion gardens, hardy potted shrubs were taken out into woodland, planted and left to take care of themselves until the war was over. The peacetime practice of sowing lots of different vegetable varieties to give a seasonal spread was abandoned; instead a number of rows were sown with one variety. Lawns were left to grow and simply cut as a hay crop. Gardeners were encouraged to use the new John Innes composts instead of making their own. Many old gardeners, however, preferred to keep to their own mix, laborious to prepare though it might have been!

In an effort to reduce hand-labour, some cultivators invested in fuel-driven machines. The larger of these were known as hand-tractors and worked by the operator walking behind and guiding progress by a pair of handles. These machines could usually be fitted with numerous attachments. For example, an 'Auto Culto' had attachments which enabled it to plough, ridge, hoe or cultivate. Despite the labour-saving properties of such gadgets, Harry says that private professional gardeners used to prefer hand-digging to machine-ploughing, not only for the 'finish' but also because hand-tractors were awkward to control, particularly when it came

Foreword of a book on cloche culture.

St George's Day – and the black-out lifted! At 9.15 I went all round the house & turned on every light and put all the 100 watt lamps I cd find, in the windows – Freda & I went out at 10.15 to look & the house really *did* blaze – but no one else in the village had lifted so much as a curtain. We felt queer! A sort of defiantly guilty feeling. The house felt sort of naked & unprotected!

From the diary of Miss C. M. Edwards, Binbrook, Lincolnshire. 23 April 1945.

to path edges. Moreover they had no reverse gear, and turning space in gardens, unlike in fields, was limited.

Reduction of labour by 'going mechanical' was not confined to large gardens. Small cultivators could buy a range of tools known as 'Planet Junior'. Unlike their engine-driven bigger brethren, these were pushed along. There were hoes, ploughs, drills and seeders. Many gardeners used the wheeled push-hoe, and a fair number of garden sheds still boast one in perfect working order.

ENEMY ACTION

Those who love a garden will have a fellow feeling for the problems faced by their wartime counterparts. It is easy to sympathize over pests, weeds and lack of time, but for those who have never experienced it, it is hard even to imagine coping with enemy action in the garden!

Yet it *was* done and sometimes with humour. In September 1940, when the London blitz began, a gardener exhibiting potatoes at a local show wrote on a card beside them: 'Dug by Goering's Gang'. They had been 'lifted' when a bomb made a 30-ft-deep crater in his garden!

Destructive in a different sort of way were bombs which covered vegetables in an evil-smelling oil. Not only were crops then unusable, but there were fears that the soil would be contaminated too. In December 1940 Ministry of Agriculture analysis showed that various kinds of oil were used in 'oil bombs', but the Ministry did not know enough about them to be able to advise gardeners. However, it could say encouragingly that an oily patch in a farmer's field did after several weeks sprout fresh grass.

Some enemy bombs landed on gardens more by accident than design. In 1940 a damaged German plane broke up over Stansted Park (a mansion where Harry had worked before the war) and the dozen or so bombs on board caused severe damage to its gardens and church.

In August and September of 1940 the sky over Kent was thick with aeroplanes as the RAF and German fighters and bombers fought the Battle of Britain. The roar of massed planes overhead became so familiar that a headgardener from Lamberhurst, writing to the *Gardeners' Chronicle* about his daily work on food production, mentioned as an aside that 'only a thrilling "dogfight" would induce us to straighten our backs'.

Other gardeners in 'Bomb Alley', as Kent became aptly named, had occasion to be less casual about overhead activity. Susan Cokayne remembers one afternoon between 1942 and 1943. She was a student at Swanley College and was working with colleagues in a field when a plane swooped and machine-gunned them. She says, 'It made us feel chary about working outside.' Muriel Wildash, who as well as working in Cornwall was a land girl in Kent, remembers a day when the ack-ack guns were particularly busy against enemy aircraft. She and the other young women huddled together: then, as Muriel recalls, 'For some reason I said, "Enough of this: in the cage!" and we all ran and got in the hedge. When we came back, there were bits of shrapnel in the place where we'd stood.'

June 1944 brought a fresh danger: the first V1 flying bombs. These pilotless bombs, launched from Calais, were aimed at London, but frequently their fuel would run out *en route* and the engine propelling them would stop. People quickly learnt that if they heard an engine cut out above them, they had fifteen seconds to run before the bomb came plummeting down. The V1s were nicknamed 'buzz-bombs' or 'doodle-bugs'.

Muriel Bushby, who worked at Warnham gardens in West Sussex, remembers the anxiety she used to feel when she heard a doodle-bug approaching. 'When you're in the peach house up on a pair of steps with a plank across, it's not a nice situation. I used to bolt down quick into the stove house.' On one occasion, when the day was very dull and cloudy, she and one of the elderly men gardeners were in the kitchen garden when a doodle-bug appeared from the direction of a nearby meadow. Muriel says, 'There was a terrible shaking through the air. It suddenly stopped right overhead. Your instinct is to go first on to the ground and this old chap and I just shot under the wheelbarrow. It did actually glide over, otherwise I wouldn't be here!' Pearl Bourhill, who worked for the London County Council on land at Epsom, recalls that the land girls who worked in the gardens there, growing produce for nearby hospitals, had their own doodle-bug early-warning system. When the bombs were about, the girls wore their tin hats (especially in the greenhouses) and one of them stood on guard with a whistle which she blew if she saw a doodle-bug coming!

Doodle-bug spotting.

The fear of bombing, rather than actual bombs, had a nuisance effect on gardeners. Instead of letting a huge bonfire pile accumulate, they had to have small, frequent fires which would burn out before nightfall. Those who let bonfires gleam into the night sky could expect police on the doorstep followed by a summons. Harry recalls a way of getting round this if you wanted the fire the next day: you put a sheet of galvanized iron over it and it would smoulder under the iron but not flare up.

Black-out regulations also had to be followed when garden boilers were stoked at night. Harry remembers that in pre-war days a 'duty man' would swing off down the garden with a hurricane lamp, but in the black-out he would take a torch with a hood or hold his hand over the light so that it filtered through his fingers. Harry himself remembers doing this when he was working in the Admiralty's gardens at Leigh Park near Portsmouth. It was something he was not loath to do for, he says, there were periods at that time when German bombers were over every night.

Not quite to do with black-out and only indirectly with gardens but interesting nevertheless is Harry's tale of the-bombs-that-were-never-found. One day, when he was stationed at Chichester barracks, he set off to visit some friends of his garden days at Stansted. He went on a push-bike he kept in the South Down bus depot at Chichester. Coming home on the road between Rowland's Castle and Emsworth, he heard anti-aircraft fire, so he stopped and got off his bike. Suddenly three bombs came whizzing through the air, each falling with a plop in a coppice wood on Stansted estate. Later Harry did inform about the bombs but says that he had to be careful because he was away from Chichester without permission. He thinks, however, that the bombs are still there!

POTATOES

feed without fattening and give you *ENERGY*

CHAPTER EIGHT

GARDEN PRODUCE

Home-produced, health-giving and able to bolster a meagre meat ration: these were the virtues of vegetables, and the Government constantly reminded people of them. Indeed, those who could grow vegetables and did not were failing in their duty to their families and to their country.

However, recognizing that growing and eating the same vegetables day in day out could be a little boring, two entirely different sources came up with the same suggestion – grow unusual ones. Old-style private gardeners used to providing such delicacies for their employers were the first to write about their plus points. Endive was useful for soup and salad, and could be cooked as a green vegetable; scorzonera was pest-free, easy to grow and could be left in the ground; salsify added variety to root vegetables and Jerusalem artichokes were prolific and would grow on poor soil. Even the rather strong-tasting kohl rabi was palatable if harvested when just the size of a cricket ball, and its leaves could be used as 'greens'. *Good Housekeeping* magazine, beating the same drum, published a book called *New and Unusual Vegetables: How to Grow . . . How to Cook*. Carter's Seeds carried a line of seeds to go with the book and advertised them as the means of producing vegetables which would provide a 'health-giving thrill, only before enjoyed in the most expensive establishments and luxury hotels'. The price of a packet of seed was 'only 3d [1½p]'. Despite this tempting offer and the plus points of unusual vegetables, probably not a great many were grown. One wartime gardener recalls, 'Quite honestly, we hadn't got time to muck about with things we didn't know.'

Potatoes *were* grown – lots of them. Their pleasant, neutral taste went with most foods, which was just as well for the Ministry of Food urged eating them twice a day. In fact to promote potatoes the Ministry created a cartoon character called Potato Pete. Betty Driver (now more famous for being Betty Turpin in the television soap opera *Coronation Street*) sang a song about Potato Pete and it was made into a record. Potato Pete also had his own recipe book which included potato recipes for every meal of the day plus suggestions for using the vegetable in snacks and sweets!

Eating potatoes saved bread and adding them to pastries and cakes saved fat. The potato was also a healthy food. It prevented fatigue and helped fight infection. Interestingly, during the First World War an outbreak of scurvy in Glasgow, Manchester and Newcastle was put down to potato shortages. The bigger a potato was, the more vitamin C it contained. Commercial growers were bound by official orders not to lift immature tubers.

Potato Pete, Potato Pete,
See him coming down the
    street,
Shouting his good things
    to eat,
'Get your hot potatoes
    From Potato Pete'.

Now hear him sing as he
    goes by,
All the kiddies are his
    pride.
Love to hear him shout,
    'Hi! Hi!'
Here's the hot potatoes
    coming by and by.

Have them in a packet,
take them home to Ma.
Have them in a jacket,
or eat them where you are.

This song about the cartoon character invented to promote potatoes was recorded by Betty Driver (below).

Facing page: A poster encouraging people to eat potatoes.

POTATO PIGLETS

6 medium potatoes, well-scrubbed
6 skinned sausages
cooked cabbage, lightly chopped

Remove a centre core, using an apple corer, from the length of each potato, and stuff the cavity with sausage meat. Bake in the usual way and arrange the piglets on a bed of cooked cabbage. (Use potato removed from each for soup.)

In January 1941 the national effort was towards getting 1,000,000 acres growing potatoes. There was even a scheme whereby the local council or War Ag. would take over and prepare vacant land. The ground, usually in 10-rod plots, was free to anyone who had paid 2s 6d (12½p) membership and 17s 6d (87½p) for a hundredweight of seed potatoes which they had to plant in their plot. In the same year Lord Woolton opened a 'model' potato bar which sold potatoes baked in their jackets.

A potato's jacket was important whichever way the potato was cooked. 'Food Facts' posed the question: 'How much potato do you lose when you peel it?' The answer: 'About a quarter (yes, really!). So you see how important it is to *scrub* potatoes, not peel them.' Just in case the message had not hit home, someone coined the doggerel:

Those who have the will to win
Eat potatoes in their skin,
Knowing that the sight of peelings
Deeply hurts Lord Woolton's feelings!

The Ministry of Food encouraged commercial growers by guaranteeing to pay a fixed price for their potatoes. Amateur growers were obviously not swayed by this incentive but responded well to Lord Woolton's enthusiasm for this vegetable. Dennis Darby of Thetford, Norfolk, a schoolboy at the time, remembers that his family's allotment grew so many potatoes that they had to borrow a horse and cart to bring home the main crop and his father made a big storage clamp for them in the garden.

SWEET POTATO PUDDING

8 oz sieved cooked potatoes
1 oz cooking fat
1 level teaspoon salt (less if potatoes previously salted)
1 egg
2 dessertspoons honey
2 sticks rhubarb, diced, or any fruit in season

Mix all the ingredients together and beat well, turning in the diced fruit last of all. Place in a fireproof dish, and bake in a moderate oven for about 45 minutes.

The Ministry of Agriculture viewed this enthusiasm for potatoes with some alarm. On 22 March 1943 it wrote a letter to the BBC which began: 'In many parts of the country gardeners and allotment holders seem to be reacting in a strange way to the Ministry of Food propaganda to eat more potatoes. Some of them seem to be determined to turn two-thirds or more of their ground over to potatoes . . .' The letter enclosed an urgent press notice telling amateurs that they should not aim at self-sufficiency in potatoes unless they had enough ground first to grow all their other crops. Despite this, some amateurs continued. As events turned out they were wise, for due to lack of labour it was impossible to lift all the commercial crops grown in 1944. By the spring of 1945 there was a potato shortage and people queued for them at the greengrocers.

The Ministry of Food's propaganda character. Potato Pete.

Potato shortages continued and in November 1947 they were rationed to 3 lb per person per week. This allocation continued into 1948 and must have struck hard at a time when the weekly meat ration was 1s (5p) and cheese only 1½ oz.

Root vegetables like carrots, parsnips, turnips, swedes and beetroot were valuable because they could be stored. In the kitchen they could form the basis of stews, pies and hotpots. Some were useful in other ways. Raw swede juice contained almost as much vitamin C as orange juice and parsnips, beetroot and carrots were sweet enough to be incorporated into a number of unlikely dishes. For example, beetroot and carrots were included in buns and cakes, and carrots wrapped in cellophane were sold as sweets. This latter trend may have started in 1941 when a Hornchurch confectioner applied to his local Food Council for permission to sell carrots as sweets. The sweet, vanilla-like flavour of parsnips was a godsend for inventive cooks. After they had been peeled, grated and simmered, parsnips could, by the judicious addition of flavouring, be made to taste of pineapple, banana or orange.

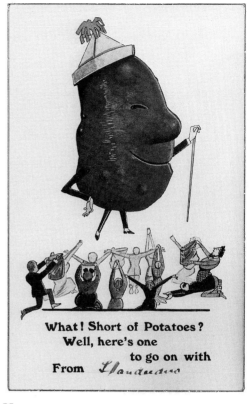

What! Short of Potatoes?
Well, here's one
**   to go on with**
From *Llandudno*

Beetroot, too, had a few odd uses – as a colour rinse on dark auburn hair and to provide a tint to marzipan. However, beetroot's main war role seems to have been as sandwich filling, where, at least for some consumers, if you had enough liquid you did not need butter. Any pleasure attached to eating beetroot sandwiches could wane with familiarity, as Harry remembers. When he was discharged from the forces, his landlady asked him if he liked beetroot. Harry, never one to tell an untruth, said he did and from then on she made him beetroot sandwiches day after day. He got to the point where he took the beetroot out and ate only the bread. It was some time after this that he finally managed to tell her, 'No more beetroot, please.'

In the winter of 1940–1 there were few surpluses in the country but carrots formed one. The Ministry of Food encouraged people to eat carrots by telling them that they contained vitamin A which would help them see in the darkened streets. In fact leafy green vegetables were richer in vitamin A, but of the root vegetables available the carrot did carry the highest amount of that vitamin. Muriel Smith of Cirencester, Gloucestershire, denies that eating carrots helped her to see in the black-out: 'I constantly sported a crop of bruises as a result of encountering unexpected obstacles.' Scientists sought to find a long-term method of keeping the enormous amounts of unconsumed carrots. They crushed some in an ordinary cider mill, clarified the juice and by evaporation turned it into treacle. The left-over pressed carrot which held a lot of vitamin A was deemed to be suitable either for fortifying foodstuffs or as an animal feed.

'Veg means vitamins, so keep your "vits" about you,' Ministry propaganda advised. For vitamin C one of the best sources was the ferny

> … After the Treasurer's Report which was very satisfactory, tea was served which included a special cake make by Mrs Bromfield. Members were asked to guess what ingredient in the cake made such an excellent substitute for fruit, the answer proved to be beetroot.
>
> *Ashmansworth and Crux WI, 4 November 1942.*

Above: Harry and Anya lifting potatoes.
Facing page: Poster emphasizing that carrots make healthy eating.

Vegetables Afloat
A note in a newspaper that sailors on board minesweepers suffered from toothache because of lack of fresh vegetables inspired the WVS to collect garden produce for them. Owners of gardens near ports were asked to help fill hampers and the hampers were taken to a WVS hut on the quay. When crews came in they were supplied with enough vegetables to last them two to three days. Grimsby, Plymouth, Yarmouth, Portsmouth and docks in Northern Ireland all received this service.

foliage of carrots. A wartime way of using this was to boil it and then use the strained water for boiling the carrots themselves. Vitamin C could also be obtained from green vegetables, provided that they were not overcooked. The way to avoid this was to use a 'conservative' (literally conserving the vitamin) method. *Cooking and Nutritive Value* by A. Barbara Callow (1945) recommended the following 'conservative' method as being very good:

> Take a saucepan with a closely fitting lid, and a vegetable fresh from the garden. Cut up large vegetables with a sharp knife before you cook them; cabbages should be cut downwards into slices about 1 in. thick, and cauliflowers should have each small sprig cut off separately; any thick pieces of stem should be cut into thin slices. Now put a small amount of boiling water and ½ teaspoon of salt into the pan. Let it boil briskly and add the cut-up vegetable, bit by bit, packing it down into the bottom of the pan. Boil for about 10 minutes – long enough for the vegetable to be cooked but not waterlogged. Keep the pan lid on firmly so that the steam does not escape. Serve at once.

To encourage consumption of greens the Ministry tried appealing to vanity: 'You can look right if you feel right and you can feel right if you feed right. An ounce of cabbage is worth an inch of lipstick.' This was

DOCTOR CARROT *guards your Health*

an interesting analogy, particularly as in July 1940 a 24 per cent tax had been put on cosmetics!

Spinach was useful to gardeners for it could be grown as a 'catch crop' between rows of other vegetables. As well as adding variety to greens, it also had the merit that the more it was cut, the more it re-sprouted.

The Ministry advised those who bought their cauliflowers from a greengrocer to ask for the outer leaves as well as the 'flower'. The leaves could be cooked by themselves like cabbage. Even the cauliflower stalk need not be wasted. Cooked until tender, rolled in browned breadcrumbs, then fried quickly or browned in the oven, it was supposed to 'have a nutty flavour'.

Peas could be given similar economic treatment. Their pods, divested of their outer skin, could be boiled and served as a green vegetable or made into pea pod soup. Even the pods of broad beans need not be wasted. Young beans could be eaten *in* their pods, and the pods of older beans used in stock for soup. Official advice on runner beans was not to slice them but to save time and flavour by simply breaking them up into 2-in. pieces.

One bean both the Ministry of Food and Ministry of Agriculture were keen to promote was the haricot. It was described as the French neighbour of dwarf or climbing beans. With their relatively high protein content, dried haricot beans were valuable when fish, meat, cheese and eggs were short. In 1941 commercial growers were asked to devote a large acreage to haricots and amateur gardeners were encouraged to try their hand at cultivating them. In Hastings the parks superintendent planted them in the floral clock instead of bedding plants, his declared object being to draw attention to their value as a winter foodstuff. As Hastings is a southern town he might have been successful in harvesting the beans, but gardeners 'north of the Trent' (as one contributor to a gardening magazine put it) found them a difficult crop to ripen. You also needed a lot of ground to get a worthwhile yield.

Haricot beans came in a variety of hues: white, green, black, buff, various shades of brown and red and even mottled. Jean Neilson of Bath recalls cooking with haricots and indeed with other dried beans available

PINEAPPLE SPREAD

I lb parsnips
I teacup water
3 oz sugar or golden syrup
2 teaspoons lemon substitute
I teaspoon pineapple flavouring

Peel the parsnips and grate them (or, if that is difficult, cut into flakes with a potato peeler). Put into a saucepan with the water and simmer until the parsnips are tender and the water reduced almost entirely. Take the pan from the heat, stir in the sugar or syrup, lemon and pineapple. Return to the heat and cook gently, stirring well. When the mixture is soft and juicy, put it into a jam dish or small jar.
Perhaps you say, 'Why the lemon as well as the pineapple?' Well, it serves two purposes. One is that the acid helps to make the mixture slightly more solid and jammy in consistency, and the second that it imparts a juicy fruity tang that is not there with merely the sugar and flavouring.

Cutting from a wartime newspaper sent by Edith Baker, Oakham, Leicestershire.

PEA SOUP

pods from 2 lb peas
1½ pints water
2–3 tablespoons peas
1 spring onion
lettuce leaves
salt and pepper
1 tablespoon cornflour
10 fl oz milk
½ teaspoon chopped mint

Wash the pea pods thoroughly and
discard any withered ones. Bring the
water to the boil. Add the peas,
pods, the spring onion and the
lettuce leaves and seasoning. Boil
for 30 minutes. Rub through a sieve.
Mix the cornflour with the milk until
smooth and add to the soup. Bring
to the boil again and boil for 2–3
minutes. Add the chopped mint and
serve.

From Cookery Under Rations (1941).

LEEK PUDDING

Potato suet crust pastry
8 oz self-raising flour
2 oz finely chopped suet
2 oz raw potato, grated

Filing
2–3 large leeks, or 6 small ones
Pepper and salt

Trim the leeks, cut in four
lengthwise, wash thoroughly and
chop into one-inch lengths.
Make up the pastry and line a
pudding basin with two-thirds of it,
leaving the remaining piece to form
a lid.
Fill up the basin with the cut leeks,
seasoning at each layer. Roll out the
pastry lid, place in position, then
damp the edges and seal together.
Caover with greased paper, place in
the steamer and cok for about 2
hours. Serve with a good brown
gravy.

in wartime. She says, 'There were mountains of them, some of colours we'd never seen in our life before!'

There is a wartime cartoon which shows a duchess lovingly touching a string of onions round her neck and saying, 'They're real, my dear!' A report in *Garden Work* magazine (18 January 1941) tells of a parcel which landed up in a dead letter office because its labels had been lost. The parcel contained 14 lb of onions and at least seventy people applied for it before it was delivered to the rightful recipient, a woman in Surrey! Such was the value of onions.

Prior to the war cheap foreign sources had made it uneconomical for growers to store onions for winter use and Britain imported 80 per cent of all the onions it consumed. With the outbreak of war, supplies from France and Spain ceased and Britain was caught with a short home-grown crop. In the springtime limited supplies could be got from Egypt and Argentina, but until 1944, when 'Dig for Victory' efforts began to provide an adequate home supply, an onion was worth its weight in gold. Occasionally nuggets could be found. Following a visit into Louth in Lincolnshire, Miss C. M. Edwards wrote in her diary on 29 January 1941:

I went into a veg. shop and bought three cabbages. The woman whispered, 'I've a *few* onions if you'd like a lb.' We hadn't *seen* one since we begged a small one from a friend on Xmas day – so she gave me three fat ones in a paper bag to hide in the bottom of my bag! The price is controlled: 4½d [just over 1½p] a lb.

The Red Cross quite cleverly turned the onion shortage to its advantage. It ran an 'Onion Scheme' whereby people could donate their home-grown ones. Gifts came from the likes of the Duchess of Marlborough at Blenheim, Lord Iliffe from Yattendon and the 'Victory Diggers' on the Bethnal Green bomb sites. When sufficient amounts had been collected, the onions were given to the NAAFIs of the fighting forces. The authorities paid their value in money which went towards Red Cross funds. Certain parts of the country had 'Municipal Onion Weeks' and set themselves a target tonnage of onions to donate to the scheme.

In 1941 the Minister of Agriculture had called for 14,000 further acres of onions to be grown. By 1943 it was estimated that Britain was growing more than it had ever grown in its history. A fair number of commercial onion growers operated in the Vale of Evesham, an area known before the war for its spring onions. However, because of the wartime shortage the Evesham growers had compulsory orders to turn 1,500 acres over to growing bulb onions. The late Ron Sidwell recalled that, despite this change of direction in their crops, the growers found a very good way of making the spring onions they still grew highly profitable. He explained:

Prices for the green salad onions were based on the slender, clean, washed articles of pre-war days. Under war conditions it was found that much fatter onions, unwashed, would make the full controlled price. A good dose of nitrogen would help the onions to put on weight until they resembled leeks. And it was possible to make £1,000 per acre without difficulty.

This figure was five times the profit the growers could make on their bulb onions!

The growers also discovered that their bulb onions responded well to nitrogen. Ron remembered:

> There was obviously a big temptation to clear the crop at midsummer as salad onions. At times the queue of growers asking for permits to pull reached out into the street from the little office above a former shoe shop. 'Me onions be gone gollynecked. They won't bottom,' was a typical assessment of the situation. And the cause of the gollynecked condition was known, only too well, by all parties.

In the kitchen, spring onions, dried onion or sliced leeks all stood in for the elusive large bulb onion. For those who had a bulb onion and used only half of it, 'Cheerful Rationing' (published by Central London Electricity Ltd) advised against putting the unused half back in the vegetable rack in case it became forgotten. Instead it suggested slicing it and popping it in the oven when the oven was switched off after cooking. With this treatment the rings would dry golden-brown and could then be stored and used for soups and stews.

According to the Ministry of Food, salad was not just a pleasant little addition to cold meat, but should be a meal for all the year through, especially in winter when fruit was scarce. The Ministry suggested winter salad recipes which used grated raw vegetables and spring recipes which included clusters of young dandelion leaves. Amateur gardeners were asked to use their coldframes for raising hardier varieties of lettuce because these too helped fill winter and spring salad bowls. Generally, however, lettuce was a summer salad crop. Beryl Robe, who worked on a large market garden in Milford, Surrey, recalls that it was the main summer crop there. She remembers very long, hot summer days spent going up and down lines of cabbage lettuces feeling each with the back of her knuckles to see if it was firm enough to cut and cutting hundreds each day.

Harry recalls the importance placed on lettuce by American troops. A nurseryman friend of his was asked by Americans stationed nearby to supply their camp with lettuce. When he enquired how many they would like each day or each week so that he could plan ahead and grow them, they looked puzzled and replied that they usually bought them by the ton!

Harry believes that his friend managed to supply the lettuce. Had the request been for cucumbers, though, it might have been a different story, for these were scarce. The reason was that the Government had decided that the nutritional value of cucumbers was low and banned their being raised in heated glasshouses. Harry says that if he had any, say, grown as a catch crop in frames or under the vines, or perhaps in a house after tomatoes had finished, they proved a very 'worthwhile' crop.

SCRAMBLED ONIONS

2 onions
1 teacup breadcrumbs
½ teacup milk
1 oz cheese, grated
salt and pepper
4 rounds of toast
chopped parsley

Parboil the onions and chop finely. Place the breadcrumbs, onions and milk in a saucepan to boil. Add the grated cheese and seasoning. Pile in heaps on toast, and garnish with chopped parsley. This makes a useful supper dish. Try with leeks when they are in season.

From a Central London Electricity Ltd 'Cheerful Rationing' card, June 1944.

I was front-page news a year ago . . . more precious than gold to those lucky enough to get a pound of me. That was because you relied on having me brought to you from abroad. Yet, if women and older children, as well as men, are sensible enough to Dig for Victory *NOW*, you can have me ALL THE YEAR ROUND for only the cost of a packet of seeds . . .

YOU SEE, I AM ONE OF THOSE CROPS YOU CAN STORE

LORD WOOLTON'S VEGETABLE PIE

The chef of the Savoy Hotel created a dish called Lord Woolton's Vegetable Pie. Some Liverpudlians believe that Lord Woolton favoured this recipe because of his connection with their city, which has a meatless stew called Blind Scouse traditionally eaten on Bally Ann Day (the day before pay day). Scouse is 'Liverpool' for stew. Ordinary Scouse is a stew of meat and vegetables. Unlike Lord Woolton's Pie, Scouse doesn't have a crust.

I lb potatoes
I lb cauliflower
I lb swedes
I lb carrots
3 or 4 spring onions
I teaspoon vegetable extract
I tablespoon oatmeal
chopped parsley
wheatmeal pastry (or extra potatoes) for crust

Cook the first 7 ingredients together for 10 minutes with just enough water to cover. Stir occasionally to prevent sticking. Allow to cool, put into a pie-dish, sprinkle with chopped parsley and cover with a crust of wheatmeal pastry or potato. Bake in a moderate oven until the pastry is nicely browned and serve hot with a brown gravy. This mixture of ingredients might be varied in many ways that may suggest themselves to the cook.

Ruth chopping vegetables for 'Woolton Pie'.

The worth of wartime cucumbers did lead to a little bending of Government regulations. One such case is recalled by Triss Male (*née* Comben) of Portland in Dorset, who worked as a land girl on a nursery in a village between Weymouth and Dorchester. The nursery raised tomatoes, but one spring all the young tomato plants got blight and had to be removed. It was too late to replace them, so her boss planted two large houses with cucumbers. This illicit crop grew to wonderful proportions, and the more they were picked, the more they grew – and they sold like hot cakes. Mrs Male's boss had to go to court as he had broken the law, but he was not fined a large amount. He had made a packet from the cucumbers and people had enjoyed them!

ECONOMICAL SALAD DRESSING

1 oz margarine or cooking fat
1 oz flour
1 teaspoon dry mustard
1 small teacup milk
1 small teacup water
salt and pepper
vinegar to taste

Melt the fat in a pan, stir in the flour and mustard and cook together for a couple of minutes. Then add the liquid gradually, stirring well. Season well with salt and pepper and add vinegar to taste. A tablespoonful of salad oil whisked in before the vinegar is added is an improvement. Store in a corked bottle.

From a Ministry of Food leaflet.

Left: Harry hangs up a bunch of haricot beans to dry.
Above: A wartime salad of young dandelion leaves; spring onions; beetroot; carrot and gooseberries. In the glass dish: economical salad dressing.

Tomatoes were far from banned; in fact market gardeners were obliged to turn 90 per cent of their glasshouse space over to them for six months of the year. They were a food which represented good nutritional value for they contained vitamins A, B1, B2 and C – the more so if eaten raw. Before the war Britain imported 3,000,000 hundredweight from the Channel Isles, Holland and the Canary Islands, but with Germany's invasion of the Low Countries and its occupation of the Channel Isles those imports were lost. To keep up supplies the Government ordered professional growers and encouraged amateurs to grow as many tomatoes as possible. Amateurs without greenhouses could grow them either in a warm spot – say, by a fence or wall – or under cloches which could be

TOMATO BASKETS

4 firm English tomatoes
2 oz cooked macaroni
I teaspoon chopped capers
salt and pepper
mayonnaise or cream salad dressing
mustard and cress
a few parsley stalks

Dip the tomatoes quickly in boiling
water and remove the skins. Allow
to become quite cold. Cut a slice off
the top of each tomato. Hollow out
the inside. Add some of the tomato
pulp to the macaroni. Mix in the
capers and season lightly. Bind with
mayonnaise, and fill the tomatoes
with this mixture. Cover the tops
with bouquets of fine cress. Add
'handles' made with parsley stalks.
Chill thoroughly, and serve on a bed
of mustard and cress.

*From New War-time Recipes for
English Tomatoes (1940).*

stood on bricks to give them the necessary height. Alternatively, the cloches could be left on the ground but the tomato plants inside them planted in a trench. Another method for amateurs was to plant out young tomato plants so that they lay horizontally in a coldframe and then to tie them to sticks laid up and down the frame.

Tomatoes are not an easy crop, particularly when you are dealing with a high number of plants. This was amply illustrated when for the television series Harry planted one of the large glasshouses in his walled garden with 126 tomato plants. The glasshouse was built for displays of flowering pot plants, but during the war years, like countless other glasshouses, would have been given over to tomatoes. First beds had to be prepared for the young plants, then canes were put to them. Each week the plants were tied and shoots removed from the leaf axils. When the first trusses appeared, Harry went through the house once a week tapping a cane against the plants' support canes. This sent a tremor through the plants and helped to encourage pollen to fall on to stigma and achieve pollination. The tapping was a good old private-garden method Harry had been taught as a boy. When it was done he damped down the floor of the house, for that, he said, gave the right atmospheric conditions to help pollination. When the third truss appeared plants were fed once a week and each had to be watered every other day.

Apart from the time and labour involved in growing large amounts of tomatoes, there was also an unpleasant side to their cultivation: their smell and their ability to stain hands and clothes. John Gerarde had spotted their odour way back in 1636, and wrote in his *Herball*: '. . . The whole plant is of a rank and stinking savour.' In Gerarde's time tomatoes were not liked at all and in fact did not become popular in Britain until well into the nineteenth century. However, in the Second World War they were *the* glasshouse crop and ways had to be found round their defects, particularly as it was then thought good practice to defoliate plants. This involved taking off leaves below the bottom truss once it had been picked so that the goodness which fed them would go instead to making fruit. One remedy to avoid getting permanent yellow hands when doing this was to smear Vaseline over the skin before starting work. With this method, when you washed your hands afterwards you did not need much soap – a bonus when soap was rationed. Harry has his own remedy: rub a really ripe tomato into your hands as if it were a bar of soap immediately after you have finished picking off leaves or gathering the fruit, then rinse your hands under the cold water tap and follow with an ordinary soap-and-water wash just to make sure that you do not turn the towel yellow when you dry your hands!

As to the tomato plant's odour, some land girls used to carry with them a reviving bottle of smelling salts. Harry did not go to those lengths, but says that by the end of a day defoliating in the big glasshouses at Nuneham Park, 'The smell seemed to be right inside you: very, very difficult to explain.' Also, oddly, 'You weren't hungry but it made you feel extremely hungry.'

At Nuneham picked tomatoes were tipped out on to a clean pine bench and weighed up into 12 lb chip baskets. Then a paper cover resembling greaseproof paper with the words 'Choice produce from Nuneham Park Gardens' was fitted through the chip handle and over the fruit. Harry remembers that all private gardens of substance used this sort of cover.

Harry no longer had paper covers for Chilton to grace his crop grown for the television cameras, and even thin chip baskets have become a thing of the past. The first picking from his 126 plants (varieties 'Ailsa Craig' and 'Best of All') yielded almost a hundredweight of tomatoes. In a small glasshouse he also grew a fine crop of 'Potentate', a wartime variety suited to a low house. Its rather 'boxy-looking' fruit is now out of fashion, but for years its earliness and heavy cropping made it a favourite with tomato growers in the Channel Isles. In fact Harry obtained his 'Potentate' seed through the kindness of Guernsey Tomato Museum.

Perhaps the nicest wartime success story regarding tomatoes is the achievement of Ryde Council on the Isle of Wight. In February 1941 the mayor, after a meeting with a Ministry of Agriculture official, agreed that the Council would pioneer a project for growing outdoor tomatoes on a large scale. The Ministry had suggested to Ryde the slogan: 'Why not tomatoes instead of tourists?' The first planting was of 15,000 plants raised in the Council's nurseries and planted by waterworks staff on a piece of neglected Council land. Such was the plants' success that in 1942 the mayor was asked to give a five-minute talk on the wireless in the *In Your Garden* series. By 1943 Mr G. Toms, the Council's tomato manager, was cultivating 7½ acres' worth. These yielded 92½ tons, and after sales to the mainland there was sufficient profit to provide 4½d (just over 1½p) relief to the rates. Tomatoes had indeed taken the place of tourists!

The Right Way to Gather Tomatoes
Early morning or late evening, when the plants are full of sap, is the best time for gathering. After gathering stand the tomatoes in a cool pantry for twelve hours before you eat them. This gives the 'flesh' an opportunity to set, and greatly improves the flavour.

From The Smallholder and Home Gardening, 10 July 1942.

Loading tomatoes at Ryde, Isle of Wight.

Facing page: Harry picking Ailsa Craig tomatoes.
Left: 'Boxy-looking' Potentate tomatoes before they turned red.

Crossing the Horse Guards Parade one morning *en route* to the office, a civil servant engaged in the 'Dig for Victory' movement was surprised to notice a perfect specimen of a tomato plant in full flower, jutting out of the wall of a Government building. Practising what he preaches, he promptly bent down and nipped off the side shoots, although his expectations of gathering the fruits in due course are far from optimistic.

From the Gardeners' Chronicle, *25 August 1945.*

WARTIME SUMMER PUDDING

Stale bread and breadcrumbs
Elderberries
Mixture of fruit (eg, blackberries,
blackcurrants, redcurrants,
raspberries), as available
Sugar

Put some ripe elderberries in a
saucepan, cover with water and
simmer. Mash the berries to get a
nice red juice and sweeten with
sweeteners or sugar. Cut a round of
bread to fit the bottom of a basin
and triangles to fit round the sides,
having first dipped them in the red
juice. Put chosen fruit mixture into a
saucepan with any left-over juice and
cook through over a low heat.
Sweeten to taste. Put a few
spoonfuls into the lined basin until
about a third full, then cover with
breadcrumbs. Repeat layers of fruit
and breadcrumbs until the basin is
full, finishing with a round of bread.
Place a saucer and weight on top of
the basin and leave the pudding to
soak overnight. Next day, run a
knife around the edge of the pudding
and turn onto a dish, leaving it for
about an hour while the pudding
eases itself down. Give it a quick
shake and turn out. If you have a
little juice left over, you can use this
to take care of any 'bald' patches.

Owing to the fact that their
British market is for the time
restricted, New Zealand is
making a free issue of one apple
a day to each of its
schoolchildren.

*From Garden Work, 19 April
1941.*

The Ministry of Food decided that fruit was not a necessary food and to save shipping cut the import of both fresh and canned fruit to almost vanishing point. As practically three-quarters of all the fruit eaten in Britain was imported, this was drastic action.

The shortfall could not be made up by British commercial growers because they were not allowed to put down any extra ground to fruit, the reason being that it took too long to come into bearing. Instead all available land had to be given over to vegetables: these would be relied on to provide the minerals and vitamins imported fruit had given. Private gardeners endured no restrictions on fruit growing, but as war continued it became increasingly difficult for them to obtain young trees or fruit bushes as nurseries had to cut back their stocks to 10 per cent of what they had been pre-war.

Anyone with fruit trees possessed a valuable asset. Potash fertilizer would have helped maximize this but it was difficult to obtain in quantity and so gardeners had to rely on pruning and spraying to help the fruit yield. It was also advisable for the owners of top fruit to put grease bands around the trunks of their trees in September to prevent insect pests climbing up to lay eggs in the branches. If this was not done, the eggs would turn into maggots which would eat the fruit.

Although derelict orchards were pulled up and potatoes planted in their place, old orchards capable of renovation were kept and teams of specially trained Land Army members set about pruning and, if necessary, top-grafting the trees.

At picking time amateurs collecting for their stores and commercial growers with an eye to sales strained to reach even the most inaccessible fruit. Nor were windfalls wasted, for there was a ready market for them. To prevent prices escalating too much the Ministry of Food fixed the price a grower could ask for each variety of fruit. However, there were some kinds for which it was not considered worthwhile to fix the price: these were known as 'any other variety', and the grower could fix his or her own price. This piece of legislation brought a great benefit to a Herefordshire tenant farmer. He had on his land some perry pear trees which yielded a small, brown pear called 'Brown Bess'. In normal times these tiny pears would have either been used to make the drink perry or simply left to rot on the ground. However, because they were just sweet enough to pass as 'eaters', the farmer sold them. By the end of the war he had made sufficient money out of 'Brown Bess' to buy his farm!

Large private gardens found a ready sale for rhubarb, and their peaches and grapes, which ripened despite the unheated glasshouses, could command black-market prices! Harry recalls that amongst the American soldiers based around Nuneham Park, word went round like wildfire that there were peaches in the garden. Several GIs turned up at the gardens and, instead of buying one or two peaches, as people usually did, they took off their hats and each bought a hatful!

If the Americans bought fruit, they also gave it, for their camp rubbish bins, which were collected by pig keepers, often yielded an untouched

RASPBERRIES
PICK YOUR
OWN
6¼d per lb

banana or orange. With the skin washed this found fruit was prized. Oranges were scarce and if they did come into the shops children had priority claim to them: adults were allowed only what was left. This was the general rule, but some grocers had their own form of rationing. Pamela Deane of Exmouth, Devon, remembers going to the greengrocer's because some oranges had come in and not being allowed any because her parents did not buy any vegetables! As she says wryly, supporting the 'Dig for Victory' campaign occasionally had unfair results.

Perhaps the most 'missed' fruit of the war years was the banana. Imports came to an end in 1940 and the last bananas to be sold were in the shops in the middle of December of that year. (Also at this time lemons disappeared, even off the black market.) Many people did not see a banana for the following six years. Mothers mashed up cooked parsnips with banana essence as a substitute and children ate it, for eventually some did not know what a real banana tasted like. Ruth remembers queuing up for the odd banana for her daughter Bertha, but when she got it home Bertha was not really keen on it because she had never acquired a taste for them! Bertha did, however, redeem herself on another score. Like all small children she was allowed tins of blackcurrant purée, and Ruth found some of these very useful for making blackcurrant tarts.

Pick-Your-Own raspberries at a market garden in Cheltenham. Over 500 people arrived in the first hour of opening, August 1941.

Most apples are not rich in vitamin C, but 'Bramley's Seedling' is fairly rich and its peel may be as rich as orange juice.

From Cooking and Nutritive Value, *1945.*

KITCHEN ECONOMY

If, during the war years, someone served you baked sultana cake pudding, you might have made the educated guess that it had started out in life as a fruit cake. However, owing to the intervention of enemy action, it had, through sudden lack of heat, dipped dramatically in the middle and had to be metamorphosed into a pudding. Stork Margarine had suggested this salvage action to housewives. The company's kitchen had looked seriously into how dishes could be saved if air raids or other emergencies necessitated turning off the oven. Mercifully, it seems that meat and milk puddings generally went on cooking in what warmth was left.

Should air raids look like being a nightly occurrence, Central London Electricity Ltd's 'Cheerful Rationing' thought it sensible to abandon main evening meals and go for high teas instead. However, as occupation of the Anderson shelter was often for hours at a time, it was sensible to take some form of sustenance. Sue Usher recalls during raids on Birmingham scooping up her sleepy son Neville and encouraging him to the shelter with a 'picnic' of weak tea and biscuits. For women who had time to plan ahead, a small publication entitled *Easy Meals for Busy Days and Nights* suggested quite an elaborate picnic. It advised packing vegetable broth or beetroot soup, some sandwiches (mashed haricot bean and Marmite is one suggested filling), perhaps pasties and some biscuits or oatmeal buns.

In daily kitchen routine, economy was patriotism. Women were encouraged to save food scraps (for pig bins); paper and rags (for recycling); bottles (glassmaking used too much fuel); bones (for soap, glycerine, glue and fertilizer); and aluminium milk-bottle tops (to build Lancaster bombers). Also for building planes, Lord Beaverbrook, the minister of aircraft production, put forward a plea on 11 July 1940 for women to donate aluminium pots and pans. The WVS, charged with organizing collection, ended up with 1,000 tons' worth. This piece of patriotism might have been in vain, as only certain high-grade scrap aluminium was used for aircraft and some historians believe that Britain had sufficient supplies of this without the need to call in pots and pans. Indeed, today's aviation experts express doubts that such a motley collection of household utensils could have helped the situation. If it *was* all in vain, it was a great pity, for later in the war buying a new saucepan was not easy: you might make an order but would have to wait several months for delivery. There were occasional bonanzas: for example, in May 1944 Woolworths secured a stock of blue enamel pots and all and sundry queued to buy them.

BAKED SULTANA CAKE PUDDING

8 oz pieces of cake
2 oz sultanas
sugar to taste
I egg, beaten
10 fl oz milk

Place a layer of cake in the bottom of a pie-dish brushed with melted Stork margarine, sprinkle with a few sultanas and a little sugar, and repeat these layers till the ingredients are used up. Mix the beaten egg with the milk and pour over the dry ingredients. Bake in a fairly hot oven (375°F or gas mark 5) for 50 minutes. Serve with custard.
Serves 4–6.

Facing page: Ruth and her 'evacuee' using the 1930's Acme 'New World' gas cooker supplied by South Western Gas Historical Society.

Above: This photograph taken on 24 July 1940 shows men sorting and stacking saucepans donated for recycling into aircraft.
Below: A Spode utility teapot. A good pourer.

Metal pan cleaners disappeared; galvanized buckets were on ration and strainers and mashers reserved for babies and invalids. A housewife with a flair for DIY could get over some shortages as old tins with holes punched in them could serve as graters, sink strainers or flour dredgers.

Care had to be taken with crockery, for replacements were difficult. The Potteries were producing only three varieties of cups compared with sixty-seven in peacetime. Shortage of workers and fuel had also put an end to pretty, decorated crockery for the home market. Instead crockery was plain white and earthenware. It became known as 'utility ware'. To save labour some utility cups were made without handles, but were economical because they could double as sugar or jam containers. Hot-water jug tops were also interchangeable with teapot lids and the general design of pieces was streamlined to lessen the risk of breakage. Spode made a teapot with an inset spout because it took less labour to produce: ironically today some experts view this teapot as one of the best 'pourers' ever made!

Kitchen economy could be furthered by adhering to countless tips which were published or given over the radio. Here is a brief selection:

1 Scrape carrots away from you, 'down not up': you waste less carrot.
2 Let an 'empty' milk bottle stand for a few minutes before washing. You will find that you will be able to drain a bit more milk out.
3 Save pieces of margarine or butter paper for lining cake tins or covering steamed puddings and baked jacket potatoes.
4 Save muslin flour bags, wash and use for straining sour milk for cheese, also for covering food against flies.
5 Apple parings can be used to make a good summer drink for children.
6 When storing tinned foods, choose the smaller sizes. This allows one to use a variety of ingredients in a dish without being extravagant.

The foregoing little economy measures were voluntary; a big economy which was *not* was fuel saving. Fuel was needed for factories and shipyards employed in war work, and to keep these supplied every private household was rationed. The Ministry of Fuel informed people that the 5 lb of coal it took to supply an electric oven for two hours could make a hundred Bren gun bullets. Housewives were particularly singled out as targets for propaganda, the Ministry informing them that they were in the front line of the 'Battle for Fuel'. Many women, who previously had not bothered, learned how to read their fuel meters. For gas and electricity the ration was based on the part of the country in which you lived (the further north, the more you were allowed) and how many rooms were in the house. Added to that was a personal allowance. In 1942 the coal ration per household was 4 hundredweight for three weeks. Gordon Veitch can remember it being as low as 1 hundredweight a month, for when his delivery of this amount arrived it looked so small that he weighed it on the household scales. It was *just* 1 hundredweight.

In addition to coping with fuel rationing, households which had gas cookers sometimes found that, following air raids, the gas was cut off or the pressure so low that it was impossible to cook on. April Badrick of

Yeovil in Somerset recalls that when this happened her mother had to resort to cooking on an old-fashioned oil heater and her father fixed up a 'spit' in front of the fire to roast their small Sunday joint. Cuts in the supply to save electricity were generally timed for mornings, so it became nightly routine to fill a Thermos flask with hot water. This was when a hay-box cooker could come into its own: porridge just brought to the boil, then placed in the hay box and left overnight was piping hot next morning.

Hay boxes had proved their efficiency in the First World War and if you had the right materials it was simple to make one. You needed a stout old wooden box with a lid – a packing case would do. The next step was to line it with three or four newspapers (about twenty sheets in all) and fasten them with drawing pins. Then you packed sweet, dry hay to a depth of 5 in. in the bottom. Next you made a mattress the same size as the base of the box and filled it with hay. Cooking pans to be put in the hay box had to have short handles, so that they would fit in, and firm lids; they had to be filled as full as possible and their contents had to be thoroughly boiling before a lid was put on and they were placed in the hay box. It was wise always to check the bottom of a pan before doing this just to make sure that there was no burning ember of soot stuck to it which would ignite the hay! Once the pan was nestled inside the box, 4 in. of hay had to packed closely round the sides and top and the hay mattress placed firmly on top. The last step was to shut the top of the box securely.

Hay-box cookery was not confined to porridge. It was useful for soups and casseroles; for old fowls and cheaper cuts of meat which needed long, slow cooking to make them tender; for stewing fruit; for finishing boiled puddings; for cooking vegetables (except green ones because the method destroyed vitamin C); and even for jam making. To make jam by this method you first boiled it in a deep enamel pan for ten minutes, put it into the hay box for two or three hours, removed it, brought it to the boil again, then replaced it in the hay box for a further three hours.

Fuel saving, like general kitchen economy, was aided by numerous helpful suggestions. The Ministry of Food advised one-pot meals. These could be made in a saucepan topped by a steamer, in a saucepan topped by a plate, or in one big saucepan which contained two or three stone jam jars. For the last method sweet and savoury dishes could be cooked in the jars, which would be stood in boiling water reaching half-way up their sides, and the steam from the water would cook vegetables hung in a muslin hammock below the pot lid.

More fuel-saving tips were:

1 Use half-moon pans (two pans on one ring).
2 Keep saucepans clean (dirt wastes fuel) and arrange oven shelves before switching on.
3 Have a complete oven meal, such as a casserole, scalloped potatoes, apple charlotte.
4 Club together with neighbours over cooking the main meal. A cooker normally used for a family of four could work for three families.

SUGAR BEET SOUP

Boil the beets (2 large roots are sufficient for soup for 6 people) for 1 hour on the stove and transfer to a hay box for 6–7 hours. Rub through a sieve, skin and all. Make a roux by melting 1 teaspoon of margarine in a small saucepan, adding a little flour and stirring to a smooth paste over gentle heat. Add 2 pints of stock very slowly and the sieved beet. Re-heat, put 10 fl oz of hot milk in the tureen and pour in the soup.

From Haybox Cookery by Eleanor Sinclair Rohde (1943 edition).

Right: Ruth shows Tracey (Joyce) how to make a hay box.

Facing page: Preserving Apple Rings
1. Ruth ignites a pile of Flowers of Sulphur. A glass jar was then inverted over the burning heap to fill with sulphur fumes.
2. Turned up the right way again the jar retained sufficient fumes to stabilize the colour of the cut apple rings when they were dropped into it. Each ring was then taken out and threaded on to a stick which had been cut to a size that fitted across the inside of the gas oven.
3. The loaded stick(s) were placed inside the oven when it had just been turned off but before it had cooled. This supplied enough gentle heat to dry the rings sufficiently for storing in a tin.

5 When all cooking is finished, switch off and use the heat left over to warm a bowl of washing-up water.
6 Cook pulses or prunes in a vacuum flask by covering with boiling water and leaving overnight. NB: Leave room for expansion. Prunes will be ready to eat next morning. Pulses will be considerably softened.

'Fruit eaten raw is soon gone, and does no good, whereas if boiled and converted into jam it goes much further, and often "comes in" handy when butter is scarce.' This advice was written in 1850, but in 1940 it rang particularly true. Ruth recalls, 'During the war people were still eating old-fashioned teas of bread, butter and jam. You used to scrape the margarine on very carefully but you could put on plenty of jam to compensate.'

With increasing quantities of bread in the wartime diet, the Ministry of Food was keen to promote jam making. Home jam makers were allowed an occasional bonus ration of sugar and during certain times of

the year could take sugar in lieu of their jam ration – the usual deal was that 1 lb of sugar equalled 1 lb of preserves. Even those who had not managed to secure sufficient sugar could still try jam making, for magazines gave recipes showing how glucose, honey, syrup or even salt could be used to bolster what sugar they had. The recipe for using salt was ½ teaspoon of salt and 8 oz of sugar to 1 lb of jam. A precautionary measure, if any sugar-saving jam would not thicken properly, was to add ½ oz of tapioca (soaked overnight in cold water) after the salt and sugar.

During the early part of the war no amount of economy could produce marmalade. There just were not sufficient supplies of Seville oranges. For a time there was no factory-made marmalade in the shops either. Lord Woolton suggested to housewives that they could make marmalade from sweet oranges and some bitters from the pub. At this one bemused woman wrote in her diary, 'But, dear man, where do we get the sweet oranges?!'

Jam was not the only preserve the Government wanted to encourage, for under wartime conditions it was considered that no home-grown produce should be wasted and after immediate needs had been satisfied women were urged to preserve any surplus. The Government took its advice from Bristol University's Long Ashton Research Station which had a special section dealing solely with home preservation of fruit and vegetables. Alice Crang headed the section and, with the help of a handful of women assistants, researched and suggested methods which were published by the Ministry of Agriculture in its 'Growmore Bulletins' and by the Ministry of Food in its 'War Cookery' leaflets. No method was ignored. Housewives were advised how to dry apples (particularly useful for non-keeping varieties), plums, onions, mushrooms and herbs; how to salt string beans; how to make pickles and chutneys; and how to bottle.

Bottling vegetables was not encouraged for fear of soil organisms causing botulism, a rare type of food poisoning with a mortality rate of

GOOSEBERRY BROWN BETTY

6 oz dried national wheatmeal
breadcrumbs
2 oz margarine, melted
1 bottle gooseberries
¼ teaspoon grated nutmeg
sugar (if necessary)
10 fl oz hot water and gooseberry
syrup

Mix the breadcrumbs with the
melted margarine and use to cover
the bottom of a pie-dish. Drain the
gooseberries and put a layer of fruit
in the dish. Sprinkle with nutmeg,
and also sugar if the gooseberries
are bottled in water. Put another
layer each of crumbs and
gooseberries, and sprinkle again with
nutmeg and sugar. Cover with
crumbs, pour the hot syrup and
water over and bake for 40 minutes
at 350°F or gas mark 4.

From Stork Margarine's Puddings with
Home-bottled Fruit *(1942).*

Two wartime members of
Barham Women's Institute in
Kent, canning fruit.

A wartime advertisement.

Summer PRESERVES
mean WINTER RESERVES
POROSAN
CAPS & RINGS
POROSAN
SKIN
POROSAN
Fruit Preserving
METHODS ARE BEST

over fifty per cent. However, bottling of fruit was fully explained, particularly four methods which did not involve using sugar. These were stewing fruit and bottling the resulting pulp; heating fruit in jars in an oven and then pouring in boiling water to cover; sterilizing by putting filled jars into a deep pan of water and bringing the water slowly to simmering point; and the Campden Method. The Campden Method was named after the Gloucestershire town of Chipping Campden where the preservation research laboratories perfected it before they were moved to Long Ashton. The method involved simply putting fruit in a jar and covering it with a solution of sulphurous acid.

Up until 1940 'Campden Preserving Solution' was sold directly from Long Ashton. In that year, however, the plum crop broke all records, and despite the Government releasing large quantities of sugar specially to preserve the crop, people also asked Long Ashton for 'Campden Solution' as it was known to be particularly suited to preserving plums. Unable to cope with the demand, Long Ashton gave the formula to manufacturing chemists, who converted it into tablet form so that it would keep better on their shelves.

As well as being good for plums, the Campden Method was suited to damsons, greengages and apples which had been first peeled and cut up. Unfortunately it made the skins of green gooseberries and blackcurrants tough. The recommended 'recipe' was 1 tablet to 10 fl oz of cold water, and at least that quantity had to be used completely to cover 1 lb of uncooked fruit in a preserving jar. After that the jar was simply sealed, although the inside of metal lids had to be protected against the sulphur in the solution by a layer of paper or smear of Vaseline. When the fruit was wanted, it was boiled for 15 minutes to remove the sulphur dioxide.

The plum glut of 1940 was the catalyst for another wartime preserving development, one which depended not so much on chemical aid as on woman-power. The National Federation of Women's Institutes informed the Ministry of Food that by setting up fruit preserving centres all over the country it could stop the waste of all surplus fruit. The Ministry agreed to release 600 tons of sugar which the WI headquarters purchased. Church halls, school dining rooms, empty cottages, derelict huts and even garages all became preserving centres. People brought along their surplus fruit and WI members, working in shifts, sorted, cleaned and cooked it. In many cases the cooking apparatus was simply a primus or oil stove. Some centres also had a canning machine, either a recent gift from America or one which had been purchased by the WI in pre-war days from a manufacturer in the Midlands. At the end of 1940 the preservation centres had produced 3,000,000 lb of jam, 150 tons of canned fruit and 160 tons of pulped fruit and chutney!

In 1941 the scheme continued but was sponsored by the Ministry of Food. This meant strict Ministry regulations, jars stamped with 'MF' and official covers tied, according to Doreen Furmidge of Harrietsham WI after she had consulted their wartime records in Kent, 'with a special knot which didn't waste an inch of string'. No more than two stones were allowed in each 1 lb of plum jam and only four in damson. An inspectress came quarterly to check the quality of jam, and fish-paste-size jars were filled and put with each batch for the purpose. The inspectress's other task was to make sure that the amount of sugar allocated to the centre matched up to the jam produced. The rule was 60 per cent sugar content, so 10 lb of jam indicated the use of 6 lb of sugar.

The year 1941 was not, however, such a happy one for the scheme. The introduction of rationing meant that WI members could not buy back their jam at wholesale prices as they had done in the previous year. In essence they were being asked to work long and hard for nothing except the knowledge that they were helping the war effort. There were grumblings, but many agreed to carry on. Another setback in 1941 was that it was a poor year for fruit, and it did not help preserving centres that

SPICED RHUBARB

The process is simple and the fruit needs to be well cooked. The extra spices are necessary, as during the longer cooking some of their flavour will evaporate.

3 lb rhubarb
2 lb sugar
1 pint spiced vinegar
a little extra clove, cinnamon and ginger

Cut the rhubarb into 1-in. pieces and simmer with the sugar, vinegar and spices till the rhubarb is transparent. Then remove the fruit and reboil the liquor until it is a thick syrup. The final pickle, when cold, should be almost a jelly. Close while still hot and it is ready to eat in a couple of days.

From Home Pickling *by Henry Sarson (1944).*

PLUM CHUTNEY

5 lb plums
2 lb sugar
3 oz salt
1 oz ground ginger
1 oz ground cinnamon
1 oz ground allspice
1 oz mustard seed, bruised
1 quart vinegar

Stone the plums and cut into quarters. Add all the other ingredients to the vinegar and bring to the boil, then put in the plums and simmer till tender. If the mixture is still too thin, continue to simmer gently until the desired consistency is obtained.

Above: Ruth canning plums. The 'Dixie' canning machine was loaned from Doddington WI in Kent. Since the war it had lain in an ammunition box stored in a barn!

the price they were allowed to pay when fruit was brought to them was often below pre-war prices. The rates for fruit were read out on *The Kitchen Front* radio programme every Monday morning. Members had to listen carefully, as in some parts of the country certain fruits were worth more than in other parts. In fact there came a stage when the announcement had grown so long and involved that an announcer refused to read it. After a certain amount of smoothing ruffled feathers all round and promises from WI headquarters that the announcement would not exceed one minute in length, the service was resumed.

Other problems of that year are revealed by a letter written by Ethel Kirby of Long Ashton's home preservation section. The letter, dated 28 July, was written from Cornwall and addressed to Miss Kirby's superiors at Long Ashton. These extracts give some idea of the dispiriting task she faced in her role as adviser and inspector:

> Inspection by paid inspectors is not understood and much objected to . . . storage is very hard as a whole and I fear great trouble when large quantities of blackberry jam are made as local shops will not be able to buy the bulk and there will be nowhere to put it when made . . . There are difficulties in obtaining the necessary equipment such as labels, covers, etc., though they have been ordered for a long time. Prices of fruit and jam have been altered and there has been much confusion about them. Food offices are sometimes helpful. Sometimes much the reverse and make the work more difficult and offend workers.
>
> Cornwall is of course very damp. I saw jam that had only been made a few weeks with mould growing on the outside of the covers. All this is not encouraging to the workers. Conditions for work in village halls are very, very far from ideal. Slow oil stoves, no water . . .

To add to this catalogue of woe Miss Kirby's car had broken down. However she did add a cheerful PS: 'I should have mentioned that in some villages the work is being carried out with really patriotic ideas.'

Matters did look up. In the autumn of 1941 the American Federation of Business and Professional Women presented four mobile kitchens to the Women's Institute. These, mounted on Ford V8 chassis, could be driven to remote parts of the country for collecting hedgerow fruits and into orchards where the fruit was literally taken from the bough, put into cans and the cans sterilized in a copper of water boiled up inside the 'kitchen'. The tonnage of fruit preserved in 1941 eventually worked out at 1,000 tons above that preserved in 1940!

Besides its contribution to the national larder, the fruit preservation scheme provided a benefit which is recalled by Constance Harris of Wellesbourne in Warwickshire. During the early war years she was asked to go along to the centre run by the WI in Over Peover, Cheshire. She remembers, 'As a young housewife I learned more from the jam-making centre than I would ever have done left to my own resources.'

CHAPTER TEN
WILD PRODUCE AND HERBS

Country people might have found it difficult to buy sea fish, and choice items had usually long left the shop shelves by the time their bus reached town, but living in the country did have its compensations. Country housewives were more likely than town dwellers to get wild rabbits, freshwater fish, rooks and pigeons. They could also take advantage of the wild fruits of the hedgerows, a particular boon in 1941 when domestic fruit crops were disappointing.

Hedgerow produce was adaptable. Blackberries could be made into pies; turned into jam, jelly or vinegar; and their leaves could be dried, crushed and put into the tea caddy to eke out the tea ration. Crab apples made marmalade and small black sloes jam and wine. Rowanberries mixed with apples provided a fine jelly; wild damsons and bullaces could be dried for use in cakes and puddings; and hawthorn berries yielded a jelly which was supposed to taste like that made from guava fruit.

Quite the most useful of hedgerow trees was the elder. Its blossom produced delicious drinks (wine, champagne or tea) and could be used in fritters. In fact Ruth made some elderflower fritters for the television series and they were a great success. But she warns that you need to pop only a few elderflowers into the batter mixture as they have a strong taste. She also thinks that a spoonful of jam is nice on the cooked fritter. The

Elder blossom.

berries of elder trees could be made into pies (sweetened by syrup and spiced with cloves); converted into wine; mixed with green apples and onion to make chutney; and, last but not least, dried and put into cakes in place of currants. As a woman who used dried elderberries in this way recounts, 'Well, they looked the right colour even if they didn't taste the same. It was the psychological effect that counted!'

Country people also had access to woodland hazelnuts, beechnuts, chestnuts and sometimes walnuts. Those living near oak woods might have been lucky enough to find wild truffles beneath the trees. These subterranean delicacies had been professionally hunted and sold as late as the 1930s. The last expert hunter was probably Alfred Collins, whose telegram address was simply: Collins, Truffle Hunter, Salisbury Plain.

Edible fungi more accessible than truffles were beefsteak mushrooms which look like pieces of liver jutting from a tree trunk. These could be made into consommé with stock or Marmite and water. Field mushrooms; their bigger brethren, horse mushrooms; young puffballs; and the brown-scaled *Lepiota* could all be used to culinary effect; so too, surprisingly, could the 'fairy ring' mushroom, and Jason Hill's wartime book *Wild Foods of Britain* gives the following instructions for using it:

> Cut off the stem (no peeling required) and cook slowly for 20–25 minutes. It is delicious cooked by the standard method and in soups, stews or with haricot beans. Its natural habit is to shrivel in dry weather and revive in damp and therefore it lends itself perfectly to drying, and a good quantity should be prepared, for they are as good dried as fresh.

Mr Hill's book makes an interesting read, and includes recipes for ground elder, seaweed, lady's smock and snails.

Another fascinating book of the period is *Wild Fruits, Berries, Nuts and Flowers, 101 Good Recipes for Using Them* by B. James. In this the Rose-Petal and Cherry Salad and the Primrose Tart sound fetching.

More mundane than flower petals, but probably more cooked during the war years, were nettles. These have long been known as a standby food for hard times. In Ireland during the potato famine of the 1840s people travelled miles to churchyards (where nettles grow well) to gather them for cooking. They are best eaten in March when young and tender, and as this was a time of year which coincided with a lack of green vegetables in wartime gardens, they came in useful for stretching a saucepan of greens. Nettles on their own could be cooked very much like spinach: that is, after washing, they were put into a saucepan with just the water from the tap clinging to their leaves and cooked for 15–30 minutes, depending on their age. Ruth says of this method that, once you have cooked them and tipped them into a colander, it is advisable to 'run cold water through them. It stabilizes the colour and keeps them nice and green.' The nettles then have to be hand-pressed dry, taken out of the colander and chopped or puréed. Ambrose Heath, in his *Kitchen Front Recipes and Hints* (1941), considered both nettle and dandelion leaves excellent: 'A poached egg on

Children picking young nettles.

a bed of dandelion or nettle purée covered with a cheese sauce is an almost perfect meal, containing every one of the foods which we are being told to eat, body-building, protective and energizing . . . and very good eating too!'

Nettles had another use than as food and this interested scientists: they could be employed in the manufacture of textiles. It was known that in the First World War the Germans had used large quantities of nettles in this way; and, as a Kew researcher noted in 1942, his experiments served to show 'that British scientists are as alive to the possibility of using makeshift materials as their opposite numbers in Nazi Germany'.

It is uncertain how successful British nettle fabric was, but the adoption of another overseas idea for using wild produce was overwhelmingly so. The rose hip had long been valued in Scandinavia and Russia, and in Germany it was planted on railway and road embankments as a national resource. Its value lay in its vitamin C content, ten times more than that of oranges. In Switzerland a wartime collection of rose hips was organized, but it was not until 1941 that Britain began to show interest in these wild fruit. In that year experiments to see how they measured up in domestic preserves proved disappointing. Alice Crang at Long Ashton found that rose hip jam did not set well and it was impossible to remove all the small barbed hairs which surrounded the seeds in the hip. These

Above: The further north they grow, the better the vitamin C content of rose hips.
Facing page: Girls milling rose hips in a machine specially invented for the purpose, September 1943.

hairs irritated the throat when the jam was eaten. She found that the best way of using rose hips for domestic purposes was to turn them into a syrup, and this method also resulted in the highest extraction of vitamin C. At this time people's normal sources of vitamin C were oranges (which were scarce), greens (which children did not really like) and potatoes. It was obvious that another source was needed, and rose hips fitted the bill.

It is not known whether it was Miss Crang's findings or the result of other experiments in 1941 which prompted the Vegetable Drugs Committee of the Ministry of Health and the Ministry of Supply to appeal for large quantities of rose hips. In that year 200 tons were collected by voluntary effort and the syrup from them bottled for children over the age of five years (the under-fives received Government orange juice) and invalids. In the following year the collection target was put at 1,500 tons and everyone who could was asked to collect rose hips. The WVS and

What is (or are) Rose Hips?
(a) Name of a famous woman spy
(b) An eastern dance
(c) Pods of the wild rose, rich in
    vitamin C
(c) Name of a Russian folk song

*From 'Food Facts' Quiz Corner,
31 December 1943.*

Answer: (c) Pods of the wild
rose

Women's Institutes proved able organizers. The hips had to be collected when they first turned red (for that was when their vitamin C content was highest) and picked with as little stalk left on as possible. The further north the hips grew, the higher their vitamin C. Hips had to be handled carefully, taken to a collection point and sent off within a week to pharmaceutical manufacturers. Collectors were paid 3d (about 1½p) per lb and many were children eager to earn pocket money. Dorothy Hinchcliffe of Murton in Cumbria remembers that the collection point for rose hips in that parish was the local school. Towards the end of the summer holidays sackfuls used to be temporarily stored there. One year, on the children's first morning back from the holidays, the teacher sat down at the piano to play the opening hymn of morning assembly. Her hands fell with a flourish on the keys, but not a sound came forth. Inspection revealed that in the holiday-quiet schoolroom mice had busied themselves eating fleshy bits of rose hip and stuffing the seeds beneath the piano keys until they were packed solid! Collecting hips for National Rose Hip Syrup went on into the early 1950s.

Although rose hips were always a priority, people were asked to collect other wild plants too. Some were for research but most were for medicine as there was an acute shortage of drugs. Although Britain had over eighty native medicinal plants, it had always found it cheaper to import drugs, mainly from Europe, but now, of course, this source was no longer available. Before the war even large quantities of nettles and dandelions had been shipped in.

The Vegetable Drugs Committee issued leaflets telling prospective collectors which plants were needed most. The top eight were:

PLANT	USES
Belladonna leaves (children not allowed to collect because poisonous)	Narcotic, diuretic and sedative
Colchicum corms and seeds	Anti-rheumatic and emetic
Dandelion roots	Tonic and diuretic
Foxglove leaves and seeds	Cardiac stimulant
Male fern rhizome	Kills intestinal worms in man and animals
Sphagnum moss	Absorbent dressing (had proved its worth in First World War)
Stinging nettle	Anti-asthmatic
Valerian root	Anti-spasmodic in hysteria and allied conditions

County Herb Committees, mainly organized by WIs, arranged collecting and drying centres, for it was important to dry plants before they deteriorated. All sorts of places were utilized for drying: in Shrewsbury, for instance, a clothes-drying room was pressed into service and in Montgomery in Wales a loft above a bakery. A member of Bocking WI in Essex remembers that Bocking used a condemned house and drying was done on netting stretched out in an upstairs room. Half- and quarter-pounds were not counted when collectors were paid because it was found that when the herbs dried they lost weight. In fact a contemporary booklet on collecting medicinal herbs states that when 8 lb of dandelion roots are dried they reduce in weight to 1 lb. Noreen Jardine of Coventry remembers dandelion roots not for their shrivelling but for their stains which ruined a new dress her mother had made for her. Her first outing in the shantung dress coincided with a school effort to dig the roots to supply a health food factory in nearby Sutton Coldfield.

In addition to the collection of medicinal plants in the wild, gardeners and allotment holders were asked to grow them. Probably only those with large areas of land were able to oblige. For example, Ellen Wray of Benfleet, who was a land girl working in a private garden in Hertfordshire, remembers that one year they grew foxgloves on what had been the mansion bowling green. Another ex-land girl, Enid Smith (*née* Keys) of Devon recalls from her work at the seed company Thompson and Morgan that areas of their ground were given over to growing medicinal plants. However, the biggest suppliers were herb farms which could grow such plants as chamomile (usually imported from Belgium), caraway, dill and gentian. Gentian, it was discovered, was the best remedy for the severe burns airmen suffered.

Herb farms certainly came into their own in the war years, for not only had medicinal herb imports been cut, but so too had supplies of herbs normally used for culinary flavouring. The canning giants Heinz and Crosse and Blackwell were in difficulties through herb shortages, and other made-up food manufacturers desperately needed herb flavourings. Doris Moynihan, who worked for four years of the war on a herb farm in Seal, near Sevenoaks, Kent, remembers that their largest crops were the culinary herbs, particularly sage, which they cut by the hundredweight for Harris's sausage factory!

Housewives, particularly with shortages of imported onions and red peppers, were also looking for herb flavourings. An article written in 1942 tells of shops doing a tremendous trade in packets of mixed dried herbs. The Ministry of Food arranged for radio talks and leaflets to explain how people could grow their own, even if it was just a windowbox collection. The Ministry also asked Miss D. Hewer, who owned the farm on which Doris Moynihan worked, to write a book on herb growing. It is worth recording which culinary herbs Miss Hewer considered the most important, however small your garden. They are: sage, marjoram, savory, black thyme, lemon thyme, parsley, mint, chives and tarragon. She writes that, for a mixture of herbs, savory and black thyme form a good background to which marjoram, parsley, lemon thyme and a very little mint can be added in varying proportions. On herbs for various foods she recommends lemon thyme (or dried balm) for poultry and veal; parsley and marjoram for egg dishes; fennel for fish; lemon thyme for stuffed marrow; basil for sausage meat; savory as being the 'correct' herb for broad beans; and parsley and marjoram or simply chopped chives as excellent in omelettes.

PRIMROSE TART

Line a buttered tart tin with thin pastry. Cover with a generous layer of sliced apples and castor sugar. Sprinkle well with yellow primrose petals and then more castor sugar. Cover with pastry and bake in the usual way.

From Wild Fruits, Berries, Nuts and Flowers *by B. James.*

Chamomile being gathered at the Herb Farm, Seal.

CHAPTER ELEVEN

GARDEN LIVESTOCK

PIGS

Ruth reckons that you can use every bit of a pig except its squeal. Its body can be turned into bacon and hams; its head into brawn; and its innards into faggots, sausages, savouries, lard and pâté. Even its trotters and tail can be pickled and boiled. Should there be the odd bit of rind or gristle left over, that can go to make jelly stock or be minced up for faggots.

Given all the above, it is hardly surprising that in the lean war years pigs were prized. Unfortunately the Ministry of Agriculture did not regard them as 'priority' animals and, to save on shipping, the amount of imported meal they usually ate was drastically reduced. Meal supplies were to be primarily for humans or dairy cattle. This state of affairs resulted in the number of pigs on farms being cut by half. Added to this, Germany's occupation of the Low Countries meant that, by June 1940, 70 per cent of Britain's usual imports of hams, bacon and other pig products had ceased. Lend-Lease bacon helped the rations, but on the whole bacon was scarce.

A combination of two factors did, however, bring home the bacon for some people. The first was Lord Woolton's 1940 statutory rulings on waste food and the second was the existence of the Small Pig Keepers' Council (SPKC). Under Lord Woolton's anti-waste campaign, owners of usable waste found in rubbish bins could be – and in some cases were – prosecuted. The SPKC was set up to encourage people to keep pigs, which would eat kitchen and garden waste, thus not only rendering it unwasted but even turning it into food for the population. The other benefit of pig keeping was, of course, manure. Once this had been stacked and allowed to ferment, it could be dug in to aid the production of garden crops.

The SPKC persuaded local councils to rescind health laws so that people could keep a pig in their back garden. A helpful book called *The Week-End Gardener*, published in 1941, reckoned that a Middle White made a good garden pig. The breed was noted for its quietness and the fact that it averaged only 13 stone when full-grown (some breeds could make 21 stone). It would also yield good-quality pork after twenty weeks.

The SPKC suggested that individual pig owners get together and form clubs. In fact pig clubs were not new; many had been started in the First World War and a few had survived. Being a pig club member brought the benefits of cut-price feed from a bulk purchase, help with the collection of food scraps and, for a 2s 6d (12½p) premium, insurance for the pig.

Facing page: A pig keeper contemplates her charges.

Soon people who did not have the room to keep a pig themselves became interested in joining pig clubs and so co-operative pig clubs came into being. With these all the stock was kept in one spot and owned by the club. Co-operatives blossomed in urban areas: for example, in June 1940 Violet Hudson, sister of the minister of agriculture, opened the first ARP pig club in Wandsworth, London. In Hyde Park there was a police piggery. A correspondent of *Farmers' Weekly* magazine, who visited the park in 1941, wrote: 'The sty that houses these important pigs was built by policemen, and built like a gaol. Evidently the police were afraid that the pigs might escape.' London police were obviously security-minded when it came to pigs, for in 1942 they put some behind bars – into the empty cages at Regent's Park Zoo, the usual occupants of the cages having been evacuated to Whipsnade Zoo.

The year 1943 brought a further extension of the pig club idea in the shape of the factory canteen club. Scraps from the canteen were fed to the pigs to fatten them for its later use.

Not all pig clubs had large membership: some were quite exclusive. For example, Dolly Wall of Winford, near Bristol, whose aunt was lady's maid to the matron of Gloucester Hospital, remembers that her aunt, the matron, the gardener and a doctor all had shares in a pig. When the pig was killed, her aunt sent some of her share to Dolly.

One of the first urban pig clubs was that formed by sixty-eight refuse collectors at Tottenham borough cleansing department in London. They started with a hundred pigs and helped to feed them by carrying on each of their lorries a special bin to collect potato peelings and other vegetable waste. The mayor of Tottenham, Alderman Morrison, gave the scheme full backing. Under Ministry of Agriculture regulations, waste, before being given to pigs, had to be boiled for an hour to destroy organisms which might pass on foot and mouth disease or swine fever. The Tottenham cleansing department obtained special equipment to steam the waste under pressure. The end product was officially known as concentrated swill, but as it was like a pasty pudding it earned the nickname of 'Tottenham Pudding'. All 'pudding' surplus to requirements was sold to other pig keepers and also to poultry owners.

Eventually other local authorities, which had already begun to boil and sell waste, bought special plants to make concentrated swill. To collect their material, councils put pig bins in the streets. The bins were labelled to remind people not to put in certain types of waste – for example, tea leaves and rhubarb leaves, which would injure a pig's health. Some oddities *did* find their way in, however. Gordon Tucker, who lives near Bath, remembers that his father kept pigs and used to get swill from the local council. On one occasion the swill yielded a pair of false teeth (difficult to get in wartime, so they advertised that they had been found, but had no reply); and on another an ebony and silver pepper grinder which Gordon and his family use to this day.

Pig ownership burgeoned, and by the end of 1942 there were 4,000 clubs. But their popularity brought a problem. In addition to scraps, pigs

were allowed a ration of imported meal; yet so much meal was going to pig clubs that very little was left for commercial pig farmers. The Ministry of Food decided to put the brakes on, for this state of affairs meant that a large section of the population was not getting any pig meat. The meal ration was halved and pig owners had either to give up a year's bacon coupons or give the Ministry half a pig once it had been killed. The other Ministry curb was to restrict the number of pigs slaughtered. Co-op clubs were allowed two per member per year and domestic owners two per year.

Pigs were slaughtered in the cold months from November to February: any later and there was a risk that the meat would go off. Pig keepers were advised to engage a professional slaughterer to come and do the deed, but they were then left with the carcass and in many cases had no idea what to do with it. The Small Pig Keepers' Council met this problem by liaising with the Ministry of Agriculture and producing instructional leaflets. So that help could be given in a more 'hands on' way, it was also decided that rural domestic economy instructresses should actually go out to show people what to do.

Contributing scraps to a street pig bin, Cheltenham, 19 September 1950. The local art school designed the placard.

Although Viola Williams was a *horticultural* officer with the Wiltshire War Ag., she suddenly found that pig cutting up and curing was to come within her remit, and to gain the necessary knowledge she was despatched to Smithfield Market. When she knew that she had to do a pig, Viola visited the owner several weeks beforehand to make sure that there was somewhere cold to keep it. A spare room with a bath was the usual place – 'I've even done a pig in a hip bath!' she recalls.

Once all the cutting up was done and the various bits assembled she usually got the owner's neighbours to help rub salt and saltpetre into the meat on both sides, particularly on the skin side. When she thought sufficient was rubbed in, she packed the pieces into the bath or whatever container had been put ready. The system was: a piece of meat, then a layer of salt, and so on. The bits that would take longest to cure, like the hams (they needed about three weeks), were put at the bottom. She tried to pack the salt around the joints, particularly the big knuckle bone and hip bone. A little saltpetre mixed with the packing salt gave the meat a good colour, but too much of it would make the meat tough.

When the meat was unpacked, most of the salt was washed off and it was dried and hung up. If there was an old-fashioned hearth and the only fuel burnt was wood, it could hang in the chimney. 'The actual smoking didn't do an awful lot for the preservation, but it did make it taste and look nicer.'

Viola's other task was to show women how to make sausages and faggots from the innards and how to make pork pies from loose bits of good meat. On the latter she says, 'Dealing with a group of women making pork pies, you really did feel that you were doing something educational which they could do themselves. Obviously cutting up a pig was something most of them would never have a chance to do, but the making of a raised pie has an art in it.' Sometimes she was given a 'thank you' present of 8 oz of sausages or a small pork pie, but as a general rule she found people liked to hang on to these small niceties: 'People weren't all that generous because meat was meat. Perhaps later on they'd part with a few rashers or a bit of ham to their friends.'

Ruth, with her country upbringing and the knowledge she gained from her work in mansion kitchens, did not need to be taught how to make the most of a pig. Two wartime dishes she particularly remembers making and enjoying were brawn and chitterlings.

Her recipe for brawn is to soak a pig's head (minus its ears and eyes) with a trotter overnight in water to which a handful of salt has been added. This helps to clear any congested blood. The next morning you wash both, cover with fresh cold water in a saucepan and add a shin of beef or some brisket: Ruth says that either of these helps to make the eventual brawn mixture leaner and meatier. You also add a carrot, onion, bay leaf, perhaps a few peppercorns or a sprig of thyme – in fact anything that will give the dish a nice flavour. The next step is to bring it slowly to the boil and simmer until the flesh comes away easily from the bones. This can take from three to five hours. Ruth then takes the head and trotter and shin/

Ruth preparing a pig's head for turning into brawn.

brisket out of the pan and puts the remaining liquid back on the stove to reduce.

Once the head is skinned (and the tongue too), all the meat and fat are chopped and mixed up so that they are evenly distributed. Ruth believes that it is helpful to put cold water in the bowl in which you intend setting the brawn an hour beforehand. This helps to chill the bowl and that, together with the small drops of moisture left on the sides after the water has been tipped out, helps to make the brawn nice and shiny and easy to turn out when set. Tip the water out and put the mixture in. Then taste the stock which has been reducing: it might need a little black pepper and salt. If you are happy that it is OK, the final step is to strain it over the meat until it *just* covers the top – any more and the top layer of fat will be too deep. Finally put it into the larder to set.

As to Ruth's other tasty dish, chitterlings, she thinks that this would be difficult for anyone to make nowadays, particularly as the main ingredient needs to be very fresh. Chitterlings are the pig's large intestine – yards and yards of it, according to Ruth. She used to get it still warm from the pig's inside, which was the best time because it was easy to clean out. To do this you cut it into yard lengths and ran cold water from the tap through each length, which you then placed in a bowl of salt water and left overnight. The next day turning began. This involved pulling each length inside out over a bamboo cane. The following day the length was taken off, turned over and pulled back onto the cane the right way. On the day after that it was turned inside out again. Three days was the usual time for making sure that they were totally clean and dry. Ruth then used to loop them over her thumb and join them together by a sort of chain stitch. Finally they were usually boiled till tender and eaten cold or fried with bacon. Ruth says that chitterlings shrink when cooked but make a lot of fat like lard. This fat was the biggest incentive for preparing them during the war, although the chitterlings themselves made a tasty dish. Ruth admits, however, that she would eat only those that she had cleaned herself.

POULTRY

Beer was not rationed, a fact which upset a number of people, including a member of the House of Lords, Lord Arnold. He argued that if its consumption were halved, there would be enough barley released to feed eighteen million hens and provide four eggs per family per week. The Government resolutely refused to ration beer and the scarcity of poultry food remained. As in the case of pigs, the return from poultry was not considered as important as that from dairy cattle and imported meal for poultry was very much reduced. The number of hens on farms fell by 30 per cent. However, as the number on farms declined, the numbers kept by people in gardens and back yards increased. By the end of the war it was estimated that eleven and a half million hens were being kept by 'back-yarders' (the popular term for small domestic keepers), whereas in 1939

Hey! Little Hen
Hey! Little hen,
When, when, when, will you
  lay me an egg for my tea?
Hey! Little hen,
When, when, when, will you
  try to supply one for me?

Get into your nest,
Do your little best,
Get it off your chest,
I can do the rest.

Hey! Little hen,
When, when, when, will, you
  lay me an egg for my tea?

Extract from a popular song of 1941 performed by Bunny Boyle and his orchestra.

Wartime gardeners were advised that the following was extra food for their hens:

Beans and peas
Sow an extra row especially for them.
Lawn clippings
Use I in. long and perfectly dry.
Sunflower seeds
Cut when ripe and beginning to fall. A 9-in. head equals 5½ oz, enough to supply one hen for a week. Excellent for laying hens.
Parsnips
Boil and mash with household scraps.
Lucerne
Feed fresh, chopped up in mash. A crop will grow for five years, and can be cut twice in the first year and four times in following years.
Buckwheat, maize and mustard
Grow for their grain or seed.
Kale
Especially 'perpetual kale'. Supplies minerals in winter.
Carrots
Use roots and tops. Cook, mince, and feed in small quantities.

there had been just five million. This doubling of numbers was helped by the Domestic Poultry Keepers' Council which, like its porcine counterpart the SPKC, dispensed advice and encouraged the setting up of clubs.

One important piece of expert advice to novices warned them not to buy stock from street traders but to go to reliable breeders or send away to established hatcheries. It was obviously advice well taken. Margaret Griffiths of Bridgnorth in Shropshire, who worked at a large hatchery in Worcester during the war years, recalls that the hatchery sent out four thousand growing (eight-week-old) pullets a week. It was part of her job to make up the orders for back-yarders, which ranged from two to eight growing pullets per order. The birds were put in large, clean, cardboard boxes which were tied with string and labelled. The boxes were taken by van to the railway station and went by train to the station nearest the customer.

Buying pullets was quite an expensive way of obtaining hens. Some people preferred to rear them from chicks and if any of them turned out to be cockerels they were grown on for the pot. This could be profitable: the *Daily Express*'s wartime *Domestic Poultry Book* made an interesting computation that within six months six day-old cockerels would provide ¼ hundredweight of table meat!

Arriving poultry took pot luck on their accommodation. Lucky ones went into purpose-built houses, but many were lodged in home-made contrivances constructed from what was available, as both timber and wire netting were in short supply. Bedding might simply be a carpet of dried leaves which had been brought from the local park in a sheet. Some hens were put into cages in garden sheds, one bird to a cage. These could be stacked up like pigeon holes so that a dozen hens could be kept in a shed roughly 5 ft long and 4 ft wide. Inner-city flat dwellers without gardens even fitted cages on to the wall outside their window. A standard 'layer's cage' had a floor which sloped, so that when the hen laid an egg it would roll gently down out of her reach. This design was particularly useful if you had to lean over a windowbox of tomato plants to collect your eggs!

Poultry meal was rationed and to obtain it you had to surrender your shell egg registration. In 1942 one person's shell egg registration equalled 4 lb of Balancer meal. Specially formulated to provide hens with protein, this meal consisted of half middlings (residue from flour milling) and bran; one quarter home-ground wheat; roughly one-fifth dried town waste; and the remaining portion was fish meal. Balancer was designed to be mixed with household waste, for it was from scraps like peelings, cores and raw greens that the hens would get their vitamins. The waste had to be chopped and boiled before being added to the meal. The ratio was one part Balancer to two parts household scraps plus a small amount of codliver oil to supply vitamin D. Anyone with six hens needed more scraps than their own kitchen could provide each day and many back-yarders got supplies from their neighbours. A neighbour or friend could also give a poultry owner their shell egg registration to surrender for meal and in return would receive some of the eggs the hens laid.

Poultry clubs advised new owners not to keep more hens than they could feed. The best approach was to aim for the maximum supply of eggs from the smallest number of stock. Perhaps this advice was not always followed: looking back, today's poultry experts believe that a lot of domestic poultry keepers gave their birds too many vegetable scraps and insufficient meal, a diet which resulted in the birds having enough protein to keep them healthy but not enough to produce eggs. This tallies with statistics published after the war which showed that, despite the increase in the number of hens, egg production up to 1944 declined until it was half its pre-war level.

Given the right treatment, hens *did* lay well, and some were even feted for their achievements. For instance, a hen called Molly was exhibited at a Victory Show on the Isle of Wight because between February 1942 and October 1943 she had laid 357 eggs. Moreover, Jean McCredie Forster, a rural studies organiser during the war, recalls that some of the poultry raised and looked after by children in Wiltshire schools were such good layers that they were entered in egg-laying trials. These were run by the local War Ag. and involved hens being sent away and records kept of the amounts they laid. Winning owners were awarded a medal.

Hens which were definitely bad layers or past their laying best were a liability in wartime. Experts advised amateurs to 'weed out wasters',

Not all wartime hen houses were purpose-built.

Facing page: Anya hanging up a bundle of cabbage leaves for her hens to peck at.
Left: Preparing a mash with poultry meal, hot water and boiled kitchen scraps.
Above: A large sunflower head supplied enough seeds for one hen per week.

though this was sometimes easier said than done. David Howard of Bath remembers that his mother kept hens during the war in their London garden. After the first one had to be killed, his father came into the house white and shaking, saying, 'Don't ask me to do *that* again!' Even with a hen safely demised and cooked, many a family sat looking at their plates, unable to eat what had become a named pet.

Dead hens provided more than meat. Their feathers could be sold for war purposes and tobacconists would buy the pen feathers as pipe cleaners. Also poultry fat was noted for making delicious cakes and scones: apparently it has a sweetness and lightness superior to that of butter.

Many country people recall that wild rabbit was almost the only meat they ate during the war years. In some cases no money changed hands and a rabbit caught in a trap or shot was exchanged for payment in kind. Ruth *did* pay for hers: most weeks she had two from a local woodsman and paid him 1s (5p) for each one. This arrangement went on all through the war years and provided Ruth's family of four with at least two meals a week very cheaply. Ruth remembers that a wartime rabbit could take on all sorts of guises: it was put into a crust and made into a pudding or a pie; you could stew, roast or casserole it; you could use it to make potted rabbit, which is like pâté, and eat it cold with salad; and sometimes, if all the meat was pulled off the bones, rabbit could even 'become chicken'!

In towns and cities people were not so lucky over rabbit. Its price had been controlled in 1940, but by 1943 shop-bought rabbit was scarce and expensive, and in some places unobtainable.

In order to ease meat shortages the Government made every effort to encourage people to regard rabbits as garden livestock. It coined the pithy slogan 'Keep rabbits – meat from waste', and encouraged the publication of such tempting facts as 'In a single tame rabbit four and a half months old there is the nutritive value of 4½ lb of best beef, shoulder of mutton or of pork.'

The Domestic Poultry Keepers' Council had the responsibility of helping amateur rabbit keepers and many districts formed a combined

A *Radio Times* announcement about a programme to help listeners with their garden livestock.

'BACKS TO THE LAND' today at 1.15 brings you more expert advice on how to turn that backyard to the best account.

poultry and rabbit club. The value of rabbit keeping was spread at 'Dig for Victory' shows. An expert would pin up posters, have live rabbits for people to see and hand out leaflets which explained how to look after them.

Two children help with the carrying at the end of an afternoon's rabbit catching in the Cotswolds.

Many people did take up rabbit keeping, for out of all domestic garden livestock this animal was the most accommodating when it came to feeding, and cheap too. As the book *Make Your Garden Feed You* pointed out, 'Rabbits can be fed at practically no cost on the wartime allotment or garden plot.' They would eat kitchen scraps; garden weeds like sow thistle; any number of green hedgerow plants; the leaves and twigs of several common trees; garden waste and certain flowers such as marigolds, nasturtiums, asters and wallflowers. Rabbits would even eat, in moderation, the tea leaves not allowed into the pig bin. Their winter menus could be taken care of by summer planning: for example, by making long grass

RABBIT PIE

1 rabbit
¼ lb scraps of bacon or pork
1 teaspoonful chopped parsley
pinch of herbs
salt and pepper
stock or water
short pastry

Joint the rabbit and wash it well.
As we've said before, we always
leave the rabbit in salted water
for an hour to make certain it's
quite clean. You can't be too
particular about this. Put it in a
pie-dish with the other things,
seasoning it well with salt and
pepper. Add a little stock or water,
cover with the pastry – you
know how – and bake two to
two-and-a-half hours

*From Gert and Daisy's Wartime
Cookery Book.*

Above: By 1943 approximately a
million rabbits were being kept
by householders.
Right: Ruth's Rabbit Pie.
Facing page: Ministry of Food
poster emphasizing the versatility
of rabbit.

Rabbit Pie

Delicious Dishes

gged Rabbit · Fricassee of Rabbit · Curried Rabbit
Roast Rabbit · Rabbit Stew · Rabbit Brawn

Rabbit in Casserole

CURRIED RABBIT

1 rabbit
1½ tablespoons flour
1 oz cooking fat
1 large onion, chopped
1 dessertspoon curry powder
1 pint stock or water
2 tablespoons tomato purée or
2 fresh or bottled tomatoes
1 large apple (if possible), peeled and
chopped
a few sultanas
salt, pepper and cayenne

Remove the head and neck from the rabbit. Cut the remainder into joints. Sprinkle with half the flour, and fry until browned in the cooking fat. Remove the rabbit and fry the chopped onion. Add the remainder of the flour and curry powder and brown slowly. Now slowly stir in the stock or water, tomato purée or tomatoes, peeled chopped apple and sultanas, and season to taste with salt, pepper and cayenne. Add the rabbit and simmer slowly for 1–1½ hours till tender. Serves 4–5.

From Stork Margarine's Rabbit Cookery (1943).

HARICOT OF RABBIT

1 rabbit
1 onion
2 carrots
1 teaspoonful pickling spices
1 tablespoonful dripping
1 pint water
salt and pepper
1 lb haricot beans
redcurrant jelly

Cut up the rabbit and fry the pieces in dripping. Fry the cut-up vegetables and put all into a saucepan with the water. Bring to the boil. Tie up the pickling spices in a piece of muslin and add these. Simmer for 2½ hours until cooked. Remove spices. Thicken the gravy and add a little browning if needed. Have the haricot beans boiled after soaking overnight and arrange them as a border on a large dish with the rabbit in the centre. Serve with redcurrant or crab apple jelly. Any remains of this dish can be thinned down with water and served as rabbit soup.

into hay, by drying nettles and mixed weeds and by saving dried pea haulms. The Government allowed rabbit club members to have bran for their rabbits, in return for which a club had to undertake to sell not less than half the rabbits its members produced to approved buyers who were buying either for meat or for breeding. Bucks did not get a bran ration, so it was usual for breeders to share one.

One of the most popular breeds for wartime rabbit keepers was Beveren. It produced good table meat and furriers liked the quality of its pelt. In fact there was a use for all rabbit pelts as both Britain and the USA had lost their pre-war sources of supply. Many pelts never found their way to furriers but supplied local needs. Muriel Smith of Cirencester remembers:

> Curing rabbit skins was strictly my job, having attended a Women's Institute lecture and demonstration. My mother was a dab hand at skinning rabbits complete, like taking off a glove. I would immediately sprinkle the skin with coarse rock salt, every day rubbing and pulling the pelt pliable. It was laid out flat during the slow curing and drying. Not until the last stage would a skin be hung on a line out of doors.
>
> As clothes were rationed one didn't waste coupons on gloves. We formed a fur working group and made gloves, mittens, slippers and hats.

With its flesh on the table and its fur on fingers, the only bit of a rabbit for which no real use seems to have been found was its droppings. This is highlighted by the following extract from a letter to the *Gardeners' Chronicle* of 9 January 1943:

> I believe that something like a million rabbits are being kept by householders. This great herd of animals must be producing a lot of manure, yet no authoritative pronouncement regarding the value of rabbit manure has been made.

No doubt, following this, one was made.

GOATS

Goats were not livestock for small gardens. They needed space, a chain to stop them wandering and constant change of grass. Their other drawback was their disposition to eat any article they could digest. However, for anyone with space enough a goat or goats could provide both meat and milk. Mary Rankin of Salisbury remembers that their billy kids provided her family with good joints for roasting and she got quite a bit of fat from under their skins. She and her husband also kept a herd of Saanea goats whose milk was sent to a London firm of milk bars. The firm used the milk to make ice cream as rationing prevented them from using cow's milk.

Facing page: Wartime advertisement for cat conditioning tablets.

CATS AND DOGS

Cats and dogs did not, of course, provide food but did have to be fed themselves: not an easy task, because bones were supposed to be kept for salvage, and tinned cat and dog meat was in short supply. In fact, grocers only sold it to their regular customers who had bought it before the war. The Ministry of Food's order preventing waste did not forbid giving meat to domestic pets, but anyone found guilty of giving too much was likely to be prosecuted.

One solution to the pet-feeding problem was to serve offal as a base and mix it with rice, cooked vegetables and toasted scraps of stale bread.

Elizabeth Craig's book *Cooking in War-Time* (1940) has some interesting suggestions for both cat and dog meals. Below is a synopsis of some of her thoughts:

"*I've had to hand in my Larder Guard stripes. Me—old Tiger—the cat that once held the Battalion record for catching mice! I feel rotten, dopey, mopey, miserable.*"

CATS

Breakfast	Large saucer of tepid milk.
Dinner	Lightly boiled liver twice weekly, stewed rabbit on two other days (mix with your own meals' vegetables and stale bread in gravy). Other days: chopped, stewed ox heart with vegetables and bread and boiled rice; cod's head or tail simmered in milk.
Emergency food	Scraps of meat stewed and seasoned lightly with salt, mixed with dried stale bread, boiled rice or thick porridge and gravy. 4–6 fl oz of milk a day.

DOGS

General	Extra dog biscuits to make up for less meat. Add rice, oats, vegetables, toasted scraps of bread.
Dinner alternatives	Stewed tripe with carrot, onion and hound meal. Crisped stale bread mixed with meat stock, dripping and chopped cooked carrot and turnip. Sheep's head broth mixed with hound meal and cooked vegetables.

"*What are they up to now? I hope they're not going to court-martial me.*"

NEXT DAY

"*Here we go, boys! They're giving me 'TIBS'—I'll soon be in fighting trim again!*"

Dogs being dogs, they did get hungry between meals. Mr and Mrs Gordon Veitch remember that their spaniel disgraced himself by wolfing down a week's ration of cakes which had been put on the tea trolley. Gordon cured him of the habit by putting a mousetrap on the bottom with a bit of cake in it. When the spaniel tried to take the cake, the trap snapped at him and he never went near the trolley again!

Finally, an ill-wind blows someone some good. Manufacturers of dog and cat conditioning pills made much of the war adversely affecting pets' health. For example, advertisements carried soulful-looking dogs bemoaning the fact that their owner's war work had cut down their daytime walks and that the black-out had stopped their evening one. After reading these adverts, of which there were many, it would have been a hard-hearted owner who could not have put conditioning pills on the shopping list.

A WEEK LATER

"*They've given me my stripes back—I've mopped up all the mice in my larder. I don't care if they drop 'em by parachute—the more the merrier! Wonderful stuff, 'TIBS'!*"

CHAPTER TWELVE
CHILDREN

Facing page: Ruth welcomes her 'evacuees'.

There were several waves of evacuation during the war. The later being prompted by flying bomb attacks on London during 1944. However the main evacuation operation was the first. It took place between 1 and 3 September 1939. During those three days 1,250,000 city dwellers, prompted by the fear that densely populated areas would be bombed, evacuated to towns and villages. The evacuees included expectant mothers and those with children under five years old, school children with their teachers, and disabled people. Evacuation on their part was voluntary, but when they arrived in the 'reception areas', householders there, unless they had a very good reason for not doing so, were bound to take them in.

Ruth's sister was late on the day child evacuees arrived in her area. She had to dress her twins, and by the time she reached the school where the arrivals had been assembled, potential foster parents had taken their pick. That is why she got Sid. It must have been some form of prescience that no one had chosen him, for Sid, Ruth recalls, turned out to be ' a very difficult child'. He had come from Stepney in London and did not at all like the country practice of eating generous quantities of cooked vegetables. In fact there was a lot of food he disliked, so it was with some trepidation that Ruth's sister put parsley sauce on the table on a day when they had bacon. Sid, however, confounded everyone by helping himself to it and saying that he liked parsley sauce, explaining, 'I has it on eel pie.' According to Ruth he loved eel pie, cockles and winkles and all the things that made them shudder: 'That was his diet, but not for us it wasn't, so we had to get between the two. It wasn't easy.'

Meal times were not easy for many foster families, or for their little evacuees who were having to come to terms with a totally different way of life. Reports gathered during and after the war tell of foster parents who found that their charges were unused to sitting down to a meal and using cutlery because the only meal they had known was a 'piece' (a slice of bread and jam) eaten on the doorstep. It was also difficult for country people to accustom themselves to the requests of some evacuated children for fish and chips, pickles, ice cream, biscuits, sweets, strong tea and beer.

Sometimes foster families were shocked to learn that a child had never seen its mother cook or had a hot meal at home. But blame could not always justifiably be laid on natural mothers for this, as just five years before the war a survey taken in London revealed that out of 125 families in various parts of the city only half had a kitchen or kitchen-parlour to themselves, while two out of every five had no kitchen at all.

On Tuesday I had an awful few moments – I got to Kings Cross at 2 pm and found the 4.5 train in and people already crowding in to it. I got a seat and watched a train on the other side of the platform being packed with children and mothers and babies (about 700?) for evacuation. They were all in, and porters and helpers were loading collapsible prams into a van when the siren went. Then we heard the thing come over and it got slower and slower. The porters bolted into the van. We turned our backs on the windows, held our breath. It fell with a great column of smoke and dust rose into the air but other buildings must have taken the blast. 2 minutes later the evacuee train pulled out into safety.

From the diary of Miss C. M. Edwards, Binbrook, Lincolnshire. 11 July 1944.

Despite initial difficulties foster mothers were gratified to see that, with regular meals and country air, their evacuees filled out. Some developed such healthy appetites that the money the Government paid foster parents was barely enough. The rate was 10s 6d (52½p) full board and lodging for one child and 8s 6d (42½p) for each additional child. Sometimes a child's allowance could be dispelled in one day when its parents, perhaps bringing some friends for a day out in the country, all arrived without food expecting the foster mother to provide hospitality.

Families fostering evacuee mothers with their little children received 5s (25p) for the adult and 3s (15p) for each child. These sums were for lodgings only, but the Government instructed intending fosterers: 'It would be particularly appreciated if you could make cooking facilities available.' And thereby was a rub, for sometimes an evacuee mother and her hostess fell out over sharing the stove. The reasons varied: standards of cleanliness might differ; pots and pans sometimes got burnt. The Government paid compensation for damaged articles, but when it became difficult to obtain new cooking utensils evacuated women were encouraged to send for their own and the Government paid the cost of carriage.

The problem of sharing a kitchen affected houses big and small. Anne Kenrick of Birmingham remembers that her aunt had evacuees billeted downstairs in the servants' quarters of her large house. When the mothers wanted to come into the kitchen and share the stove, her aunt's cook found it hideous. In small households it was sometimes the practice for the evacuee mother to cook her food after the hostess had prepared her family's meal and then, either because of lack of room at the table or through natural reticence, to carry it up to her room and eat it in isolation.

For some evacuee mothers the state of isolation extended to their entire day: householders had no obligation to include them in activities. One woman endured this kind of treatment when she was evacuated from London to a seaside resort with her toddler and baby. Her hostess was a tailor's wife who cleaned everything with paraffin and the house reeked of it. She was not allowed to stay indoors but had to wander about all day pushing the pram. Once a man came up to her and shouted at her to go home because she was taking 'their food'. She seized her toddler's sandcastle bucket and beat the man on the back of the head. When she got home there was a policeman waiting, but when she told him what had happened he laughed. She returned to London soon after that, preferring to risk the bombing than put up with any more.

The belief that evacuees suffered feelings of alienation is re-inforced by information from Jean Neilson, a schoolteacher in Tottenham during the war. Her school was evacuated and when their train left London they had no idea where they were going. Jean says, 'We only knew we had to stay there until Hitler was defeated!' Their destination turned out to be Long Sutton in Lincolnshire. Jean admits of their stay:

We did feel that we were a nuisance and we had to have
discussions with the children because they wouldn't eat the food

---

DOCTOR'S DINNER

A wartime meal for 2–5-year-olds suggested by a dietician, as containing proteins, carbohydrates and fats.

Lentil porridge
Grilled sardines
Plain boiled rice

To make the lentil porridge, clean the lentils, just cover with cold water, add a good pinch of salt and simmer in an uncovered saucepan until soft. The sardines are, of course, tinned ones, and easily grilled in their own oil.

This combination of three valuable foodstuffs may be served in many different and attractive ways.

From Child Feeding in Wartime *by Margaret Cheyne (published by Good Housekeeping).*

the villagers served up to them. We had to cajole them and had little talks about people who lived in different parts of the country having different food and customs – we had to make it a geography lesson. These discussions used to take place after assembly when we asked how they were – had they slept well? There was a stand-up strike against apple pie. I said, 'What's the matter with apple pie?' and they said, 'We like apples and don't want all that wet stuff around them.' Another thing they wouldn't eat was faggots.

Some areas eventually set up communal feeding schemes for their evacuees. These had the dual benefit that the children ate happily among their friends and the evacuee mothers, who helped prepare and serve the food, had an interest. Unfortunately communal feeding was not as universal as it could have been. This was because it had to rely on voluntary help and sometimes a suitable building could not be found. There could also be local opposition – for example, in one district the lady from the big house (who of course had her own cook) said, 'It will be bad for local people. Our country folk have always done their own cooking and communal kitchens will produce bad habits in our women folk.'

Perhaps if Jean's pupils had stayed longer in Lincolnshire communal feeding might have been organized for them there, but by Christmas 1939 they were back in Tottenham. Jean remembers that teachers had to be recalled as unevacuated children and those that had drifted back to the city early were running wild in the streets. She resumed the teaching of nutrition and cookery that she had been engaged in before evacuation. However, she found that because of this, in addition to teaching she had been 'commandeered' to cook school dinners.

The Education (Provision of Meals) Act had officially started school dinners in 1906, but the wartime Government, concerned that children might not be getting the right nutrition, especially as many mothers were out all day doing war work, were keen to expand the service. Jean says that she was supposed to give them half the nutrition they needed per day in their midday meal and if she did not get it into the first course she had to get it into the second. 'I used to have a 7 lb tin of orange jelly made from real oranges,' she says. 'I had to get it into them, not quite without telling them . . . I used to put it into custard after it had been cooked so that the vitamin C wasn't destroyed.'

The lunch was to cost no more than 4d (just over 1½p) per pupil and Jean had to teach a lesson while she was preparing it. Sometimes in the middle of her lesson the siren sounded and the children went off to the shelter. Jean had to stay: 'They didn't bomb teachers,' she comments wryly; and continues, 'If we'd been cutting up vegetables for stew and suddenly the children all had to disappear, I'd run off to the staff room and ask another member of staff to get someone to look after her children and she came to help me. If we'd been making steamed pudding, I'd rush around, mix every basin and set them in the oven.' After the raid she

Sheila Gray of Langley in Berkshire recalls her wartime cookery lessons:

I can remember making rock cakes with a knob of margarine and, believe me, they lived up to their name. I can also vividly recall trying to make a stew with a 1-in. square of corned beef – that was the allowance the school had for each person in the lesson. After the class I carried the stew home in a big dish. Really it was a few vegetables floating in a large amount of opaque, slightly greasy water. I had the dish in a basket and spilt the liquid all down my school gaberdine. As you can imagine, my mother was not amused: the headmistress was adamant that we had to have a uniform and it was very difficult to get as clothing coupons were rationed.

J.H.DOWD

PRIORITY

The Ministry of Food feeds a family of 45,000,000. In this family THE CHILDREN COME FIRST. Oranges ... milk ... extra eggs ... school meals. And now—on December 8th—a new scheme has come into operation: A FREE REGULAR DISTRIBUTION, TO ALL CHILDREN UNDER TWO, OF COD-LIVER OIL COMPOUND AND OF FRUIT JUICES (black-currant juice or purée at first, orange juice later). Cod-liver oil contains the growth-promoting Vitamin A and the bone-building Vitamin D; and the fruit juices are rich in the protective Vitamin C. Three essential vitamins in concentrated and convenient form. The scheme may be reviewed at the end of March, but until then THERE IS NOTHING TO PAY.

The Vitamin Welfare Scheme

This scheme was introduced to make up for a possible lack of vitamins in children's diet resulting from fruit, butter and eggs being in short supply. Started in December 1941, it granted children up to the age of two blackcurrant syrup or purée and cod liver oil free of charge. During 1942 the blackcurrant was replaced by Lend-Lease orange juice which mothers had to pay for. Eventually any expectant mother or child under five who had cheap or free milk became entitled to cheap or free orange juice or cod-liver oil.

Not every mother took advantage of the scheme, and of those that did some found it difficult to make their children take the cod-liver oil. One enterprising solution to this problem was to put a mixture of cod-liver oil and malt into a cake. The oil acted as shortening and its flavour was covered by the malt plus added cocoa.

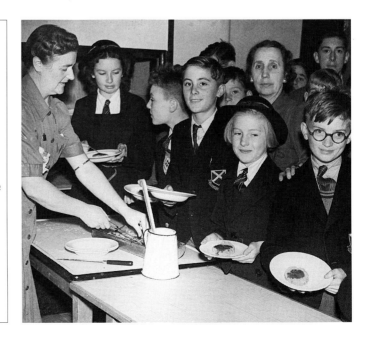

pushed the cooked food on a trolley to the dining room which had space for 400 children. She recalls, 'It was a mystery to most people how we got the food on the table and into the children.' On occasions when the children had to stay in the shelter she gave them soup and dry food as there was no room for them to use knives and forks.

Jean's school had a rural studies teacher who taught boys from the age of seven how to manage an allotment. Produce from the allotment sometimes came her way for school dinners, but she could not rely on it as she had no idea what vegetables would come in and often children would take them home. Occasionally a small boy would present her with one or two parsnips and she would incorporate them into the next lunch and he would proudly think that they had made everyone's meal!

Facing page: School mealtimes.
Below: 'Dig for Victory' poster.

WHAT DOES YOUR GARDEN GROW ?

It was not an unusual arrangement for a school to have allotments, for food growing became a regular part of the wartime curriculum. Some school children did manage to supply substantial amounts to their canteens but generally school produce was more likely to be prolific when a professional gardener was employed. When Viola Williams was the gardener at Sunny Hill School, Bruton, in Somerset, she fed 240 pupils a day but had to plan the crops carefully to avoid gluts occurring in the holidays. Her previous employment had been as headgardener at Cheltenham Ladies' College, where the principal decided that the school playing fields should be dug up and potatoes planted. Unfortunately the ground was so appalling that the potatoes did not stand a chance. Some

Below: A wartime gardening lesson.
Facing page: The family photograph which was displayed in Lewis's store window.

good did come of the exercise, though, for when eventually the fields were laid back to grass, the beautifully 'done' soil rendered them absolutely superb.

Not all school children were enthusiastic about food growing. Josephine Redgwell of Petersfield, Hampshire, who was educated at Pate's School in Cheltenham, says that her mother remembers her fury at having to weed an allotment in Pittville Park. This had to be done after games and after school hours. They were given no tools or wellingtons but were expected to use their hands and wear their ordinary school uniform which included a white blouse.

Conversely Robert Trangmar of Powys learned his love of allotments from his wartime school days. At his Brighton school pupils had the option of doing sport or gardening. He opted for gardening and had a 23 × 7½ ft allotment (a quarter of the standard size) dug on local playing fields. He bought his own seeds and worked on it on his own on Saturdays, taking the produce home.

Children also helped on their parents' allotments and in one instance this family activity became an enduring image. Margaret Short of Llandysul, Dyfed, recalls that her father had three and a half allotments and a photograph showing her father, three brothers and sister (Margaret was a toddler at the time) was displayed in the window of Lewis's store in Manchester. The photograph was 8 × 4 ft and stayed on display all through the war.

CHAPTER THIRTEEN
CATERING

HOTELS AND RESTAURANTS

During the war hotels and restaurants were allowed to stay open. For his part Lord Woolton countered the view that they provided 'luxury feeding' with the argument that people needed some relaxation, and they were therefore permitted to enjoy a restaurant or cafe meal without surrendering any coupons. The draw of an off-ration feed led people to eat out more frequently than they had before the war. Existing restaurants were never fuller and new eating places started up.

The Ministry of Food did, however, make some rulings which affected high-class restaurants in particular. In January 1941 Lord Woolton announced that he was planning to make it obligatory for a customer to have only one basic dish per meal. It could be meat, fish, poultry, cheese or eggs. Up to this point those who could afford it had been eating restaurant meals of five or six courses! Later in the year he also issued an order that no meal was to cost more than 5s (25p), although some top hotels were allowed to charge a cover price to help defer their overheads.

BRITISH RESTAURANTS

In the autumn of 1940 heavy bombing on London and other centres prompted the Ministry of Food to ask the London County Council to open up what in the previous war had been called national kitchens or national restaurants. Their purpose was to cater for people whose home cooking facilities had been damaged by air raids. The LCC consequently opened two hundred such establishments, which were known as Londoners' meals service centres.

At the same time Lord Woolton, mindful of the capabilities of his Liverpool business friends, called in Sir Bertram Chrimes, managing director of Coopers, a large food store, to organize a wartime meals division in the Ministry of Food. He also sent for another Liverpool contact, Oscar C. Waygood, head of the engineering department at Lewis's, the department store where Woolton himself had been managing director until he was asked to become minister of food. Woolton knew that Mr Waygood's department had done a lot of work on the design of large-scale kitchens and the equipment they needed – it had revised the Liverpool store's restaurant and planned one for its Leeds premises. When Mr Waygood, known as 'OCW' to his work colleagues, arrived at the

I lunched in a British restaurant. It was plentiful but not very appetizing, cabbage cooked in the old way – all the goodness boiled out – good soup – lots of potatoes, also cooked to a mash – meat nothing to grumble at – suet dumpling baked but burst and bakewell pudding with abominable custard – tea also abominable. I was interested in the numbers (one of my tickets was 95,000), also in the clientele – a woman and child, a lot of young men in overalls, 3 soldiers, a good many shopgirls, a few old men (poor) and a sprinkling of elderly middleclass men, shopkeepers of the smaller type I think, who couldn't get home for dinner. Pity it wasn't nicer.

From the diary of Miss C. M. Edwards, Binbrook, Lincolnshire. 16 December 1942 (after a visit to Scunthorpe).

Facing page: Queuing in a British restaurant.

Ministry offices, the permanent secretary Sir Henry French explained to him that it was Mr Churchill's wish that the workers in Britain be well fed and that there should be feeding centres around the country. Lord Woolton wanted his department to produce layout drawings for three different-sized kitchens capable of producing respectively 100, 250 and 400 hot meals at one sitting.

At this time, owing to the war, only four staff remained in Lewis's engineering department: OCW, his secretary, a draughtsman called Harry Lambert and an office boy. Harry was asked to prepare the drawings as quickly as possible. He headed his designs 'Proposed layouts for kitchens for Community Feeding Centres'. When these were handed to Winston Churchill, according to Harry, 'I am told that the first thing that caught his eye was the heading I had given the drawings, and that he looked over his glasses down the table and said (and I quote), "They are *not* Community Feeding Centres, they are British restaurants," and that's how the name was born!'

> Went to lunch at Mrs Massie's British restaurant – an excellent meal, *much* better than Scunthorpe. Clientele a wonderful mixed bag: a parson and wife, some service men, working lads and girls, elderly clerks, mothers with small children, shopgirls, shoppers, etc. etc. All classes except the smart or would-be smart set.
>
> *From the diary of Miss C. M. Edwards, Binbrook, Lincolnshire. 16 December 1943 (after a visit to Lincoln).*

The plans were revised to make the original arrangements slightly less elaborate and copies were sent to councils all over the country. Councils were given financial assistance to help them set up British restaurants but had to pay back the loan over the rather precise period of eight and a third years at the rate of one per cent per month. They could also obtain some of their equipment from a Ministry 'pool'. Their choice had to include a water-storage tank and solid-fuel ranges and boilers, so that even if air raids damaged the main services, the restaurants could still operate. When it came to installing all the equipment they could call on the Ministry for technical advice. That advice came from OCW who had been seconded to the wartime meals division (although he kept his office at Lewis's). He was allowed to use his secretary for Ministry business and also use Harry Lambert for drawing work.

As it turned out the work load on OCW was so great that he asked Lewis's Stores if Harry could take on some of it. Lewis's agreed to Harry covering areas which were within reasonable travelling distance of Liverpool. Harry recalls: 'Though I may be stretching the story somewhat, I think I planned kitchens in an array of buildings which varied from ladies' boudoirs to churches, but it conveys an idea of the variety I had to contend with. Still, we got by.' There *were* some odd conversions: for example, in Nottingham, the divisional food officer capitalized on the shortage of poultry and used some battery hen houses as British restaurants. Eventually the Ministry supplied pre-fabricated buildings which could be erected on a vacant site.

With a view to making the interior of British restaurants as attractive as possible, the Ministry appointed an art advisor who could advise on decoration. At some restaurants local art students were asked to paint murals, and in London there was a scheme for loaning pictures from a central source, then swapping them for a different selection.

In January 1942, to save time and manpower, most British restaurants began to operate on self-service lines. The food was arranged on hot-plates on a long counter and served on crockery that was likely to be utility

Left: Lord Woolton admires a French cafe scene painted on a British restaurant wall.
Facing page: A placard showing a typical British restaurant menu.

ware as most of this went to caterers. Customers purchased the necessary tickets (or, to save paper, plastic tokens) from a pay desk near the door, then collected their food. A typical meal consisted of soup; roast joint and stuffing, potatoes, swedes, watercress; Bakewell tart and chocolate sauce. All this would cost approximately 1s 1d (5½p), and could be washed down with a cup of tea costing 1d (½p). Customers were encouraged to take their empty plates to a hatch before they left.

INDUSTRIAL CANTEENS

On 17 July 1940, as part of a Government campaign to promote communal feeding, Lord Woolton lunched at the Grosvenor House restaurant in London and invited the press along. His object was to show them that 600 people could be served a three-course meal for 9d (3½p) per head.

In November of that year the Ministry of Labour and National Service made it compulsory for factories employing 250 people on Government work to set up a works canteen. The thinking was that the country was dependent on manpower to produce munitions and if that manpower was not fed well it could not do its job. The Government-only limit was lifted in 1943 and other workplaces came under the same rule.

Industrial canteens were divided into two categories, A and B. Category A canteens were those which served heavy-industry workers like dockers, quarrymen, steel workers and miners. Category B canteens served other industries and included transport cafes.

Colliery canteens came under the Ministry of Fuel and Power. A communication from the Miners' Welfare Commission written in September 1944 gives an interesting account of what some South Wales miners could be served in their canteen:

(a) Twopennyworth* of meat per meal (double the British restaurant, cafe and normal canteen allowance).
(b) Generous allocations of butter, margarine, fats, etc., sugar, cakes, flour and confectionery.
(c) Four times the normal allocation of ordinary canteens of hams, bacon, etc.
(d) Highest scale allowed in the way of teas, beverages and rationed foods.
(e) Points allocation for canned meat, fish, fruit, preserves, etc.

*All category A canteens gave their workforce 2d (1p) worth of meat per person per meal. Category B gave 1½d (just over ½p) worth.

Lord Woolton asked employers to make their canteens as cheerful as possible and to provide music. Many works managers took this message to heart and invited the BBC wireless programme *Workers' Playtime* to their premises. Its artistes, many world-famous, were transported on buses and often travelled miles to factories in the heart of the country. Once all the programme team was at the venue, engineers rigged up a small wooden stage in the works canteen, slung a microphone from the roof and the show began. The team did three 'live' lunchtime shows a week in front of audiences which ranged from 500 to 4,000. However, millions more shared each show for it was broadcast and heard in factories all over the country.

THE PIE SCHEME

During the harvest of 1941 the Women's Voluntary Service in East Anglia ran a scheme of delivering pies to harvest workers: extra rations to help boost the workforce to get the crops in as quickly as possible. The scheme was so successful that the Ministry of Food agreed to other WVS regions adopting it, not only at harvest time but also throughout the year. The Ministry took no part in the organization of this but did ask divisional food officers to encourage the setting up of pie and snack schemes, as they were called, for they were seen as valuable assets to rural workers who did not have the benefit of works canteens or British restaurants.

At first WVS members or the local baker made the pies and they were delivered to the fields in an assortment of conveyances ranging from bicycle baskets to small hand-carts. Ex-land girl Triss Male of Portland, Dorset, who was on the receiving end, comments appreciatively: 'Because land girls came under the Ministry of Agriculture workers, we were allowed fresh meat pies each week, as were the men. Very good they were, too, made by the local baker with a special meat ration.'

A WVS handcart on its delivery round.

Pies turned out to be more popular than the snacks side of the scheme, and in November 1942 nine pies were sold for every one snack. When the scheme grew bigger, the pies were made by commercial manufacturers or by the nearest large British restaurant. However, the WVS, often helped by the WI, still undertook their sale and delivery – no small feat as over 1,000,000 pies were sold each week. Dolly Wall, who was a member of the WVS at Winford, near Bristol, remembers that pies were delivered to a house in the village once a week and she used to go there every Friday afternoon to sell them. When people came to buy, they left their order for the following week.

Farmworkers who could not get a hot meal during their working day and were not served by a pie scheme were entitled to extra rations of sugar, fats, cheese, tea and preserves at their busy times – that is, during harvesting, lambing and potato lifting. These were supplied to the farmer so that he could provide the meal. Unfortunately some employers did not bother to apply for or collect these extra rations, a fact which provoked the bitter comment in the *Land Worker* of January 1944 that farmworkers were 'forgotten people . . . all they give us is a little extra cheese'.

EMERGENCY CATERING

The devastation wrought by bombing raids demanded a special kind of catering. The following pages outline some of the forms this took.

MOBILE CANTEENS

Mobile canteens owned by local authorities and voluntary organizations (the YMCA and Salvation Army, whose canteens were normally used to provide refreshments to troops) were called in after raids. These served food to emergency workers and householders who had lost the means of preparing their own food. For the first forty-eight hours refreshments were free, but after that they were full cost to all who could pay.

The WVS manned a substantial number of mobile canteens, often with great courage, as an extract from Charles Graves's fascinating book *Women in Green* shows. After one of their canteens was blown into the dock basin during a bombing raid on Liverpool, its driver said: 'I was that annoyed. There I was, bobbin' about in the icy cold water with me equipment biffin' me in the face. I was that annoyed . . . She did not say that she had to be pulled out by the hair, having gone down twice. But that is what happened.'

QUEEN'S MESSENGER CONVOYS

Queen's Messenger convoys were owned by the Ministry of Food. Each one consisted of a mobile water tank; two lorries, each containing 6,000 meals; two kitchen equipment lorries; three mobile canteens and four or five motorcyclists. The units, whose colours were blue and silver, received their name through Lord Woolton asking the queen's permission when

Left: Emergency workers get
mugs of tea from a WVS mobile
canteen.
Below: Queen's Messenger
mobile canteen and motorcycle
dispatch rider.

their formation was merely in the planning stage. Apparently the queen was so taken with the idea that she insisted on paying for one complete convoy. The American people, through the British War Relief Society, paid for seventeen others.

Queen's Messengers, which began operating in spring 1941, were staffed by WVS volunteers helped by Quakers. A unit usually worked in daylight hours, moving in as soon as possible after an air raid. It was designed to serve drinks and simple meals, such as hot soup and snacks, to the maximum number of people. As with ordinary canteens, refreshments were free for the first forty-eight hours.

EMERGENCY MEAL CENTRES

During February 1941 all local authorities with a population of 100,000 and over, and local authorities in the Greater London area, were asked to provide emergency meal centres. These were not necessarily to cater for homeless people, but for those who could not cook at home because a raid had cut their supply of gas, electricity or water. In March the scheme was extended to places with populations of 50,000 and over and, a short time later, to any vulnerable town.

The centres were to come into operation immediately after a raid and could be set up in schools or church halls using the existing furniture, whether it be school chairs or benches. Each centre had to have coal-fired boilers so that tea and soup could be prepared, and larger centres could have cooking ranges. One other requirement was water-storage facilities which would hold a reserve equalling ½ gallon per head of the area covered or, in high-risk places, 1 gallon per head. When they came into operation the centres were manned by volunteers, many of them schoolteachers.

Immediately after a raid they served tea, sandwiches, soup and stews. After forty-eight hours, when numbers had decreased, roast and baked dishes were served to people still there.

If, after a very severe raid, emergency meal centres could not cope or had been destroyed, the local authority covering the area had the power to ask local caterers to supply food either on their premises or to be taken from them and served elsewhere. For example, in Nottingham the director of feeding, who was on the city council's emergency committee, asked fish and chip restaurants to provide food if need be. He also arranged for bakers, restaurant proprietors, butchers and greengrocers, plus their staff, to merge into a scheme to supply food to the community as a whole.

REST CENTRES

The Ministry of Health ran rest centres for the homeless, providing food on the same lines as emergency centres. Generally they did not open until after a raid, but in London some were permanently manned.

Many rest centres were in rural areas, as through fear of bombing some city dwellers would rather walk out into the country at night than stay at home. Sometimes these rural centres were just village halls where the WVS or WI served hot drinks and biscuits. Occasionally goodwill on

---

EMERGENCY MEALS

Quantities sufficient for 100 persons.

Meat Stew with Mixed Vegetables
10 lb meat (bully beef, etc.)
5 lb dried beans or peas
10 lb onions or leeks
20 lb carrots
or
30 lb mixed vegetables
65–70 lb potatoes
1 lb oatmeal or national flour
1 lb parsley (chopped)
water or stock
1 lb cooking fat
25 lb national bread
1½ lb margarine

Cocoa (⅓ pint per person)
6–7 oz cocoa
2 galls milk (fresh or household)
¾ lb sugar
2 galls water

From Canteen Catering, prepared and issued by the Ministry of Food.

the part of the hostesses was tested when young men went over to the village pub until ten o'clock. The feeling was that if they were old enough to be doing that, they were old enough to be doing something useful!

COOKING DEPOTS

Cooking depots were large kitchens set up in 1941 on the outskirts of areas vulnerable to air attack. Their purpose was to supply meals to emergency feeding centres, rest centres and anywhere else which needed emergency food. The depots could be housed in an existing building or in a pre-cast concrete structure erected specially for the purpose. They were equipped to produce 3,000 meals of soup, roast joint, two vegetables and a sweet over a period of four to six hours, or 6,000 emergency meals of soup and stew. Volunteers were on standby to help the paid workforce if emergency meals were needed.

Cooking was done on special patent cookers which combined the principles of a coal-fired range with a steam-raising plant. In case the mains supply was cut, each depot had a store of water. Food was sent out in two sorts of insulated container which kept food hot from four to six hours: one was cylindrical and came in three 1-, 3- and 5-gallon sizes; the other was rectangular. The rectangular container took baking tins straight from the oven and was usually packed with roast meat, other oven-cooked dishes and baked and steamed puddings.

When not cooking emergency meals, many cooking depots supplied lunches for schools, works canteens and the smaller British restaurants.

BRICK-AND-MUD STOVES

As a back-up to central cooking depots, the Ministry of Food suggested that a small brick-and-mud cooking stove be built in each street of vulnerable areas. The idea was that householders could use this if gas or electricity supplies had been cut. WVS members and Girl Guides demonstrated how to make the stoves from bomb-site material. However, on occasions even these emergency stoves proved inadequate, for householders found that their food had either been destroyed or was too full of dust and splinters to be cooked.

SEMI-MOBILE COOKING UNITS

Semi-mobile cooking units were kitchens which could be unpacked from lorries, set up and be capable of cooking food for up to 5,000 people. Their purpose was two-fold:

1 When an area had been particularly badly bombed, to provide it with food over and above that supplied by cooking depots.
2 To serve any area not covered by a cooking depot – for example, non-industrial places which had been secondary targets.

The kitchens were designed by Lewis's engineering department (which had planned and advised over British restaurants). Lewis's transport controller, Colonel Jerrett, advised them over the kind of lorry suitable.

SHELTER CATERING

Mobile canteens manned by volunteers toured some London areas and fed people in public shelters. It was a dangerous job to be out at such times. When it became apparent that people were having to spend long hours in shelters, the Government asked local authorities to arrange for hot drinks and snacks to be on sale within the shelters.

The standard air-raid shelter canteen was a counter with storage cupboards and electrical power points for heating appliances and insulated urns. It was operated by voluntary organizations or caterers and prices and operating hours were regulated by the local authority. If, after a heavy raid, a shelter canteen was unable to cope with demand, the local council could supply it with stores from those set by for its emergency meals centres.

The London Passenger Transport Board organized catering for people who used underground stations as shelters. On 14 November 1940 the first special 'food train' brought foodstuffs to stations from depots in the suburbs. Food trains did their distribution run during the day and supplied eighty stations, which had power points installed to heat food and drinks. Provisions were sold to shelterers between seven and nine o'clock in the evening and from half-past five to seven o'clock in the morning. Because of the lack of space people could not come up to a counter, so instead food and drinks were distributed by attendants.

Above: A row of boiler-like army 'kitcheners' (with steaming chimneys) form the basis of this emergency canteen set up in Liverpool city centre.

CHAPTER FOURTEEN
OCCASIONS

CHRISTMAS

With greetings cards double their normal price because of a 100 per cent tax, a shortage of decorations and food on ration, a merry Christmas needed forethought. Ruth remembers the regime:

> You started collecting your stuff for Christmas around September time, collecting a little bit of fruit with your odd coupons and putting it by and making a little bit of mincemeat at the last minute. It was always a last-minute job, that, because you put in perhaps more apple than you should, which made it ferment.
>
> The Christmas pudding got its dosage of carrots which actually made it very light, but cook them long enough and they turn dark. Carrots also went into the Christmas cake. You couldn't really survive without carrots. They were one of the mainstays of life.

Ruth is thinking of these 'mainstays' as making the more traditional ingredients go further, but a carroty Christmas could bring another benefit: it could save you fuel. For example, in 1944 when fuel rationing was at its most stringent, Helen Burk's booklet of Christmas Fare for 'Mr Therm to Cook' gives the recipe for a 'one-boil' pudding. She says that it will save five to eight hours' fuel in every home where it is made.

As to the Christmas roast, although some advice leaflets recommended a cheap cut of meat pot-roasted to make it tender, Ruth recalls that people did their best to get a cockerel or chicken. Hers came from a cousin who kept hens which Ruth had supplied with scraps throughout the year. Other people obtained their Christmas poultry in a more underhand way. Dolly Wall tells the following story:

> One year we had four cockerels to fatten up for Christmas. The grain was black market from the farmer. Six o'clock one morning just before Christmas there was a terrible squawking. I jumped out of bed, banged the door bolt back and rushed out, but

---

CARROT (CHRISTMAS) PUDDING

The dry ingredients can be prepared a day in advance. The pudding itself should be mixed first thing on Christmas morning and put on to steam or boil 3–3½ hours before required.

I teacup self-raising flour
I teacup fine breadcrumbs
I teaspoon ground mixed spice
¼ teaspoon bicarbonate of soda
¼ teaspoon salt
½ cup sugar
2 tablespoons dried egg (dry)
I teacup shredded suet or margarine
I teacup sultanas
½ teacup chopped raisins
½ teacup chopped prunes
1–2 tablespoons marmalade or chopped candied peel
I teacup grated raw carrot
I teacup grated raw potato
2 tablespoons golden syrup
½ tablespoon liquid gravy browning
lemon or orange squash to mix

Mix together the first eight ingredients in the order given. Add and mix in the fruit and marmalade, then the carrot, potato, syrup and liquid gravy browning. Finally add just enough lemon or orange squash to make a firm mixture which drops from the spoon when you give it a little jerk. Mix all very well.
Two-thirds fill a thickly greased pudding basin with the mixture. Cover with margarine paper and a cloth and boil or steam for 3–3½ hours. Serve with a nice custard sauce.

Note Boil or steam this pudding very hard for the first hour. You can then reduce the heat considerably.

EGGLESS CHRISTMAS CAKE

4 oz carrot, finely grated
2 tablespoons golden syrup
3 oz sugar
4 oz margarine
1 teaspoon bicarbonate of soda
½ teaspoon almond essence
½ teaspoon vanilla essence
4–6 oz dried fruit
12 oz self-raising flour
1 teaspoon ground cinnamon
1 small teacup milk, slightly warmed

Cook the grated carrot and syrup over a low heat for a few minutes. Cream the sugar and margarine until light and fluffy. Stir the bicarbonate of soda into the carrot and syrup mix. Then beat it into the fat and sugar, using it as if it were an egg. When well mixed, stir in the flavourings and fruit. Lastly fold in the flour and cinnamon; add a small teacup of slightly warmed milk to make a moist dough.
Put into a greased cake tin. Smooth the top and make a deep hole in the centre. Put it into a hot oven; then turn the heat very low (the equivalent to milk pudding heat) and bake for 3 hours.

CHRISTMAS ICING

4 level dessertspoons sugar
6 level tablespoons household milk (dry)
2 tablespoons water
colouring and flavouring

Mix the sugar and milk together. Add the water and beat till smooth. Add the colouring and flavouring and spread on top of the cake.

our cockerels were still there. Whoever it was had taken two belonging to a farmer at the back of the chapel. After that we brought ours in and put them in the kitchen in a big box with wire over. But can you imagine four cockerels in the kitchen cock-a-doodle-doo-ing!

Turkeys were more difficult to come by. Commercial poultry farmers could not make a profit on them as the Ministry controlled their price, and so there was little incentive to rear large numbers of these birds. In 1943 it was estimated that about one family in ten had managed to buy a Christmas turkey. Their lack was something 'Gert and Daisy' tackled in *The Kitchen Front* wireless programme. 'Daisy' bemoaned the fact that she was unable to get one and 'Gert' suggested that instead she ask the butcher to bone her a leg of mutton which she could treat like a turkey. The script went like this:

GERT Have bread sauce with it and stuff it with the whatnot – no, shut up, Daisy. I suppose you could imagine your leg of mutton was a turkey. Often me and Bert used to eat whelks and kid ourselves they was oysters. But I must say I shall miss old Bert carving this year. Talk about all-in wrestling. They both used to finish up under the table. Of course, you know, there's just as much goodness in the joint. I mean, that's if you use your imagination.
DAISY . . . Reminds me of Old Mother Butler, mutton done up as lamb. Well, come on – give us your recipe for your murkey.
GERT Murkey, what's murkey?
DAISY What we're going to have for our Christmas dinner – half mutton, half turkey: murkey.

The Kitchen Front programme gave other advice for Christmas fare. Margaret Allen of Wallingford, Oxfordshire, states:

I wish I could remember the recipe from *The Kitchen Front* one Christmas for icing for the Christmas cake, which we followed to the letter and the result was most impressive – but, alas, when we went to the larder next morning to admire it, it had disappeared, soaked into the cake presumably!

This was probably the standard Ministry of Food recipe which Ruth used in the television series, when there was much anxiety over getting the cake photographed before its icing departed from it completely! The recipe is given left.

Ruth's fruit cake beneath the troublesome icing was a surprising success. She made it from a wartime recipe supplied by Christine Bebbington of Ledbury, Herefordshire, whose grandmother used to make it regularly. At first appearance the recipe seemed very austere as it did not include any eggs, but Ruth was agreeably pleased with the way the cake turned out.

Fig:1. Seeds and Seed Potatoes make good presents. If you are undecided what to buy purchase a Seed Token from a Seedsman, for your friends to make their own choice

Fig:2. Gardening Books make an ideal present, especially for the beginner — or what about a year's Sub-scription to "G.W.A"?

Fig:3. A set of Cloches, a small frame, or tools, would delight any keen gardener.

Fig:4. Why not a bag of fertiliser or lime; or a supply of wash. Rustic wood garden furniture is still available.

PARTIES

Just before Christmas 1939 Winifred Simpson of Rotherham, West Yorkshire, bought a McVitie's Christmas cake. It was iced and wrapped in cellophane, and it remained that way throughout the war years even though it graced any number of tables spread for soldiers' coming-home or birthday celebrations. Mrs Simpson's daughter Sheila Gray remembers that this useful cake was even employed as a sort of friendly blackmail: viz., 'We'll bring our cake if we can come to your party.' A few years after the war it was finally divested of its wrapper and eaten. It turned out to be very good and Mrs Simpson wrote an appreciative letter to McVitie's, who sent her back some biscuits.

Sheila also remembers that most of the family parties were held in the house of the owners of the biggest Morrison shelter because the top of that made a good table which seated a lot of people!

At formal parties, flowers (if the hostess could acquire them) were arranged on the table. An article on table decoration written in 1940 light-heartedly suggests that it would be in keeping with the times for hostesses to hang a white rose over the table. This is a reference to the Greeks having consecrated roses to (among other gods) Harpocrates, the god of silence, and to the Roman practice of hanging a white rose over the heads of guests who were then honour-bound not to repeat or give any information they had learned at the table.

After 1 November 1942, it became illegal for flowers to be sent by rail (they took up room needed for troops or food), so people had to use

Useful Christmas presents for gardeners. From a wartime edition of *Garden Work* magazine.

If it is not possible to buy ordinary table jelly before Christmas, powdered gelatine melted in sweetened fruit juice (from bottled fruit) is a very good substitute.

A home-made sponge cake, bottled plums, and a custard made with dried eggs are all the ingredients needed for an excellent trifle, which is, however, more attractive if it is topped either with table jelly or with dabs of apple or blackberry jelly.

Tips from a wartime newspaper feature, 'Good Things for Xmas'.

their ingenuity over decorations. The magazine *Picture Post* suggested using branches and berries gathered on country walks, and said that a pitcher of evergreen oak or a container of ivy was suitable, particularly when American guests were expected as they used evergreens in their homes.

As an aside, the combination of table decoration and Americans created a very odd wartime incident which has stuck in the mind of Constance Harris. One day, when she was in her garden at Over Peover in Cheshire, an American soldier came and asked for some flowers. She said, 'Help yourself,' and he began to pick the heads off her polyanthus. After a bit she ventured to ask if they would not be better with their stalks *on*, but he said, 'No, I only want the heads.' The next day the same soldier came running up to say that her flower heads had decorated the table at which Winston Churchill had sat to have dinner. Constance philosophically comments that she doubts whether Churchill noticed them.

Central London Electricity Limited's 'Cheerful Rationing' card for January 1945 announces, 'Let's have a party', and suggests to those who take this advice to make it a friendly fork party where guests help each other. The menu could be:

> *Kidney patties*
> *Creamed chicken or white meat cones*
> *Cheese boats*
> *Mock chicken sausages*
> *Sandwiches or filled rolls*
> *Salads*
> *Stuffed dates*
> *Shredded cabbage*
> *Salad bowl*
> *Norwegian prune pudding*
> *Ice cream*
> *Marzipan fruits*
> *Whipped jelly*

And for drinks? Perhaps the wartime cocktail (left) invented by 'N.S.' of Finchley, London, who sent the recipe to the *Daily Telegraph*, which printed it.

HOLIDAYS AT HOME

A wartime newspaper article that advised taking a Whitsun holiday picnic either in the garden or on the allotment, sensibly pointing out, 'It isn't so far to carry the food,' was not quite as unadventurous as it might seem, for, travel being difficult and discouraged, people *had* to spend their holidays at home. In fact 'Holidays at Home' became a much-quoted phrase and the Ministry of Food issued a leaflet called 'Suggested Menus for Holidays at Home'. This thoughtfully began:

> We all know that holidays at home can be great fun for the holiday makers. But what about mother? Too often she has to spend long

---

**ORANGE BITTERS
COCKTAIL**

Take 4 Seville oranges, remove the pips and cut in slices. Add 2 pints of water, boil for about 1½ hours, then strain off the liquid and add sugar to taste. Use this with gin or whisky. A fine drink.

Save all the cartons you can. These can be filled with jellied foods which are easy to carry because they do not spill.

A tip for packed meals from Food Facts *from the Kitchen Front.*

hours in a hot kitchen, trying to cope with the tremendous appetites of the rest of the family. This is all wrong. Mother needs a change from the kitchen just as much as father needs one from the office or the children from school. How can this be managed?

How indeed? The Ministry's solution was to plan a week's worth of meals with every midday one as a picnic to be eaten in the garden, park, countryside or, on wet days, at home, and to bake on Sunday and Thursday evenings. For example, Thursday's lunch could be:

Mock hamburger wrapped in greaseproof paper
and carried in a tin
Green salad carried in screw-top jars
Bread and butter
Sweet sandwiches (a mixture of margarine, golden syrup, strong
coffee and cocoa spread on bread)

An enterprising recipe leaflet of June 1944, working on the adage 'A change (of menu) is as good as a rest', suggests that if you cannot actually travel to your desired holiday location you can have dishes at home which will remind you of it. For instance, those yearning for Wales might eat Welsh cakes or Carmarthenshire pikelets.

Sheila Gray remembers spending her holiday in Clifton Park, Rotherham. There notices reading 'Holidays at Home' would be on display and many people took along their sandwiches and sat in deck chairs. A marquee had been specially erected for afternoon and evening tea dances. This had a rough wooden floor and Sheila's mother used to complain that her daughter, dancing away on it, wore out her shoes at a rate of knots.

One day, about lunchtime, before the afternoon entertainment started, Sheila was in the kitchen at home with her mother and, looking out of the window, they saw a German bomber rising up after having screamed down on to the park. Sadly it had bombed the marquee and its surroundings, the pilot presumably having mistaken the set-up for an army camp.

ENTERTAINING AMERICANS

American service personnel arrived in Britain in January 1942. Although there were private hospitality schemes to introduce them into British homes, it was not a venture hostesses undertook lightly. First they had to overcome their feeling that their own rations would not provide tempting enough fare for their guests; then they ran the risk that, through service duty, the Americans would let them down without warning (apparently this often happened); and lastly there was the dilemma over what to serve them if they did come.

Fortunately, as usual, cooking columnists, seeing a need, met it. The first thing they advised be tackled was coffee. This had to be freshly ground, for as one magazine noted, 'Americans are great coffee drinkers

Sidebar:

SUGGESTIONS FOR SANDWICH FILLINGS

Sardine and watercress
Marmite and chopped celery or shredded lettuce
Salad cream and any cold chopped vegetables
Cold potato, salad cream and chopped parsley
Grated raw carrot and grated raw beetroot
Mustard and cress
Lettuce and spring onions
Cucumber and lettuce
Chopped apple and celery
Purée of butter or haricot beans flavoured with anchovy essence, curry powder, meat or vegetable or any other flavouring liked.

From Cookery under Rations *(1941).*

and it's no secret that they don't find the coffee over here much to their taste.' Then there should be plenty of salads on the table and a dish of grated raw vegetables called coleslaw. This was doubly useful advice, as such dishes did not require cooking and so saved fuel. Hot food could be American hashed potatoes, hamburgers, American sausage pie or carrot and potato chowder, any of which could be followed by apple pie or Harvard pudding.

If American guests were coming to tea they could have chocolate pin wheels or American muffins; it was helpfully pointed out to the hostess that the latter were not like British muffins but more like queen cakes, and the Ministry of Food published a recipe for them.

Supper could be an American sandwich, a substantial piece of bread toasted or fried and topped with the filling of your choice. In fact these sandwiches, with an assortment of toppings, began to appear in street snack bars. Irene Veal, who compiled the *Radio Times' Wartime Recipes* book, wrote that she first encountered them at lunch in Piccadilly.

This entertaining was not one-sided, as Joyce Basey, who joined the WRNS in 1941, can confirm. As a leading Wren cook, she travelled to Rosneath Castle in Scotland to organize the kitchens for the Royal Navy who were moving in as American servicemen moved out. She recalls that on the night before they left the Americans threw a party for the civilian cleaners and their children and that there were bananas and oranges and also sweets by the ton for the children. In the 'hand over' few weeks she and her petty officer lived like ladies, even using butter to mash their potatoes! In fact all the new inmates eventually benefited, for the Americans left cellars of white sugar and tins of dried onions and potatoes.

AMERICAN HOT SANDWICH

Toast two slices of bread, spread one with Marmite and butter, and sprinkle with chopped watercress. Spread the second slice with the same and place buttered side down on top of the first slice. Cover with two crisply cooked rashers of bacon, sprinkle with some bacon dripping, and add, if liked, a suspicion of grated cheese. Place in the oven for 2 minutes before serving. Cut in two. When tomatoes are available one or two button tomatoes or halved tomatoes put the finishing touch to this dish. Eat with a knife and fork.

Above: Ruth's American Hot Sandwich (substituting mustard and cress for watercress).
Right: American servicemen find hospitality returned at a thanks-giving party given by British children.

WEDDINGS

In addition to their catering legacies American servicemen also left behind thousands of brides! British girls *would* marry them, in spite of local newspapers publishing off-putting 'regulations' about such matches, for example:

> A woman marrying a member of the United States Armed Forces will not be allowed to accompany him on his return to the United States; will not become a United States citizen by virtue of her marriage to him but will be subject to the general laws as to immigration and naturalization.

In fact, it was not only Americans whom girls were wedding: a lot of marrying went on altogether during the war years, for who knew what tomorrow would bring?

Many of these marriages were by special licence, the fee for which was £2 14s (£2.70) in Newbury, Ruth's nearest town. If you had been getting married there, you might have had Ruth catering for you, because she earned herself a reputation as a wedding caterer. It had started out with doing a friend's wedding and gone on from there.

Ruth remembers that getting reception ingredients together demanded ingenuity. She had to apply to the food office in Reading for an allocation of rations and soon learned to double the guest list. For example, if it was a wedding for fifty, she made the figure one hundred. Even then she was still given only 2 oz of tea which, diluted in an urn, made pretty weak stuff. Ruth remembers that friends and relatives of the couple were always helpful and used to collect and save food to contribute. They would save their coupons for Spam and for American tinned sausage meat. Once the sausage meat was delivered to Ruth she made it into sausage rolls, using the fat in the tin to make her pastry. People would also contribute fruit for the wedding cake – not that a tremendous amount was needed, for wartime wedding cakes were small affairs. She cannot recall making one bigger than 10 in. in diameter and usually it was only 8 in. When it was cut, a portion averaged out at 1 in. square.

Ruth remembers trying to make a wedding cake with dried eggs – unsuccessfully: 'It all sort of caved down in the middle, so I made another one and that did exactly the same. I came to the conclusion there wasn't the right material in the dried eggs to hold the cake up. We scratched around the village for the odd eggs and it was fine with them.'

Owing to the shortage of almonds, Ruth had to make mock marzipan (see right), but preferred the recipe which included semolina rather than soya: 'It made the marzipan more like real marzipan; it had that little gritty texture. It's a nice recipe which you can use today if you want to and it's cheaper than using ground almonds.' Unlike real marzipan, which she would have put on to the cake three weeks before the wedding day, Ruth put the mock marzipan on just two or three days beforehand – any earlier and it would have dried too hard to be pleasant eating.

RUTH'S MOCK MARZIPAN

4 oz margarine
4 tablespoons water
2 teaspoons almond essence
8 oz semolina
8 oz sugar

Heat the margarine and water in a saucepan. Add the almond essence. Put in the semolina and work it round till it has absorbed all the water and margarine. Stir in the sugar. Remove the saucepan from the heat, turn the mixture into a basin and leave to cool but not to get cold or it will harden. Spread over the cake.

As to icing, the Ministry of Food had taken care of that, for on 5 August 1940 it had banned icing on wedding cakes. Instead Ruth generally used what had covered her own 1942 wedding cake. This was a very nice cardboard cover decorated with crêpe paper. It had a little vase on top which could be filled with real flowers. She used this cover for cakes throughout the war and, she says, it always made a nice-looking cake. She adds, 'As long as you've got a nice cake underneath I think we could well use something like that today because so many people don't like icing!'

VE CELEBRATIONS

On Monday, 7 May 1945, the BBC informed listeners that the following Tuesday and Wednesday were to be public holidays; at 3 pm next day Churchill would announce the complete surrender of all German armies.

Tuesday, 8 May, Victory in Europe Day, dawned wet and thundery. Many people flocked to the shops to stock up for the holiday. Bunting was strung across streets and flags hung from windows. Church thanksgiving services took place and in some towns the Home Guard paraded in the streets. Victory party preparations were well under way. More often than not two or three local women had collected money for the food, bought it and were organizing its cooking. Food for the afternoon was for children's parties: jellies, custards, blancmanges, sandwiches, tarts, cakes large and small, ice cream and often a 'victory cake', iced in red, white and blue.

At 3 pm Churchill made his broadcast, church bells pealed and children and adults wearing coloured hats and red, white and blue rosettes sat down to tea. In the towns the tea tables were in the streets or in hotels, in the suburbs under the trees of large gardens, and in the villages in the village hall.

After tea many village children took part in sports on the green or local cricket pitch or, where it was raining heavily, inside the hall. Town children also had specially organized entertainment, and usually before a child went home, whether it was in town or country, each was given 1s (5p), an orange, a bag of crisps or some sweets.

The evening saw social events for adults: suppers in halls, radiograms put out into streets to accompany dancing and fireworks and bonfires at nightfall. Countless of these bonfires were topped by an effigy of Hitler. A lot of people brought out drinks that they had been saving for the peace celebrations, which was just as well as some pubs had to close because they ran out of supplies. Many a person's evening ended with renderings of 'Auld Lang Syne' and the national anthem.

Despite the celebrations, the war was not entirely over. Victory over Japan did not come until 14 August and rationing was to grow more austere as the bulk of food supplies was diverted to war-ravaged Europe.

Facing page: Ruth reveals that wartime wedding cakes were not all they seemed!

Ruth spent the night before VE Day preparing and packing food for the children's party and sports afternoon which was to take place in the village cricket field the next day. She recalls:

My mum sat there, my dad must have been about. There was also my friend, Mrs Elliot from down the road, Mrs Allen, myself and my husband Bill. We'd made rounds of sandwiches and some cream biscuits and sat till four o'clock in the morning putting the food into special bags which had a Union Jack and the American flag on the side. The bags were greaseproof and you've never heard anything like the noise we made all sitting there stuffing this food into them!

On VE Day Harry was in Nuneham Park gardens doing duty in the glasshouses. That night he had a victory drink in the Harcourt Arms with one of his fellow gardeners and a friend of the latter. Fairly late in the evening someone came into the pub and said that the Roebuck Inn at the next village still had beer and the villagers there had lit a bonfire on the green. Harry, his mate and his mate's friend set off for the Roebuck where they met up with more friends. Finally the three set off for home, but going past the bonfire Harry's mate's friend got slightly burnt and the other two saw him home.

At this time Harry had been at Nuneham only a month or two and knew very few people but thought he ought to go next day to see how the injured man was. When he knocked at the door the man's niece opened it. It was a momentous occasion, for this was Harry's first meeting with Jane, the girl he was to marry. He classes this as his best memory of VE Day.

Below: Ruth's VE cake.
Right: 'Evacuee' Paul enters into the spirit of the occasion once the camera starts to roll!

CHAPTER FIFTEEN
AFTER THE WAR

After Harry was appointed headgardener at Chilton in 1947 he married Jane. It was an old accepted custom that intending headgardeners should 'marry when suited' and thus move into the headgardener's cottage. Indeed, Harry hoped that he would again pick up the traces of many of the customs of the pre-war years in private gardens. For a time he did.

It was not an easy start, as large gardens had suffered during the war years. Lack of labour had meant that glasshouse repairs had been neglected, paths were overgrown and plants had run wild or been lost altogether. One of Harry's first jobs at Chilton was to pull out the untended vines. He planted new ones, for the owners wanted the garden restored and Harry was pleased to do it, seeing his new job as a great opportunity. Seeds and plants were hard to come by but friendly seed-firm representatives visiting the garden to sell their stock also carried news of gardeners who were willing to barter. For example, the rep. might have been to a place where the gardener had saved a stock of a certain plant and would part with some of it in exchange for some cuttings or seed from Harry's garden.

By degrees Harry built the garden back up and was pleased when his employer expressed an interest in exhibiting at shows. He recalls, 'It was wonderful and we thought it was going to go on from strength to strength.'

Meanwhile flower nurserymen and florists were also seeing a gleam of revival, for in the grey post-war years there sprang up an interest in flower arranging. Demonstrations were given, flower-arranging societies were formed and it came to be regarded as an art form. It was one which needed ingenuity, because vases, being unnecessary items, were not being made. Exhibitors heated gramophone records until they were soft enough to mould into vases or used the most elegant-looking kitchen casserole dishes they could find!

The latter choice was in fact quite effective as there was some very attractive new kitchen ware currently being made. No doubt its presence had a good deal to do with the Council of Industrial Design. Set up in December 1944, this worked with designers to raise the standard of design of all the goods made by British industry. In the immediate post-war years the Council looked at kitchens. There was a definite need for a re-think on kitchen design which, up to this point, had been paid little attention, with the result that most existing kitchens were monuments of inconvenience.

Post-war building of new houses also presented a golden opportunity for implementing new kitchen designs. The war had in fact helped further one new trend – for kitchen-diners. Families who previously had retired to a dining room to eat had discovered during the war that labour and fuel were saved by eating in the kitchen instead. Designers evolved a 'dining-room kitchen', which had an alcove for the dining table and chairs and concentrated the kitchen equipment together in another area.

Concentrating equipment was one of the basic aims of new kitchen design. Efforts were made to position table, cooker and sink as conveniently near to each other as possible. Cupboards, instead of being placed around the room in ones and twos, were built up to the ceiling. This trebled storage capacity in small kitchens. The top cupboards were for little-used utensils.

Pre-fabricated units also helped save space in smaller kitchens. Their standard height was 36 in. and they could be fitted together so that there were no dirt-catching ledges or crevices between them. The tops of the units also provided a work-surface far more convenient than that offered by the pre-war kitchen cabinet, with its pull-down front.

Sinks and draining boards became moulded into one piece, easy to clean and cutting out a dirt-collecting join. Pillar-type single taps with one spout for hot and cold water abolished the need to drag containers from one side of the sink to the other.

Kitchen units were not cheap but could be bought singly and added to. You could also take them with you if you moved house. Because timber was in short supply the first ones were made of metal with various finishes. People starting their kitchen from scratch were advised to buy light-coloured units: cream, dove grey or plain white. Colour could be provided by cheerful handles on doors and drawers and pretty-patterned curtains, although the new soft plastic ones needed thinking about as, once drawn, they excluded air. Colour could also come from the walls: tiles were unobtainable, but distemper or enamel paint did just as well.

An electric clock on the wall was inadvisable in the early post-war years, for there was still the danger of power cuts. At this time refrigerators were rare and expensive, so many of the most up-to-date kitchens had mesh-sided food safes. Even mundane kitchen equipment was in short supply, for trade in exports had priority over the home market.

The president of the Board of Trade in Clement Attlee's post-war Government was Sir Stafford Cripps, better known to the populace as 'Austerity Cripps'. People remembered his 1942 statement to the House of Commons to the effect that 'personal extravagance must be eliminated altogether'! In 1945 it was difficult to be extravagant. On 17 August, three days after victory over Japan, America ceased its supply of Lend-Lease goods to Britain and world wide there was a serious shortage of food. At home the minister of agriculture urged allotment holders and gardeners to keep digging. The slogan 'Dig for Victory' now became 'Dig for Victory over Want'. Even bread and potatoes became rationed and in 1947 fat supplies reached their lowest point of the entire period since the outbreak of war in 1939. However, by 1950 most shortages had been made good and in 1954 all rationing ceased.

Looking back, some people believe that their existence on wartime rations made for a healthy diet. Others admit that though they did not starve – for there was bulk in the diet – they were constantly hungry, especially for protein.

Dorothy Hollingsworth is in an eminently suitable position to give the definitive view on how rations affected people's health. Not only is she a member of the executive committee of the Board of the British Nutrition Foundation, but in 1941, as a young scientist, she joined the Ministry of Food's statistics and intelligence division. Her work at that time was involved with the Ministry's Wartime Food Survey. This was carried out very much as surveys are today: families were asked to fill in a form for a week, writing down what food they had bought and how many meals they had taken at home and out. The object was to see if, despite wartime deprivation, people were getting sufficient adequacies of diet and to try to assess what they needed and what would happen if rations changed – for example, if the meat ration were reduced. According to Miss Hollingsworth, the surveys showed that the nation *did* have an adequate diet – plenty of bread, potatoes, green vegetables and carrots, all providing good nutritional value. It was also a healthy time for you could not consume excess calories if there were none available!

In spite of people's moans about food being boring, the work carried out by the Ministry of Food was a highly successful application of nutrition knowledge, and it was the first of its kind in the world. It resulted from the necessary combination of the political will to do it (you need to have help from politicians, says Miss Hollingsworth), linked with scientific knowledge. After the war nutritionists from many of the Commonwealth countries came to Britain, such was the Ministry's reputation for having done a good job.

However, the public had not been completely re-educated nutritionally, as Miss Hollingsworth recalls: 'We thought we'd done it, solved all the problems; but we hadn't, for as soon as rationing finished there was a tremendous rush to get more sugar and fat!'

The Wartime Food Survey changed its name to the National Food Survey and in 1990 celebrated fifty years of existence. A paper written for the event comes to the conclusion that changes in the British diet have brought fat and sugar intakes back to their wartime levels – so messages do get through eventually!

Harry carried on as headgardener at Chilton until the mid-1960s when it was obvious that, with the price of heating oil rising alarmingly, it was no longer practical to keep the glasshouses in the kitchen gardens heated. 'I realized that it was never going to go back to what it had been and knew that I had to settle down and make different arrangements, to make changes and go along with the times. I've tried to do that all through the years,' he says.

With the help of his wife, Harry began to run the kitchen-garden plots as a nursery business. It was a route which countless private gardens had taken, either directly after the war or in the intervening years. Chilton, through the interest of its owner and Harry's enthusiasm, had staved off this end longer than most. Harry enjoys his nursery business but says of his headgardener years which followed the war: 'The end of the forties and the fifties were a great time for a chap like myself and I am always pleased that I worked and took advantage of it.'

The war has left legacies for both kitchen and garden. The radio programme *Gardeners' Question Time* follows in the footsteps of the 'Dig for Victory' Brains Trusts and Growmore continues to hold its reputation as a good all-round fertilizer. In the kitchen some women still use a favourite wartime recipe and wish that English rabbits were more available. A few miss sorting out their refuse into salvageable bits and at least one continues to buy her groceries in the order in which they were listed in her ration book, despite today's well-loaded supermarket shelves. Then there are popular myths. One in particular puzzles Ruth: 'They kept saying we were better as a nation when we were at war than we had ever been – was that propaganda or wasn't it? I've never worked that one out!'

5 February 1953, a happy day for children – sweets finally came off ration!

BIBLIOGRAPHY

•

BOOKS

Canteen Catering, Ministry of Food (?1942)
Cookery Under Rations, M. Pearson and M. M. Mitchell (Longmans, Green & Co., 1941)
Cooking and Nutritive Value, A. Barbara Callow (Oxford, 1945)
Cooking in War-Time, Elizabeth Craig (Literary Press, 1940)
Daily Express Domestic Poultry Book, Eunice E. Kidd (Daily Express)
Daily Express Wartime Cookery Book (1940)
Dainty Dishes for the Queen, Scottish Education Dept. (HMSO, 1944)
The Englishman's Food, J. C. Drummond (Jonathan Cape, 1939, revised 1957)
Evacuation Survey: A Report to the Fabian Society, edited by Richard Padley and Margaret Cole (George Routledge & Sons Ltd, 1940)
An Experimental Study of Rationing, R. A. McCance and E. M. Widdowson (Medical Research Council, 1946)
Fare-Ye-Well with Ladies of the Realm, Countess of Effingham (Hutchinson & Co. Ltd, ?1944)
Feeding the Family in War-Time, Doris Grant (George G. Harrap & Co. Ltd, 1942)
Feeding the People in War-Time, Sir John Orr and David Lubbock (Macmillan & Co., 1940)
Food and Agriculture in Britain 1939–45: Aspects of Wartime Control, R. J. Hammond (Stanford University Press, California, 1954)
Food Facts for the Kitchen Front, with foreword by Lord Woolton (William Collins)
Food Values in Wartime, Violet G. Plimmer (Longmans, Green & Co., 1941)
Food Without Fuss, Josephine Terry (Faber & Faber Ltd, 1944)
Fowls and How to Keep Them, Rosslyn Mannering (Cassell & Co. Ltd, 1940)
Friends of the People, The Centenary History of Lewis's, Asa Briggs (B. T. Batsford Ltd, 1956)
A Garden Goes to War, Stephen Cheveley (John Miles Ltd, 1940)
Gert and Daisy's Wartime Cookery Book, Elsie and Doris Waters ('Gert and Daisy') (Withy Grove Press Ltd)
Good Housekeeping's Unusual Vegetables: How to Grow . . . How to Cook (Good Housekeeping Magazine)
Hard-Time Cookery, (Association of Teachers of Domestic Subjects, 1941)
Haybox Cookery, Eleanour Sinclair Rohde (George Routledge & Sons Ltd, 1943)
Herb Gathering, Barbara Keen and Jean Armstrong (Brome & Schimmer, 1941)
History of the Second World War FOOD III Studies in Administration and Control, R. J. Hammond (HMSO and Longmans, Green & Co., 1962)
Home Pickling, Henry Sarson (C. Arthur Pearson Ltd, 1947)
How Britain was Fed in War Time Food Control 1939–1945, (HMSO, 1946)
Isle of Wight at War 1939–1945, Adrian Searle (The Dovecote Press, 1990)
Kitchen Front Recipes & Hints, Ambrose Heath (A. & C. Black, 1941)
Lady Sysonby's Cook Book, Ria Sysonby (Putnam, 1948)
MAFF: 50 Years of the National Food Survey 1940–1990, edited by Dr J. M. Slater (HMSO, 1991)
Manures For the War-Time Garden, S. B. Whitehead, DSc, issued by *Amateur Gardening* (W. H. & L. Collingridge Ltd)
Market Gardening, Percy Artiss (W. H. & L. Collingridge Ltd, 1949)
Meals with a Difference (winter edition), issued with the approval of the Ministry of Food (Gass Company publication?)
Meals for School Children, (London County Council, 1942)
The Memoirs of the Rt. Hon. the Earl of Woolton CH, PC, DL, LLD, (Cassell & Co. Ltd, 1959)
Our Towns – A Close-Up, a study made during 1939–1942 with certain recommendations by the Hygiene Committee of the Women's Group on Public Welfare in association with the National Council of Social Service (Oxford University Press, 1943)

Pictorial Poultry Keeping and Gardening, Walter Brett, FRHS, 2nd edition (C. Arthur Pearson Ltd, 1942)
Potato Pete's Recipe Book, Ministry of Food
Practical Gardening and Food Production in Pictures, Richard Sudell (Odhams Press Ltd, 1942)
Preserves for all Occasions, Alice Crang (Penguin Books Ltd, 1944)
Report of the Food (Defence Plans) Department for year ended 31 December 1937, (HMSO, 1938)
The Stork Wartime Cookery Book, Susan Croft (Stork Margarine Company)
Talks on Vegetables and Fruit, C. H. Middleton (George Allen & Unwin Ltd, 1940)
The Unbroken Front – Ministry of Food 1916–1944, Sir Thomas G. Jones, KBE (Everybody's Books, 1944)
Up the Garden Path, Peter Ender (Herbert Jenkins Ltd, ?1944)
The Vegetable Garden Displayed, (Royal Horticultural Society, 1941)
Vegetable Growing, the Country Life Home Front Series for Intensive Cultivation (Country Life Ltd)
The Wartime Vegetable Garden, Eleanour Sinclair Rohde (Medici Society Ltd, 1942)
War in the Countryside 1939–45, Sadie Ward (Cameron Books in association with David & Charles, 1988)
Wartime Recipes, collected by Irene Veal as published in the *Radio Times* (Letts Quirke Diaries Ltd)
The Week-End Gardener, C. S. Goodsman (John Crowther Ltd, 1943)
What to Give Them? McDougall's Wartime Cookery Book
What's Cooking? Recipes for the Keen & Thrifty, Ruth Lowinsky (Secker & Warburg and Lindsay Drummond, 1945)
Wild fruits, Berries, Nuts & Flowers, 101 Good Recipes for Using Them, B. James (Medici Society Ltd)
Wise Eating in Wartime, Ministry of Food (HMSO, 1943)
Women in Green – The Story of the WVS in Wartime, Charles Graves (William Heinemann Ltd, 1948)
Women's Institutes, Cicely McCall (William Collins, 1943)
The World Food Shortage, (HMSO, 1946)
Your Garden in War-Time, C. H. Middleton (George Allen & Unwin Ltd, 1941)

PAMPHLETS AND LEAFLETS

'A.R.P. Home Storage of Food Supplies', Bulletin No. 3, issued by the Canned Foods Advisory Bureau (?1939)
County Borough of Reading 'Advisory Bulletins', written by Horticulture Advisory Panel (1942)
'Dig for Victory' advice leaflets, Ministry of Agriculture
'The Doctors Tell You What to Eat in War-time' (BMA)
'Domestic Preservation of Fruit and Vegetables', Bulletin No. 21 (HMSO, 1947)
'Easy Meals for Busy Days and Nights', Director of Education, Liverpool (March 1941)
'Fertilisers During the War and After', E. M. Crowther, DSc, FRIC, Bath and West Southern Counties Society Pamphlet No. 13, 2nd edition (July 1948)
'Food from Overseas – Recipes', Food Education Memo No. 4 (HMSO, 1941)
'Nutritive Values of Wartime Foods', (HMSO, 1945)
'Pests and Diseases in the Vegetable Garden', Growmore Bulletin No. 2, Ministry of Agriculture and Fisheries (HMSO)
'War Cookery' leaflets, Ministry of Food

DIARIES

Miss C. M. Edwards (courtesy of Archives and Manuscript Department, University of Reading)
Mrs Kate Vickers (courtesy of Miss Enid Usher)

JOURNALS AND PERIODICALS

The Gardeners' Chronicle, various wartime editions
Garden Work, various wartime editions
Home & Country (magazine of the National Federation of Women's Institutes), January 1946
Journal of the Royal Horticultural Society, January–December 1942
The Landgirl (Women's Land Army magazine), various editions 1942–47
Newbury Weekly News, various wartime editions
The West Kent Women's Institute News, February 1946

MISCELLANEOUS

'Cheerful Rationing', recipes and hints on monthly cards issued by the Electrical Association for Women, 20 Regent Street, London SW1, for Central London Electricity Ltd, 1940, 1942, 1943, 1944, 1945
'Stork Margarine Cookery Notes', issued by Stork Margarine Cookery Service
Sutton's Seeds catalogues of First World War and Second World War
'The Yorkshire Kitchen Front', weekly recipe cards issued by the Yorkshire Council for Further Education

INDEX
●

PICTURE CREDITS

●

BBC Books would like to thank the following for providing photographs and for permission to reproduce copyright material. While every effort has been made to trace and acknowledge all copyright holders, we would like to apologise should there have been any errors or omissions.

BBC Photograph Library pages 37, 42 *top*, 43 *right* & 141; **Michael K. Benson** pages 36, 196, 199 & 206; **Mrs Pearl Bourhill** page 139; **Mrs Muriel Bushby** pages 86, 90 & 114; **Jennifer Davies** pages 8, 61 *bottom*, 73 *bottom*, 103, 105 *both*, 125 *bottom right*, 130, 132, 144, 148, 149 *left*, 153, 158 *bottom* (by kind permission of the City Museum & Art Gallery, Stoke-on-Trent), 161 *right*, 164 *both*, 165, 168, 176, 181 *both* & 216 *both*; **Fred Daw** page 31 *top*; **Harry J. Dodson** page 13; **E. T. Archive** pages 109, 140, 145 & 185; **Mrs Lillian Harbard** page 83 *both*; **Hulton Deutsch Collection** pages 10, 15 *main picture*, 16, 18, 24 *left*, 34, 40, 44, 73 *top*, 94, 95, 98, 107, 108, 121, 158 *top*, 167, 169, 175, 183, 192 *top*, 198, 203 *both* & 220; **Imperial War Museum** pages 28, 52, 72, 84 & 102; **Institute of Agricultural History & Museum of English Rural Life, University of Reading** Pages 23, 155, & 201; **Long Ashton Research Station** page 135; **Mrs Doris Moynihan** page 171; **Dorothy Pembridge** page 88; **Emilio Ponti** pages 92 & 93; **Popperfoto** pages 56, 65, 120, 127, 192 *bottom* & 212 *right*; **Mrs Beryl Roke** page 82; **Mrs Lilian Ross** pages 162, 172 & 184 *top*; **Mrs Margaret Short** page 195; **Syndication International** page 26 *photo* Guildhall Library, London; **Topham Picture Source** pages 67, 89, 119, 179, 193 & 194; **Mrs N. Waller** page 79; **Raymond Weeks** page 151; **Weston & Lois Weedon Horticultural Society** page 43 *left*.

The remaining photographs were specially taken for BBC Enterprises Ltd by Robert Hill and John Jefford.